THE BAYOUS OF LOUISIANA

BY THE AUTHOR OF

LOUISIANA HAYRIDE

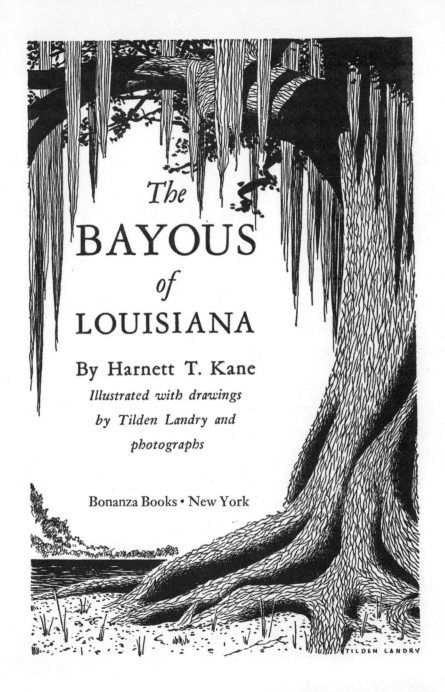

The

BAYOUS

of

LOUISIANA

By Harnett T. Kane

Illustrated with drawings
by Tilden Landry and
photographs

Bonanza Books • New York

Contents

PART III. "GARDEN OF EDEN"

PART IV. WHERE THE BUGGIES ROLL

Illustrations

The bayou won't ever give up the merchant-on-wheels.

For All Saints, the graves are lighted along the water.

An amiable angel keeps watch.

THE BAYOUS OF LOUISIANA

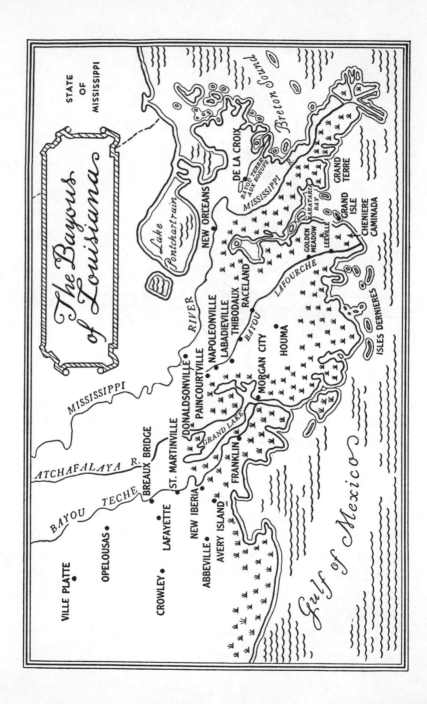

The Bayous of Louisiana

Pattern—in Water and People

IT IS A PLACE that seems often unable to make up its mind whether it will be earth or water, and so it compromises. The result is that much of moist lower Louisiana belongs to neither element. The line of demarcation is vague and changing. The distinction between degrees of well-soaked ground is academic except to one who steps upon what looks like soil but finds that it is something less.

Here is a fringe of a continent, land in the slow making. While it is found in the South, much of the traditional South is not found in it. Few states have so great a volume of water in so many forms. And in all this water the predominant form is the bayou.[1]

For nearly two centuries and a half Louisianians have been

---

[1] Pronounced bi'oo by most Louisianians who do not live near one; bi'a by most of those who do.

defining that slow word. The first Frenchmen who gazed in wonder at the curious green spread of their newly established colony and took the term from the Indians, had their difficulties. Old André Pénicaut, ship's carpenter, called the bayou a body of "sleeping water." Le Page du Pratz, planter and writer, sent word to the armchair travelers at home that it was a "dead" stream with little or no current that he could determine. The early Americans, who came late to Louisiana, smiled not only at the funny, peculiar-talking people but also at many of their little waterways, and like irreverent infidels they described them as creeks.

Peculiar to its place, the bayou is the product of an oversupply of water pouring over a yielding soil, seeking and finding many courses toward a lower level. Several things in one, it serves as a means of drainage in an area that cannot have too much drainage; an agency of balance, maintaining equilibrium among lakes, rivers, marshes, bays, and swamps, and between one bayou and another. The bayou is, too, a way of life, of access to the things of living for several hundred thousand men and women who live on or near its banks. Unlike streams for which it has been mistaken, it seldom dries up, because it does not depend for its flow upon such things as springs; its waters derive from other near-by bodies, or from the rain, or from the highly impregnated ground itself. Those original Frenchmen were in error in that the bayou has its flow, but one that is governed by its own rules, and it takes its own time in its movement. It is not set in its ways. It may flow in two directions, depending on the forces that bear upon it. For most of a day it may move east into a lake; with dusk may come a slow pull from the opposite direction, and it will turn to the west. Slow, serene, it has no rush and scouring passage; its philosophy is in the old Gallic tradition of the agreeable life. It enjoys in leisure the scene through which it makes its quiet course. Under the circumstances, mesdames et messieurs, can you suggest a better method?

The bayou is not necessarily a small watercourse. Some of these waterways are deep and powerful, have been described as rivers; others are narrow cuts, four or five feet of water or less. When two of them meet, the place may be so wide that from one bank it is hard to recognize a friend on the other; in other instances a man can almost touch the reeds of both banks as he glides through—though in a frail bayou boat this is not a recommended practice.

The majority of the bayous are notable for things other than size. Prodigal in number and in combination, they make a kind of lacework out of land, curving, twisting, curling back on their own curves, branching to meet others, splitting and resplitting. No adequate list of them has ever been made. Some are streams of renown, celebrated in gallant song and gay anecdote. Others are familiar only to the three or four families who live upon them in their houseboats and who may have named them after Grand-père.

In the latter case it is mainly these few who know the secrets of their cobweb meshes of water lines. Only one who had spent years in tracing and retracing their patterns could be expected to find his way about them. In such terrain it is not difficult to lose one's way at a turn. Hemmed in by grass and sedge and palmetto, without a foot of wholly certain land within sight, terror may come quickly; sometimes, death. Occasionally, even long-time residents are reported missing in the lower marsh reaches.

The bayous and their points of confluence have shaped the life and the history of their area and of their people, setting the design within which men have moved, made their livings, and enjoyed their world. Along the line of their movement came settlement, for these waters have been the highways of their country; paths of armored conquerors, of grand seigneurs and silent, bearded fur hunters. When the soil is like a cool pudding that quickly swallows the track of those who pass over it, men use the routes that nature has provided. Travel by land was tedious, unsure, and sometimes a matter of hazard through thousands of miles. Today railroads have been extended into the bayou country, their stilt bridges straddling some of the waters arid soft spreads. Modern roads literally float over what the engineers curse as liquid mud, highways constructed at costs that may seem fantastic. But there is not enough money in all Louisiana to provide roads throughout the area, and for a large segment of the population water must still be crossed and followed in their daily passage. The automobile has never taken the place of the pirogue—lower Louisiana's version of the canoe. This pea shell in wood can, as the local phrase has it, "ride on a heavy dew."

The bayou reaches are younger by millions of years than the rest of the South—than other parts of Louisiana. When most of the continent was dry land, the deep waters of the present Gulf of Mexico lapped over them. Land appeared only gradually, by infinitesimal stages, and largely as the gift of the waterways that moved southward. The central river— which the Indians called the Meche Sebe, and their successors the Mississippi—forced its way down through a deep, irregular valley. In its lowest reaches it shifted and wandered over many miles of yielding half-land, building up sets of side levees and thrusting forth tongues of land, then finding a new course of easier grade and beginning the same process again. Some of the present-day bayous are reduced successors to the master stream, flowing between abandoned levees; others are carriers of Mississippi overflow. But the bayous follow their own rules, and though some are descendants, others cousins of Father Mississippi, many are unrelated. For hundreds of years before white men arrived, the central stream held its present lower course unchanged, and its civilization has been separate and highly distinct from that of the bayous.

The bayous build their own banks, push downward their own tendrils of land. Their ridges of side earth are thick mounds or thin strips, depending on the age and course of the stream. For many miles these double lines of dikes are the only land to be found, dry strings above the wetness. On their borders, where they think themselves sufficiently protected, men place their cabins, as pioneers occupying outposts into a water-covered, water-threaded world.

From the hills of North Louisiana the land slips gradually downward to meet the Gulf. Soon all is flatness; levels are only a foot or two above sea level, and scattered over the surface is a mesh of interconnected bayous and shallow lakes, canals, inlets, cuts, and cut-offs. To those of other sections, the quality of the water is curious. The crystal-clear rivers of, say, the New England coast, are missing, as is the rock-bordered flow of the creeks. This liquid is thick, dark, stained. Earth-steeped, the color is frequently a heavy brown or purple, almost a black. Drop your hand a few inches below the surface, and it cannot be seen.

The bayous reach the sea along the 1500 or so miles of the Louisiana Gulf coast, torn and irregular, changing from land to water to land with the years. Behind the sand of the shore line are the salt marshes of Louisiana; no state has so wide a spread—their minimum extent ten to fifteen miles, greatly widening at a point in the center of the coast into swamps that reach nearly a hundred miles upward, and merging here and there into the fresh-water. To the sides are the drier prairies of the state, wide and thickly grassed flatlands, once wet, now marked by small meandering streams.

It is a fecund area. From the bayou and its land comes rich produce of the thick black soil, the warm air, and the dormant waters themselves—a varied life on stem, on paw, on wing, on gill, that is sometimes overwhelming in range, in teeming numbers, and in lush variety. Nature is in a free-handed mood. From these places of concentrated fertility, the washings of many soils, come jumbo shrimp and Spanish moss and tabasco peppers imported from Mexico; soft-shell crabs, alligators, and diamond-back terrapin; salt in great buried pillars; the largest number of amphibious creatures of any part of the continent. Equally at home on the soil or in the water, many such animals slip in and out of categories: swimmers they are at one time, overland travelers a little later, like the alligator; placid breathers on the water bottoms in one season, creatures that must live on the surface or suffocate by the next, like the crawfish. Fauna that live normally a thousand miles apart pass each other in the marsh. Birds whose usual habitats are separated by a continent fly together over the swamp. And the soil produces three crops a year—some localities boast of four.

As South Louisiana is a place apart, the South Louisianian is an American apart. He is apart from other Americans, from other Southerners—from other Louisianians as well. He is bounded on one side by the Gulf, on the other three sides by men as different from him as are their territories from his. To the west is the sandier, drier Texas and the sandier, drier Texans; to the east, the less prodigal Mississippi and Mississippians; to the north, well within the state borders, are the other

Louisianians, much closer in nature and attitude to their other-state neighbors than to him.

France settled the original South Louisiana, primarily with the help of French Canada and Spain. The United States settled North Louisiana, with contributions largely by England, Scotland, Ireland. There is much of France, something of Spain, and a scattering of other mixtures about the lowlands—in complexion, in Continental turn of phrase, in the shrug that says more than a harangue. One finds the rural South of America in these other areas surrounding the lowlands; and when the two meet, each knows that he is, somehow, not quite of the other's kind.

The bayou lowlands comprise less than half the state, shading gradually into the others. Above them are the upland piny hills, often thin-soiled and scrawny. Through the state runs the high ridge of the Mississippi and its immediate valley, opulent land and richly cultivated. Toward the southwest the soil becomes less fertile as it approaches the Texas plains. Thus circumscribed is Bayou Land: an irregular triangle, beginning on the Gulf coast inside the Louisiana boundaries, moving north and east along the marshes and prairies to the central Atchafalaya swamps and small streams, then reaching and crossing the Mississippi, then moving southward, skirting the city of New Orleans to reach the wavery eastern coast line of the state. Within these limits you may move at will in almost any direction and you are on a bayou or within hailing or pirogue distance of one.

The lowlander is generally Gallic, Catholic, and tolerant in many things. The uplander is markedly non-French, Protestant, and little inclined to compromise with his convictions. The former is normally calm, intermittently excitable, and romantic in temperament. His northern brother is tight-lipped and drawling. The one is quixotic, understanding, with laughter in his eye, a joke on his tongue. The other is a man whose strength may be that he makes few allowances, one to whom the lowlander's simple joie de vivre is as foreign as are the words.

Through South Louisiana the man or woman of the bayou is most often an Acadian, though at many points the name does not fit. The story of the Acadians is one of a phenomenal people, of a tenacity and determination that are unspectacular but nonetheless fervent. They came to the area as refugees from Canada, expelled in the middle of the eighteenth century for national and political reasons. It was planned that they should be widely separated, dispersed among the American colonies. But these French Canadians would not be broken. Many died, but those who lived held fast to their hopes and to their small possessions. Few thought of far-off Louisiana when they were taken from Nova Scotia. A scant band or two came here by chance, and it was the first place to which they were welcomed. These fertile acres near the Gulf became the promised land of the Acadians; to them they came until their Acadia of Canada was re-created.

The first colonists to reach Louisiana at the close of the seventeenth century had been men who came from France—military officers, merchants, some of them members of the nobility, and yeomen. Their mecca was the Mississippi, its valley the site of their plantations, and their city, La Nouvelle Orléans. Their children and their children's children were the Creoles, their culture urban or that of the plantations about the delta. A half century or more afterward came the Acadians, in small, tattered groups. The city and most of its lower valley were already filled, but beyond lay the almost untouched, widespread region of bayous. It was the opportunity for which the Acadians had prayed. They were a quiet, rural people, who wanted largely to be left alone. A series of accidents had brought them to one of the few places on the American continent that would permit them to realize that wish.

They had suffered, their families torn apart by hostile outside forces. That must never happen again. Always at the back of their thoughts has been this resolution, that here, in Louisiana, their small part of the world shall remain a citadel. They found themselves in a locale remote from other parts of the colony, and they rejoiced. They had, and still have, twin gifts of simplicity and humor, and they set to work to re-create everything as it was with them before—their small farms, their fields, their holdings of cattle, their meeting places for talk and song. The bayou became their place, their ways fitting to it and changing with it through the years. The product is a culture without parallel in the United States—a curious, untypically American design that is warm and rich in values, fitting no mold but its own.

The world heard little and saw nothing of the Acadian and his bayous. He remained in the back country, developing his own habits, his own economy, his likes and dislikes. His contacts with others, even of his own territory, were few; he lived on his own resources. He acquired, with the years, not possessions but peace. Let others concern themselves with problems and abstractions and systems of money; the Acadian worked and played as in times gone by, behind his protective barrier of bayou and distance.

There ensued a near-miracle of growth and resolution. A band of a few thousand became the mass of the lowland population, spreading over thousands of miles. It was a quiet triumph, victory in obscurity—a demonstration of the power of the human will. Others of different history and background might have turned in disappointment from this half-lost country. The Acadian saw more than water, fretted over things other than wet feet. He tugged at his land and his water edges, changed them, improved them, and extended them, turning semi-liquid "wastes" into small flowering gardens. Some would have accepted this territory only as a place of temporary refuge; the Acadian took it for home, raising levees, clearing streams, digging canals, and otherwise altering the face of the terrain. Then he turned to marsh and water and air for the promise of wealth that each held. His became an economy of the little collector; he drew from nature the things that she had ready for hungry man. He fished, trapped, hunted, picked moss, made a series of part-livings through the year. Others, of other groups and other nationalities, have come too into his haven in more recent years, and have adopted his pattern. The country remains one of small men, at small occupations.

Yet it has not been a process of mere transplantation. In this near-tropical land the Acadian has gradually fitted his habits to his necessities and become another man in many respects. What developed through the years was not standard French, nor was it Canadian, nor even the French the Creoles of the city knew. And let none say to him today that he is not an American, and a good one. He has been on his soil since the Revolution, and he means to stay there. As a matter of fact, he fought in that Revolution, on the American side— under a Spanish commander who led Louisiana Frenchmen against the British to help the colonists. Some of the Acadians are officially Sons of the American Revolution. His people have served, and well, in all of his adopted country's later wars, and in times of peace as well. They have contributed their sons to the ranks of Louisiana governors and lawmakers and soldiers.

The case of the Acadian, in fact, may be one of the answers to impatient and intolerant men who cry, in the name of "Americanism," for quick and complete absorption of all differences into a common whole. Such partisans, desiring a leveling down to a flat monotony, forget that the ideal of the nation's good life is the sum total of many contributing forces, of many origins. Assimilation here has been less than complete; and this has not necessarily meant a loss to Louisiana or to America.

But through the years most of the Acadians have lived in the background of Louisiana. The state's being had long seemed centered on the capital city and on the line of Greek-templed mansions that extended along the river from a point below New Orleans high up past its borders. Here was the kingdom of cotton and of sugar, the tradition of black slavery and white gentility. In time the plantations spread to a few of the bayous, and great sugar houses and pillared homes appeared among the places of the little men. But largely, the bayou dweller has faced away from the river and its influences.

Changes have come with the advance of train and bus and schoolhouse; and each passing year and each war, with its introduction of Acadian youth to the world beyond, bring nearer the eventual amalgamation into the American mass. Yet today, to an extent that may seem incredible, there still flourishes the tradition of a France-in-America. A man may be a fifth-generation citizen but unable to speak English. On the streets of many villages, in the bayou front yards, at the stores, the national tongue is the exotic one. A caller may spend a day, as I have done, going from one farm to another without finding a family in which l'anglais is known. A non-French stranger in the rural parts, wishing to do business, may be in a predicament; bilingualism is much more than a trade asset— it is a basic necessity.

Some years ago the state department of education thought it advisable to adopt a stringent general ruling: No French must be spoken in classroom or playground, by teacher or pupil. The natural speech of the French section was, alas, all too natural; children, it was feared, were learning English too slowly, and under handicaps. The boy (or girl) who goes to school for the first time from an outlying area has often found himself in a terrifying environment. He has heretofore heard hardly a word of the strange tongue, English. The teacher, who herself had first known French and even now heard it always at home, was tempted to resort to it daily with those who knew little else. Similarly, a state law requires that court proceedings be in English. Attorneys speaking the one tongue, who ventured into French country, were dismayed to find that testimony, addresses to the jury, remarks of the judge, and the interrogations were all in French; sometimes the records as well. Even today it is frequently impossible to abide by the law all of the time. A full English-speaking jury cannot be found; and witnesses cannot learn English, Monsieur, simply because they happened to see a shooting, or be there when a man fell off a shrimp lugger.

In the Second World War, draft boards sent to the Army youths whose knowledge of English was rudimentary. "Je ne comprends pas" was a literal statement of fact when offered after receiving orders at camps, however much a sweating sergeant doubted it. French-speaking officers were called upon in some instances to drill Acadian recruits in the early stages.

The Acadian speech through the years has become, like its user, something to and of and by itself. It is a dialect; more accurately, a set of dialects, that makes for an adventure in listening. For it has been compounded during three centuries in France, Canada, and Louisiana, out of isolation, resourcefulness, and a sense of humor. For generations the Acadians have been away from their native country; along the curving paths of Louisiana's Acadia the listener hears terms common in French villages of the late 1500's. Local peculiarities have appeared; some words have taken new endings, others have been extended or cut off, or sounds have been transposed. The Acadian will drop a word or several words whenever he can. It is a kind of French with a Southern accent of its own, of variations within variations. The language differs from one place to the other, depending on the province of France that predominated in the settlement, and on local influences. Acadians at the state universities frequently ask each other, "How do you say that where you come from?" The bayou man has enriched his language with borrowings from many groups— the English, the Spanish, the Indian, and, like other Louisianians and other Southerners, occasionally from the Negro. Beyond that, he has made up lively terms of his own to describe sights and things that were new to him. "Tac-tac" (tock-tock) is his word for popcorn. He has looked at the spotted sandpiper, noted his polite bobbing up and down, and dubbed him "Chevalier de Batture," gentleman of the river shore. He has examined the gnarled "knee" of the cypress tree and called it "boscoyo," a brawny bucko.

The Acadian wrestle with English may be illuminating. He advances upon it with the same flourish of hand and voice which he gives his native language. When he wants emphasis, he finds ways to get it. The fish, it is little-little. The magnolia is white-white; and white-white, to my way of thinking, is a lot whiter than that limp term, very white. Yet more positive is the term I heard one lowlander use: "It was black, I tell you, black like God damn." That, mes amis, sounds uncompromisingly black.

"I like that, yes," he assures you. "I don' want any, no." "I laugh till I bus', me." Gender of words, in French and in English as well, is frequently a matter of unconcern. "My maman, he is sick," says the boy. He takes you through the house: "This room, she is pretty, don' you think?" Singulars and plurals are employed with grammatical whimsicality: "He is a nice gentlemans." "In Lafayette they got lots of big building."

A little girl once caught my arm and pointed: "Look at my little dog, how he is cute." A man explained that he was going to test his prowess in the water: "I'm going to take myself a mile swimming." When I repeated a rumor about his part of Louisiana, he assured me: "That is not true, no. It is only a say-so." When a matriarch of a large family told me of a long-past hurricane, she said: "The win' came to us— jus' like a music."

As in the home country and in other places, the Acadians mix their language and English with considerable verve. I ask a friend how he feels; he answers: "Joliment all right." When we say good-by, he adds: "Futez-moi un ring" (give me a telephone call). Again, when I sought out an Acadian whom I had met in New Orleans, the neighbors called to me: "Il est gone away."

Me, I don't know anybody quite like the Acadian; and I wouldn't be willing to change one accent's worth, or one fine free chuckle, in the interest of all the dull conformity in the world. As for that word Cajun—a modern shibboleth—the

French contracted Acadian to 'Cadien, well-accented, and the Americans Americanized it to the easier style. In many cases an Acadian may use the word in speaking of another and to another in conversation, but woe to the outsider who tosses it about. To quote a common Louisiana saying, it is the kind of word with which one accompanies a smile, and a friendly one at that. Too often it has been used by others as a term of disparagement, with a superior smirk. The word has acquired strong social implications. As Dr. T. I. St. Martin has suggested, the city Frenchman uses "Cajun" for the town man. The town man grins, "Oh, those Cajuns down in the village." The villager applies it to one along the stretches of the big bayou, the latter to his fellow on the little bayou, and he, to anyone in the far reaches of the swamps and the Gulf. Still, there are men and women—prosperous attorneys, professional men, and in at least one case to my knowledge, as handsome a grande dame as graced any Louisiana parlor—who are proud of the word and of their connection with it. To them it is a heritage.

I have been seeing bayous and bayou people all my life. The place is not my home, but that of a good next-door neighbor. I was born and have lived in the midst of that contrasting civilization, always within walking distance of the Mississippi's banks. I knew bayous before I understood what they were, and I was saying Cajun before I knew what the word meant. For the first seventeen years of my life I was acquainted only with the South of Louisiana. (There was also the Gulf coast of adjoining Mississippi, where the family spent vacations, but that is largely a less dramatic continuation of the flat Louisiana stretches.) I must have been eighteen or so before I saw a hill, and promptly called it a mountain and was snickered at for my exclamation. The unending evenness of this bland and rockless land was the norm to me. It was only later that I heard others of other places comment and ask about the peculiarities of my strange country; and then I did some questioning and some learning of my own.

This process continued when, as a newspaperman, I traveled the bayous and the marshes. The Archbishop was blessing the shrimp fleet. We went, the photographer and I, partly by car, partly by motorboat, partly by pirogue. In the middle of the night, a telephone call: silent trappers had just poured leaden death into a party of Federal deputies. We went. One rainy morning a message from Southwest Louisiana, a broken connection: "The whole place wipe' out; dead people all aroun', Jesus Chris', aks 'em to sen' some doctors . . ." Again we went, over water-covered roads that highway policemen were reluctant to let us try; and we saw terror and pain borne in chill silence, and quiet resignation to the inevitable. On happier occasions there were "fais-do-does"—"go-to-sleep" is the literal translation, and an ironic term, since the dance continues all night—and the not entirely grim work of checking a new claim to champion fatherhood and motherhood in an area that counts twelve children as a fair start. Now and then there was the sharing of good wine with some of the priests and monsignori, and with at least one bishop of the territory. The more I saw of this place and people, the more I came to appreciate them. From conversations over gumbo, or at the wheel of luggers on the amiable waters, I absorbed, consciously or unconsciously, bits of places, ways of speech, quirks of behavior, the look of the waters that bad September; that long ride back, from dusk to midnight, from the pass that became a bayou and then a lake and more bayous, and finally a river.

Then one day in 1940, Wilbur Goubeaud, who travels about the bayou country and knows the qualities in it that appeal to a good, observant Brooklynite, had an idea. He passed it on to my publishers, and they relayed it to me; and all of us concurred at the start, and then did some disagreeing and finally some agreeing. Meanwhile I had recollected, not always in tranquillity; I had revisited the place on a series of trips from bayou to bayou, and sometimes I visited sections of it for the first time; I renewed earlier acquaintances and made new ones. Friends helped with suggestions, with remembrances of their own. But largely these pages represent what I saw or re-saw during these past eighteen months and what came back to me from those previous journeys: prairie cowboys who herd their cattle in French; grand'mères who can hunt and fish as well as their grandsons; men who live by repairing buggies for others who know no other way to travel in their backlands; operators of night clubs under thatched roofs (not a Hollywood-Florida architectural fillip, that, but a simple adaptation to the scene); bayou politicos, thicker to the square yard, perhaps, than anywhere in the world; and sweet-faced Evangelines who did not wait for a Gabriel but married the other boy down the way.

There were trips on Gulf trawlers, days of combing iridescent wonders of the deep from the crowded nets; a half-week with moss pickers, spent in tearing that dusty product from the cypress, then in "picking" and cleaning and drying it for the trade; a time with several operators of stores-on-wheels, riding along the bayou highways, offering bargains in housegoods; and weeks in Acadian homes, during which I learned more of a people who like life, who are social beings above all. Not always was it idyllic, of course, for at many places want and despair wait in the shadow: or sudden anger cracks over long-drawn-out discouragements. The bayou man is friendly but he is not docile; aroused, he can move into the fray with all the warmth of his Gallic nature. He has a history that has been often vivid, often violent. Blood has wet the banks of these sleeping waters; civil war has been threatened in clashes of tempestuous men, with feuds in the swamp, sudden terror in the shade of the shell ridges. At the fringes are tragic mixtures and shadings, hybrids and hybrid deeds. And fabled as the land are some of its people, past and present, individualists who, like the animal and water life about them, slip in and out of classification. I heard of them and their doings, their tall tales and legends, around the oil lamps as the old ones spoke above the clatter of rain on the palm leaves outside.

Some of these things were of the sort that are remembered a long time: an All Saints' eve in a cemetery along the waters, flickering candles in rows before each whitewashed grave; a country Mardi Gras, masked and painted men riding the roads, skylarking with greater abandon than their cousins in New Orleans have done; the cold horror that came when one matriarch described the creeping of the storm waters as she and her infant daughter waited for death in the enveloping dark; and that prairie buggy wedding, with the groom, who had used only the buggy as a means of transportation during all his previous life, due to leave after the honeymoon to join an armored tank division. And, too, the experience of being taken several times by war-conscious Acadians for a particularly subtle Axis agent. I won't forget the stout, mustachioed grandmother who watched in silence while her daughter displayed the mud chimney of their house; who broke out as I was about to leave, to ask the others if I didn't seem to be entirely too curious, probably a parachutist who had descended in the marsh.

More serious, for a moment, was the report quickly turned in against me when I photographed a brief, rickety causeway on the swamp edge near a drowsy village of ten houses. It was one of the most remote spots in the territory; I would have surmised that there was not a law officer in a day's travel. Before dusk of the same day, an armed deputy sheriff and assistant made a brusque appearance; the natives had recalled a warning that saboteurs were anxious to obtain information on all bridges. Luckily, five years earlier I had traveled over the same territory when the state introduced "dental barges," bringing such care by boat, the only way it could reach these outlying stretches. The deputy had been in those earlier pictures and remembered my face if not my name. So I did not dine that evening on prison bread, but all of us had duck and claret and talked about war and politics and people.

Out of our houseboat window we could see the slow flight of a pair of white egrets among the cypresses; in intervals between the clamorous choruses of a thousand frogs, the tired lapping of the water made other places and other events— New Orleans, Washington, the war, the peace—seem very distant. Yet in the Gulf, only a few miles from here, men had recently met flaming death in pools of oil from tankers sinking in the blue waters; and the deputy's assistant, a day earlier, at almost the same spot in which we had anchored, had bumped something with his boat and found that it was a life preserver. The man lashed in it had died; and that was for the best, the assistant decided, when he looked a second time.

But the bayous are, for the most part, places of more pleasant implications. Many times in the past months I have heard, in slightly varying forms, the story of the lowlander who met up with the Virginia lady and mystified her with his speech and manner. At last she observed that he was like no other Southerner whom she had ever met. To this the bayou man replied: "Ma'am, if I'd be born any further to the South, I'd be a sof' shell crab right now."

It is to him and his brothers, these free French-Americans, who escaped soft shells by so small a margin, that these pages are dedicated.

Part I: *The Wet Front Yard*

§ 1. *Passage to the South*

IT STARTED one clear spring morning on the Mississippi
bank opposite New Orleans, at an entry to the bayous that
is a gateway and a wet one—Harvey Canal. On one side
of the mound of earth was the mighty river of coffee-and-
milk waters, surging to the Gulf; on the other, many feet
lower, a quiet, darker, slower flow, the beginning of a curling
route of mixed waters, their eventual destination the same.
We turned our backs on the Mississippi for another scene and
civilization, to which this canal and its connecting ways were
appropriate points of introduction. Along this course for more
than two centuries has moved a sizable segment of the life
of the bayous; over it will pass a greater, more fruitful part
of their future. It is the major line of heavy water trade for
the southernmost areas fringing the Gulf—a fabulous passage
through the years.

The locks closed, the water boiled, and our small, square-bottomed steamer churned forward, feeling its way. Quickly there slipped away the last of the buildings that told of the nearness of the city. The land declined in level from the levee crest, and soon it was only a few feet high. When white men first came, in the early 1700's, this earth to the left and right was a swamp, the low, unsought ground back of the alluvial deposits. Since then thousands have worked and many have died to cut this wide ditch and to drain off the excess waters. Today long and neat rows of crops spread over the soil, and here and there stands a house, sometimes as old and solid as if it had been there since the colony's early days.

But this triumph of agriculture was short-lived about us. After a few miles the land sank further and signs of man disappeared. The swamp pressed close. Even in bright morning and in this season, it was a place of shadowy gloom. Guardian of its quiet waters, the grotesque cypress stood firmly planted, with its swollen trunks, its tall arms reaching wide to shut out most of the light, and hung with shadowy, triangular-shaped drippings of moss. The eye could penetrate only a short distance within. There, at the noon hour, in the dimness, the trees held out half-curtains of the gray growth, meshed bits hanging toward the water surface and their own reflections. At many points several feet from the tree, crooked objects jutted out of the still liquid, pointed or knobbed at the end—the "knees" of the cypress, seemingly without owners, thrust from below into the air.

From the steamer deck I could make out reflections on the shiny black surface. Water hickory stood next to locust, tupelo to bald cypress, and among them were ferns and creepers, palmettoes and vines, some green, some gray-white, all persistent in their thick, unending growth. Slanting lines of light cut along the trees, glinting on leaf or bark, or falling on the water; and they made the surrounding dark seem the heavier. Here a smaller tree had dropped and was almost submerged; about it others had risen, young and bright-hued, as if living off the dead thing. A great one had slipped but was caught and held as it had fallen against the others; and there it stayed, slowly whitening in the air. High upon it, out of a heavy drapery of green vines that covered all of one side, flamed a single orange flower, then a cluster of them, and below, among the green spikes at the edges of the trees, the indigo iris raised an aristocratic head. A few blossoms fell upon the water, neither sinking nor moving.

All was hushed, the silence of the swamp. The only sound was at the edge, as our vessel churned forward. Once an alligator lifted its head, then drew its leathery hide from an elevated point a few feet from us and disappeared under the water. A gap came in the swamp, a "road" cut for the use of woodmen and others. Now, slowly along it came a heavy skiff piled high with moss just pulled from the trees, to be taken after "curing" to a dealer who would in turn sell it to city men who would use it for the stuffing of mattresses, for airplane seat filling, and similar purposes. The small, dark man who paddled the boat waved a hand excitedly at us.

"Comment ça va, Capitaine? Wait!"

The Captain grinned and waved. David (Dov-veed, they pronounced it) Ledoux had news. The steamer's motors were halted while David, perspiring, and with gestures, told it. A few miles down, at that big bend—where the lil' Cancienne boy got drown, you know—well, a barge had hit right into the bridge; we'd have to be "cafful-cafful." The Captain, appreciative, asked about the moss picking and the Ledoux children, and David went back to the swamp. "I'm glad it wasn't worse," sighed the Captain. A year ago a God-damned lugger had caught fire and sunk right in the middle of the channel. Only the very smallest of boats had chanced the narrow margin that was left. It was a calamity for five days; he had had to tie up along here with everybody else, and lost a week's money. The smashed bridge seemed a minor matter in comparison.

The Captain frowned and pointed. "Maybe you wouldn't believe it, but that's our worst trouble." His finger was directed at a narrow line of fragile green and lavender flowers on each side of the canal, that bobbed lightly as we passed—water hyacinths, "orchids of the bayou." Somewhere behind us, on the route, one or two had crept into the scene almost unnoticed, and now they were thickening and widening as we went, reaching toward the center of the channel. A few yards forward was a circular mat of the plants, a floating garden of tight-packed, waxlike leaves. From the glistening bulbous centers protruded upthrust blossoms, pale bunches of delicate, perfumeless bloom. I managed to reach below the rail and catch a handful. They were easily crushed, more water than green cells. Below each plant extended light, colorless strings of roots, for several feet. The flowers faded quickly; in a few minutes they were limp on the wet deck. It was hard for me to realize that I held in my hand a major threat to navigation over most of South Louisiana.

This beauty is in heavy over-production and must literally be plowed under. Wherever there are bayous, the hyacinths intrude, an ever-invading, advancing army—a fragile subversive. Lakes, bays, small waterways and large ones are entered and overgrown almost in a season. Unless something is done, within the next few years they will be impassable. The matted leaves can cover a spread of water so completely that it seems like land. The man with the paddle finds passage impossible; even a heavy motorboat can be stopped by this flowered barrier, its propeller hopelessly enmeshed. The wise pilot does not attempt to penetrate a waterway so blanketed.

As we moved among the hyacinth pads, the Captain and I talked of the confusion among Louisianians as to the history of the hyacinth. Though generally regarded as a native product, it is not that, nor is it even an old import. Authorities differ as to the date, but all seem to agree that the state began to see it in large quantities only during the late years of the last century. The International Cotton Exposition of 1884 in New Orleans offered a widely admired display—interestingly enough in view of later developments—with the cooperation of the Japanese government. According to some, the plant is a native of Japan and was introduced from that source into Latin-American countries; the display in this instance was from Venezuela. "Samples" were given to visitors, who placed them in their ponds and waterways. Others believe that the movable gardens of hyacinth drifted into Louisiana from Florida. In any event, what was at first a pleasant rarity soon became an opulent curse. In the warm, shallow waters of the Louisiana lowlands it found a lush affinity, its long tendrils anchoring lightly to the banks of the waters and multiplying day by day. Bits broke away and found new places to conquer.

The consequence has been a transformation in surface appearances over much of this area. Waterways have been completely covered and choked so that they have become "hidden" lakes and passes; large bays have lost half of their open water and are rapidly losing more of it. The Captain talked long and with vigor. "See that place?" He indicated a clear spread of green. "When I was a young fellow I could row for hours around there. Now I couldn't get a pirogue into an inch of it." Men like him went to Congress a few years after the hyacinths became prevalent, and since then millions of dollars have been spent by the government to wipe them out. Many and ingenious proposals were made: that steam be poured upon the water plants from spouts, withering them on the spot; or that the hyacinths be scooped up, dried, and turned into cattle feed. At first the government tore out the hyacinths by the roots, using boats for travel about the bayous. Then poison—an arsenic spray—was attempted, and worked well. A fleet of poisoners patrolled the waters. But farmers complained that their cattle, too, were being killed when they ate the plants after the vessels passed. In recent years hyacinth "chewing" has been adopted as the approved method of destruction. "There's one of them ahead of us," the Captain observed.

A long barge was in action. As we watched, it was spitting forth bits of the broken stuff. An underwater conveyer was pulling the plants into a hopper, where heavy rollers worked over them and turned them into a mash. Behind the vessel spread a line of the digested hyacinths. Most of it floated but, the Captain explained happily, it would be saturated in a few hours, sink, and this stretch would be clear for a time. I remarked that the government apparently was merely nibbling —more or less literally—at the problem, and he agreed. It must confine its work to the main bayous and continue to experiment, and meanwhile the water growths spread in every direction.

The bayou orchids have one natural enemy, salt. Wherever that element enters the water they sicken and drop to the bottom. On thousands of routes such as our present one they were floating southward to their death. At the moment they were disappearing about us, and with them the swamp trees. The canal was bringing us to the twisting turns of a series of bayous and other waters—Big Barataria, Little Barataria, Bayou Dupont, Lake Salvador, Little Lake (which is a large one), and many cuts between others, all interconnected and complex. Slowly we were moving into the marshlands, the uncertain area of unending grasses. The last cypresses lingered with us for a time, in twos and threes, and then a narrow single file around the bayou curve, into the edge of the lake, surviving with difficulty in the brackish water that will eventually kill any tree. One old sentinel finally stood alone, lost and isolated. The salt had already done its work. The leaves had long since gone, most of the branches had dropped away, and all that were left were the trunk and two shorn arms. To one of these clung a small wisp of moss, held against the trunk by the force of the wind; on the other sat a silent, dark bird that seemed to have missed its way. As we passed, it flew ahead of us.

Now the steamer had to itself a world of flat and lonely silences, a scene little different from that which the crawling monsters and winged lizards of other ages must have inhabited —land that is only partly finished, its composition shifting by the mile. From our deck all seemed solid. At the bayou edge, we knew, there was usually a ridge. Over considerable stretches, too, there is marsh that is practically land—heavily matted, capable of negotiation on foot without difficulty, though subject to occasional inundation. A heavy peat forms below. In the dry season it may be set aflame by hunters. But in other places a spread that appears much the same may be water in disguise. The "prairie tremblante" is quavery land, as its name indicates; something that looks secure but is not— the terror of the novice, occasionally the embarrassment of the expert. All seems safe, a spread of thick grasses which obviously has a solid base. And it has—a foot or more of mud and vegetable matter floating above many feet of mud and liquid. Most trappers know at a glance which parts of such ground will support them, at least momentarily until they can step to another. Alligator grass, salt cane, oyster grass, cattails—each one carries a meaning: that the prairie is either fairly firm or almost certainly dangerous. Where that kind of growth appears, keep away, m'sieu. That one likes wet. That other, that will do. It won't go where things aren't dry. "Walking prairie" is an important trade asset; the marsh man can traverse large areas with a minimum of strain and wet trouser seats. But even the best-trained among them will sometimes slip beneath the surface. He knows how to get to safety better than the amateur, of course, using elbows and arms until he has a firm hold and can pull himself up. All that remains then is to find a dry spot and scrape away humus, roots, and ooze.

Everywhere the relationship of grasses and earth is shifting. Dr. Richard Joel Russell of Louisiana State University has described the process of slow conversion to firm ground. First is the easy movement over the still water of the hyacinths and their companion growths of alligator grass. Mats attach themselves to shore or join other mats and eventually cover the surface. Below drops the dead vegetation, thickening at the bottom of the water. The mats also grow heavier, providing a base for the invasion of other plants at the top. The work of filling takes place in both directions; eventually a few feet of clear water may stand between a heavy ooze twenty feet deep and a heavy surface cover of plants, grass, and dead matter. Bit by bit the margin of liquid is reduced. Russell concluded that once a distance of only two feet is left, "instantaneous plant invasion" is imminent, and dry earth will soon be there. Transformations are occurring with fantastic rapidity. "The last half century has witnessed greater changes in the Louisiana marshland than probably took place during the twenty centuries preceding." And for this, the hyacinths and associated growths are responsible.

About us rustled a thriving bird life, for here is one of the great bird concentrations of America. A third of all winged things of the continent move about these lowlands the year round, or use them as a place of refuge. It is a bird depot for millions that fly north and south. Plunging exhausted from the sky, many remain here for the winter among the reeds. Others, seeking a warmer locale, move hundreds of miles across the Gulf to Latin America. The southern part of the marshes is a paradise for hunters—the nearest thing left to the old pioneer abundance of game. That day the gulls and terns came in long flights, high in the air. Other birds hovered about the steamer, while some perched among the sedges in the distance. Once we heard the whirring of thousands of wings and caught sight of a descending flock that turned an area many yards wide into a white circle in the surrounding green.

The scene varied little for a time, a series of flats clinging closely to the water, cut by countless openings of streams and an occasional lake. For an hour at a time there would be no sign of human occupancy; then a turn would bring us upon a solitary shack in the wet wilderness, perched atop a foot or so of ground on the water's edge. Its roof was thatched with palmetto, long ago well dried in the blazing sun, and it stood upon stilts, a necessary precaution. If it had once known paint, that was now well baked away or washed away. Not less weatherbeaten was the smiling man who hurried out of the door at our approach and waved hello and good-by. Occasionally, where a fair-sized levee raised itself, ten or twelve houses made a small settlement; almost always with a huddle of boats to the front—pirogues, luggers, a houseboat or two.

On such circumscribed points men and women had turned to agriculture whenever they could, working every inch of dry soil susceptible to tillage. These families nursed small strips and mounds of earth where they found them, though they might sometimes look at the surrounding moistness and wonder how long it would hold off. This luxury of a few yards of ground meant also a few head of cattle. Cows swam from one dry ridge to the next and chewed at the edges of the greenstuff. Sometimes the owners had built double lines of fences across the shallower parts of the water, to make certain that the stock would not venture into places that were too deep. Once we saw a pair of youths who were alternately swimming and using their pirogues to drive home their recalcitrant cows, while their mother stood in the doorway and called out directions. In another place, where water crept high, several families had chickens cooped in small boxes attached under the house floor. A small boy held up a wriggling crawfish to us and babbled happily; what he said was incomprehensible but definitely French.

The Captain nudged me and called my attention to the water. Its color had lightened and seemed to lighten further with every mile or so. We were approaching the Gulf by degrees. Up the bayous moves the brine, and the Captain explained that it varies with season, month, and day. In times of low water, or during dry spells, the blue waters push far inland. When flood time comes, the bayou flow moves rapidly southward, the darker currents forcing out the Gulf water. But always the brine water creeps in when it can, its

Eugene Delcroix

There is silence, and a sense of mystery, in the cypress swamp.

Percy Viosca, Jr.

Caught, perhaps for days, on a hyacinth-choked bayou.

Dan Leyrer

Man with the rake, in a field of drying shrimp.

The Grand Isle tree is twisted, driven, scalded by the spray.

The place is half-land, half-water, or combinations of the two.

"A pirogue—she can travel on a dew."

Thatched against the sun, propped against the wind.

The Archbishop gives blessing to fishing fleet and families.

"Le Bon Dieu will proteck us . . ."

"You got to know how to grapple for the oysters, yes."

Home on the half-shell—oysterman's house on an island.

Farm Security Administration

Everybody works around a trapper's hut.

At five, he can tell you about fur-stretching.

tinge to be detected as much as a hundred miles or so from
shore line on occasion.

With the waters moves a constantly shifting life. Many
Gulf fish swim up the bayous for miles, and plants that are
salt-resistant press inward. As the brackish waters slacken,
some disappear, but there are variations and eccentricities.
Salt forms are found far inland; fresh-water types move un-
expectedly toward the sea. One element invades the other; the
two crowd and shift. Sometimes the native takes a fresh-water
fish in his bayou at dawn, a salt-water one by night. He calls
a salt fish by the name of a fresh-water one, and vice versa;
the state's list of fish is, accordingly, a conglomerate and con-
fusing one.

From time to time there would appear, some distance off
in the wide marshes, elevated areas three or four feet high, or
slightly higher. These were inland "islands"—rises of sand,
shell, and earth above the surrounding wetness, products of
changed conditions through the centuries. Once they were
fringes of the coast, barrier beaches along the Gulf. Then the
shore line advanced farther to the south and they were left
behind, stranded. Some are short and narrow, others as much
as eighteen miles long and two miles wide. Surmounting them
are rows of oak which have fixed root in the first earth that
will support them so close to the coast, to cling tenaciously
in a setting that is not always encouraging. From the trees
comes the name of these ridges—"chênières," oaks. The tree
fights hard here. By its nature it withdraws from salt—only
a few feet below the ground is a saline base—but once it takes
hold, it gives up only after a bitter struggle.

We talked, the Captain and I, of the chênières and their
histories. On some of them very early Indian tribes settled,
as the best points in this region. In the shells and sands are

found traces of past habitation. It is believed by some that here human sacrifices to the sun gods and others once took place. White men have, like the Indians, found the chênières pleasant places of habitation. On one of them we saw pigs spending the heat of the day under four upright posts, protected by a thick palmetto roof. It was a tropical sty. Near-by were outdoor garages for old automobiles—no sides to the structures, but sturdy palmetto tops. With perhaps only a mile or so of roadway on the chênière—and that only a glue-like spread in bad weather—there seemed little use for such machines, even before gasoline rationing, as the Captain chuckled. But an alert salesman had caught the trapper or shrimper just after a good season, and a man with a car m'sieu —ah, he is a man with a car! See how she shines! [1]

Past chênières, past bayou bank settlements, past inlets and outlets, we had gone only part of our way. The traffic was dense, with heavy barges, vessels bearing machinery, luggers of sea food, and pirogues. Oil companies had cut their own canals to the main route, adding further to the movement, their ponderous ships moving along with the shallow-water boats of small fishermen. In the confusion of transportation, our dinner was set before us. Over shrimp jambalaya—a combination of rice, peppers, shellfish, tomatoes, and genius with a French accent—we talked of the congestion, and of the earlier days of this passageway; and that led to the subject of the d'Estréhans and the Harveys, who made it possible in the first place. I remembered some things, the Captain made

[1] On one of the chênières remote from such things as tax collectors, when a man bought a new car he did not bother about an annual license for it. One was enough. A visitor to the island found six machines, each with a license for a different year—1933 through 1939. It is a pleasant thought. . . .

his own contributions, and the cook and the helper added their own. Out of it came a biography of a ditch.

The old French colony was not well settled, its capital city only recently founded, when a small canal was dug in the early 1720's between the Mississippi levee and the Barataria route, over which we had just come. The land was part of an extensive grant by the king to Jean Baptiste d'Estréhan des Tours, royal treasurer and comptroller of the colony. It was perhaps intended primarily for drainage, but from the first, men with goods to transport saw the value of this direct route; its possession was to make possible a princely life for its owners. By 1737 Monsieur d'Estréhan realized that the waterway called for expansion. Near his plantation was the small settlement of Mechanickham, later Gretna, populated by German settlers who had come to Louisiana when John Law's "Mississippi Bubble" floated over Europe. The canal owner would give a short tract of ground to any man who would help enlarge his passage. For the purpose, small white farmers or laborers were preferred to Negro slaves. Men sickened and died in these swamp waters. A slave cost good money; a white man represented no investment. His life was his own to lose. Many accepted the offer, and used wooden spades to cut a line extending more than five miles, twelve feet wide and four-and-a-half feet deep. The work took four years.

And now the route's full potentialities were on the way toward realization. Out of the swamps Monsieur d'Estréhan took heavy supplies of timber, and from his fields he shipped the fruit of his orchards and truck gardens, dairy and other products. At the same time, in both directions, moved trappers, Indians with goods to trade, men shipping shrimp, fish, furs, indigo, and other produce. Sometimes there was other cargo—men and women seeking homes in the lands now opened. It was the easiest passage to a vast territory to the south and west of the Mississippi.

The d'Estréhan fortunes grew. For nearly two centuries the canal remained in the hands of one family, in constant use, despite wars, hurricanes, and steady enlargements. In time another d'Estréhan appeared, a grandson who was to exceed his predecessor's breadth of enterprise—Nicholas Noel d'Estréhan, planter, manufacturer, and, not least, art enthusiast and individualist. For his wife he ordered a residence along the canal which was described, even in that day of expansive living, as "baronial." Years were spent in its construction. He put up a museum next to it, and imported a variety of paintings and statuary from France. His neighbors snickered at the thought, and called it "d'Estréhan's Folly." He believed that children should learn art, and he took them often to visit the place, always taking care to have the statues draped in advance—in long Mother Hubbards. In the meantime, work proceeded slowly on the magnificent building, and Madame d'Estréhan died before the last ornamentation was installed. In tribute to her, he ordered it closed forever. No one ever looked inside its boarded doors; eventually it burned down.

Another, less quixotic episode of this d'Estréhan survives. Part of the German settlements, occupied by some of the children of those who had dug his grandfather's canal, took his name, and he was a patron of the people. As Alice Rightor McCall recounted the incident, one day one of the men of the settlement was accused of taking a d'Estréhan skiff. The master sent a slave after him and, deciding that the culprit was not properly respectful, ordered for him the same treatment which he might mete out to a slave. The German was bound and lashed by the slave driver. Angry feeling arose among his neighbors. The victim was persuaded to sue, and won a $10,000 judgment. D'Estréhan was infuriated. He gave that part of his property near the German settlers to the state, ordered that his name was never to be used in connection with it, and wiped it and its residents from his sight.

Monsieur d'Estréhan had four children—a son, Azby, and three daughters, Adele, Eliza, and Louise. One day the father—who, incidentally, had lost an arm in a sugar-mill accident—summoned Louise to his presence. She was in her early teens at the time, and was the most able of the four children. He told her that she was from thenceforth to handle his accounts for him, taking charge of his office near the canal. Louise left early girlhood behind and became a business woman. Sitting on her high stool, she worked at accounts of traffic, at upkeep of other large affairs, and, in time, the further widening of the family water passage. One day her father brought in a friend, Captain Joseph Hale Harvey. A thorough man of the sea, Harvey was a bon vivant, eternally joking, eternally making bets. Once, he said, he was challenged to a duel. As recipient of the demand, his was the right to select weapons. He sent word, "Harpoons." The duel never took place. But to Orleanians the Captain was best appreciated for his remarkable accomplishment in getting a meal out of the old miser McDonogh. The Scotchman never had a dinner guest. It was generally understood that he ate at a table with a large drawer in which, if callers came, he could quickly secrete his plate. Harvey made a wager, picked his time carefully, called, and sat down. He talked interminably, outsat McDonogh, and got part of the meal. Quel homme!

Louise was not quite sixteen when a servant brought her a message. She was to marry Captain Harvey. Mrs. McCall's version is that the instruction was even more explicit: she was to put on the wedding dress that her father had ordered for her. Louise, trained to obedience, nodded and did not ask Papa a question. She and the Captain, twenty years older than she, had nine children. The canal was hers when her father died.

For his young bride, Captain Harvey did a properly sumptuous thing. Like his father-in-law in his day, he felt that his wife was a jewel which required perfection in setting, and he built for her, in 1844, his conception of it—an English castle. It was a schoolboy's chromo. No architect was needed, for the Captain knew what he wanted. He made another wager, that he could finish it in three months; and he won. He used non-slave Negro artisans of near-by "Free Town," who were among the best craftsmen in Louisiana, and he smiled happily at the result. Three stories of unprecedented height and size for its surroundings, "Harvey's Castle" had battlements, bastions, casements, and, as everybody said, the canal for a moat. All that was needed, some smiled, was Elaine, the lily maid, in a pirogue, paddling along with the trappers.

The Castle was the wonder of the area. Navigators used it as a guide mark. From its ornamental turrets the family could see the river's curves and the winding waterways for many miles. Inside were thirty rooms, some eighteen feet high, and enormous corridors as large as the outside porches. The central hall, extending through the depth of the house, gave entrance to the grand double stairway of walnut. The first floor offered the "red parlor," in crimson brocade, with chandelier and fifty red candles. On the second floor was a replica of this room in green, complete to candles. Legends grew up about the gardens, with their conservatories and their statuary. Many were certain that the paths were paved with silver dollars. This was denied. But life was free-handed at Harvey's. A private boat carried guests across the river, docking at the entrance of the grounds, for a long promenade through a double row of oaks. Presiding over all the grandeur were the Captain and his wife, "Queen Louise."

Like the d'Estréhans, the Captain worked at the canal, expanding and enlarging it. In time he conceived a new plan—construction of locks between the canal and the river. During most of the period, produce was unloaded on one side of the levee, carried over the top, and reloaded on the other. An ingenious scheme had been devised, the "submarine railway," horsepowered. Boats slipped up to the levee and were maneuvered into place over a low-slung holder. This was pulled along tracks that reached out of the water, up the mound, over it, and into the water at the other side. It was effective, but time-consuming. As for locks, many feared that with such a connection high water might mean that the raging Mississippi would pour over the surrounding country. Eventually, however, the Captain obtained legislative permission to place the locks. For years preliminary work went on. Quicksand developed; Civil War and Reconstruction intervened; the Castle was occupied and damaged by Federal and parish forces. With a decline in general business, canal receipts fell off. The Captain died, and his widow found herself alone with a considerable family, a considerable debt, and mounting problems.

Now beyond middle age, Louise Harvey put to use the things she had learned as a girl in her father's office. She left her red and green parlors and took over active management of the canal and other affairs. In a day when woman's place was still well restricted, she called on other businessmen, borrowed from banks, and made investments. She formed a land company of her own, a ferry firm. She became known again as "Queen Louise," but for different reasons. At seventy-six, she was scaling ladders to watch new work at the canal. Through it all she remained serene and unharried. It was said of her that she "never raised her voice in anger to her children, and always wore silk"—indeed a tribute. At the turn of the century she was able to inaugurate a program that she had long held before her—to bring back the family fortune by the construction of her husband's locks. And then she died.

Another Captain Harvey saw the project through, over a period of years—Horace Hale Harvey, who resembled his father in some respects. Born in the Castle, he lived his early years about the canal. Its water was mixed with his blood, he said, and he was never rid of it. He called himself "a self-made man despite Papa's efforts to educate me." Sent away to school, he ran away repeatedly, to return home, until the old Captain told him, "At least I can make you the best damned canal man and poker player in the world." The son said that the father made good the second half of the promise; bayou and river people said that he succeeded in the first. He took over the canal and it thrived, with a quick increase in transportation through the locks.

But the old Castle, cracked and shabby, had fallen on bad days. The Harveys gave it up. For a time it was a pleasure resort, and again, though under dissimilar circumstances, special boats made the trip to it across the river. When the venture failed, the Castle became a rookery. Its many rooms were rented as tenement quarters. The chandeliers and mantelpieces had long since been removed. Shutters fell and were not replaced. On the porches women did their washing. The great stretch of liveoaks over which visitors made the impressive approach also went, as the town crept up about the remains. One day, in 1924, I stood between the Harvey Canal and this great pile of rococo grandeur, and saw workmen attack it with their implements. The foundations of this ninety-day quick-construction job were in perfect condition eighty years afterward, all cypress sections intact. But no one wanted a decayed castle; and besides, there was a pressing new need for its site.

Horace Hale Harvey had been working in another direction. Other protected inland waters stretched to east and west, from the Atlantic to the Texas coast. He and others advanced a concept—an all-water, protected route for cheap transportation along or near the Gulf and the Atlantic Ocean. For years there were talk, and organization, and agitation. In 1925 the Federal government purchased the Harvey Canal and locks, and since then many millions of dollars have been spent in improving the waterway and developing it and other parts of the vital Intracoastal Canal system of the South. Today a widened, deepened water highway extends through the Louisiana lowlands, over lakes, over bayous, over cut-offs, into Texas. And men have learned the value in war—greater even than in peace—of this safeguarded channel through a teeming territory. Others meanwhile work for eventual completion of "the longest canal in the world," from Boston to the Rio Grande, through the bayous of Louisiana.

That was why, late that afternoon, as we left the Intracoastal route, we drank at our table to the d'Estréhans and the Harveys, pères et fils, and their works.

§ 2. *Fury on the Gulf*

THE SCENE warmed with the soft wind from the south as we approached the Gulf and the quasi-tropics of Louisiana. The sense of the sea grew stronger, the land wilder as it dropped toward the water level. The way ahead was a puzzle in geography, Barataria—a bay without shore, in the way most people think of that term. It is a wide, protected body of inland water bounded by clusters and clumps of islands, peninsulas, and remnants of earth. In every direction run streams and streamlets, passes, bayous, inlets, all twisting about rises of sand and earth. The bay is about fifteen miles long, five or six miles across at its broadest. Its branchlike connections give access to a highly confused terrain covering 400 or so square miles. Unless one knows the route, it is almost impossible to find a path through water that shoals and deepens but seldom drops to more than six feet or so; and often this labyrinth has dead endings and circular windings on which a man may wander bewildered for many days. Our path lay due south, but we knew that with the proper native pilot we could turn in any one of a dozen directions and ride the water as long as we desired, remaining out of sight of others if we wished, yet finding, when we asked, a quick stopping place within easy reach of a small town or settlement.

Few strangers who come to live in this area can master its secrets. The residents say simply that one must be born here to get the feel of the slow waters. And if he is a native he can make his way even in the dark.

About us was a place of tawny sand and fast-growing palmetto, of Spanish dagger plant, and the sudden blooming of scarlet flowers to match the richness of all hues in this environment. The sky came far down, a covering that seemed to hang close over the day, brightening early and remaining illuminated until late; and the sun beat with fervency upon the luminous green of the vegetation. Even at the end of the afternoon we had to shade our eyes. The native learns to squint against the violence of this light as he moves about his daily work, and to stay in the deep shade when the day is at its most ardent.

In a few moments we skirted through a pass, reached the Gulf, and advanced a few miles into its calm. Soon the land was lost to view behind us; so like a low table is the coast line that one must be close upon it at most places to distinguish it. Then we slipped along the shallow shore waters and picked out the many points of beach that can be reached only by water of Gulf or of bayou. Today, as on most days, it was a restful vista. Yet quietly in process before us was an unending struggle. No other part of the Gulf edge is such a battlefield of elements, all working for change, upbuilding, disintegrating by turn, wearing, scouring, or depositing.

At the water's edge the long ridges of sand are the first barriers against other forces. Behind them are reaches of shallow water, caught in lagoons or bays, with slight inlets leading to the Gulf. In them animal and plant life stir, and the thickening mixture sometimes becomes land. And meanwhile other agencies are at work. Over much of the coast is felt the powerful influence of the Mississippi. For long centuries the stream has been dropping a heavy burden of soil, miles deep, upon the lower end of the state. A slow sinkage of surrounding earth results, a tilting of the land at both sides. Along the coast, and particularly its eastern part, subsidence is vanquishing other forces, and the outlines are grotesquely irregular—thinned peninsulas, sinking strands of land, "split islands," which are twin turns of ground stretched into the water with an opening between, identified by geologists as disappearing remnants of stream banks where once there was dry land. In some cases the ends of other levees have dropped into marsh or water and the waiting Gulf has advanced into the lower channel, turning bayou mouths into bays.

On the lower ends of the bayous residents are forced to retreat on successive occasions. Many have shown me the places, miles down, where their grandfathers lived. Nearer are the sites of the old homes of their fathers, homes in which they themselves were born; and they can relate how, as children, they were waked in the night and taken to places of safety. One dusk, in storm or in flood, the water reached suddenly higher. Only a foot or two, but that meant the difference between a dry ground and one lost under a slow current. How long will the present settlers remain in the places they have chosen? Who knows? It will be time to worry when the bad day comes. At one point a smiling native took me along an old road that followed his bayou. The peninsula of earth gradually narrowed, then it reached a spot at which the water began. For a foot or so ahead the fading marks of an old pathway could be detected under the wavery surface; then it was gone. The minnows and the salt fish were now its only travelers. He pointed ahead: "That used to be a plantation down there—big-big." Now it was water. "She's going fast." He shook his head and shrugged. There seemed to be nothing else to say, and we went back.

The shore is spotted with thousands of islands, long archipelagoes, or single strips of sand. As elsewhere, the water takes and gives, but the taking is by far the greater. Some of these islands "travel," building at one end, losing at the other. Often, however, the wear is at both extremities, and wind and water may tear away stretches of several hundred feet within a day. Some storms have lashed small islands to fragments. Less spectacular, but equally effective in the end, is the slow sucking away of sand year by year.

Most of these uncounted islands are inhabited only by birds. Unknown or forgotten lines in the water they appear, seen from a distance. But there are a few whose histories have been connected through the centuries—four islands in particular— as places of terror and pity, victims of the violence of man and of nature.

Where Barataria Bay meets the Gulf, three bars of tawny sand and soil have been built in irregular outline. In the center, Grand Isle, smallest but sturdiest of the group; at her sides, Grand Terre and Chênière Caminada. Miles to the west is the other, Isle Dernière—Last Island. Eighty-five years ago each was a place of warm excitement, crowded with men and women who sought the pleasures of a resort on these Gulf-bathed spots, watering places of the pre-Civil War South. Today three of them have been smashed as if by a heavy fist. Grand Isle alone remains and holds together.

The bay's entrance lies only forty miles or so south of New Orleans by straight line. But the early Frenchmen, preoccupied as they were with the Mississippi, paid little attention to the section. A few great grants were made to men of prominence or favor, but little was done by them to develop the wide acreages. A fort was established, to guard these vulnerable stretches from the Spaniards or other enemies, and this was placed in the center of a circular levee which held off the marshy areas in all directions. A few men ventured into these distances—adventurers, trappers, explorers—who sometimes did not return because Indians or the locale had taken them as victims. With the beginning of the Spanish regime, in the 1770's, the area became of more interest, and several grand attempts were made at development in the manner of the indigo and cotton estates on the Mississippi—duchies about the fringes of the Gulf, slaves on the beaches. An account is extant, too, of one François Anfrey, a Norman, who went on a trip to the Gulf reaches, visited the present Grand Isle and, like a sagacious Norman, decided that what he saw was a good thing. Returning to the capital city, he applied for and received all or most of it in a grant—a stretch seven miles long, a mile wide at its widest, shaped somewhat like an oyster shell.

Monsieur Anfrey tried agriculture and cattle. Others about him operated on a larger scale. They set up spreading sugar plantations and sent down overseers, with instructions to produce crops as large as those in other parts of the colony. But the ground was too salt; a sudden wind often bathed the fields in brine. There were auctions, and the first supervisors and slaves departed. But others came, with different projects and different crops. Among them was Jacques Rigaud of Bordeaux, a shrewd man, whose realism limited his ambition. Others appeared and disappeared; Rigaud remained, and the Rigauds never left the island. They are there today, and from their holdings, reduced but sufficient, they support their families.

Next to Grand Isle, separated by less than a mile, was a chênière, then known as the Isle of the Chitimacha, after the Indians who had populated it. Francisco Caminada, wealthy Spanish merchant of New Orleans during the years of the dons, acquired it and it has borne his name since then, though all signs and evidences of his ownership soon disappeared. (The natives pronounce the name in a rush, with the accent on the last syllable.)

The islands dropped from attention after a time, and the great enterprises were forgotten. A new kind of settler moved downward, in place of slave and master. These were quiet men, obscure men, who had no means to acquire large holdings: Frenchmen, Acadians, Spaniards, a German or two, who had lived on less desirable grounds that the plantations did not take, on bayous which they wished to leave. Their needs were small—a share of food, a wife, a glass of wine on occasion. When they found a short stretch of Gulf ground that they liked, they took it; who was there to oppose? Some of the Indians remained, and from them the newcomers learned ways to live in this strange scene. From the sea and the low-lying lakes and bayous they took succulent fish, such as they had never seen before. They discovered oysters and shrimp, and they moved about the marshes and caught fur animals. From the sea the waves washed broken trees and bits of lumber, and these the men fashioned into small huts, always with a porch or galerie so that they could rest and sleep in the soft air. Some built their quarters upon the shore of their islands. After a high wind and water, they learned better; the best place was always as far in as possible, on the highest elevation that could be found. The families made their salt in iron pots, condensing the brine water. And the wives and children, working at the soil while the men were away, tried to raise edible things as best they could.

The days were long for the men of the Gulf. They rose early for the best fishing; they relaxed in the day's great heat; they worked again in the cooler hours of the afternoon. Occasionally they went out for long periods on the waters or in the marshes, and when the skies darkened and lightning struck, the women wept and prayed before their shrines. The rains, and the furies that accompanied them, came suddenly and savagely in the fall season. Then hurricanes, born in the West Indian waters, roared upon the Gulf and threw themselves against the soft barriers. Again, however, it was only the welcome downpour of the summer months, raging for an hour, then gone; and on such days the men and women listened to the beat on their roofs and were content with their uneventful lives.

About Barataria Bay, among the mazes of water and land, the settlers learned the best passages, and eventually some devised new and quick ways to get to the center of the colony's population, to New Orleans itself. Before long they were filling their boats with fish, well wrapped in green leaves and covered with grasses to protect them from the sun, and with oysters and other products for ready sales. They reached the city through d'Estréhan Canal, and they offered their wares at the wharves or as they walked through the streets. They had a well-known cry—"Bar-a-tar-r-ia!" The housewife or the housekeeper hurried to the street, eager to buy before the supply was gone.

Just how the name of Barataria was given to the place is something of a mystery. It was applied from an early date in the state's history; before 1830 a mapmaker had set it down. Some have noted that Sancho Panza gave this title to his far-off island domain in Cervantes' "Don Quixote," and it has been surmised that the early colonists in good (or bad) humor chose it because the locale was so inaccessible. But there are other possibilities. As Lyle Saxon has pointed out, the term is found in Old French, in Portuguese, and in Provençal. Sometimes it denotes a thing that is cheap, inexpensive; again, it connotes trickery and double-dealing. A more specific suggestion is provided in one of the modern definitions of a related word, "barratry"—theft, desertion, or sinking of a ship by its officers and men. Any one of these interpretations could appropriately be applied to the vicinity.

For meanwhile another kind of enterprise was passing up the waters. When it started is not known. But some of the swarthy people of the Gulf were carrying the products of small-scale smugglers—silks and furnishings and assortments of wine, and any other items that came to hand. Men of many nationalities, who lived in countries to the South, were ever ready to provide such goods; or the more daring of the Gulf dwellers might not be averse to a bit of piracy on occasion. The repressive commercial policies of France and then Spain encouraged men to engage in such enterprises. Grand Isle and its surroundings seemed designed by nature for trade in contraband.

Before long, others outside Louisiana learned of this small heaven of obscure dealings. For years the Caribbean had been a lake of pirates, spotted by nests of men who preyed on the rich prizes of the Spanish Main, the newly mined gold of Mexico and Peru, and the other wealth that poured into the holds of vessels moving between Old and New Worlds. Martinique and Guadaloupe provided the main headquarters. The life was a careless, dangerous one, free of hindrance, rich in reward. But the early 1800's saw trouble for the freebooters. England captured their retreats, and they realized that they had to give up the trade or find a safe harbor. They knew where to go.

The people of Grand Isle and the surrounding places would waken in the morning to new neighbors, who had moved in during the night and were there to stay—a crew of many hues and many dispositions. Some of the leaders of the local smugglers looked with disfavor on the new arrivals, and acrimonious and bloody quarrels ensued. These were settled, usually, in favor of the new men; or, perhaps, the old Baratarians were taken in by the others. The rest of the islanders went on with their fishing and other minor pursuits much as before. The freebooters thrived. To the south, Colombia rebelled against Spain; ever on the alert for a worthy cause, the newcomers cast their lot with the new country, at long distance. Presto! they were privateers with letters of marque, license to attack the vessels of His Most Catholic Majesty. If, by accident, the ship was not always that of Spain, eh bien . . . a man can make a mistake, can't he?

Ships disappeared in the Gulf, and their crews were never found. Louisiana was American now, since 1803, but the tolerant French population did not turn Yankee. Used to dealing with men of Barataria, they saw no reason to give up their old habits. Besides, the new masters in Washington were, unaccountably, forbidding importation of slaves; the Baratarians were always ready to provide supplies of the black flesh.

In New Orleans two men of France appeared. One was Jean Lafitte, elegant, knowing, and mysterious; the other, his elder brother, Pierre, sturdy and discreet. In the special morality of the mixed metropolis they took unparalleled roles. They began as middlemen for confederates on the Gulf; they ended by taking over the trade. Until that time it had been a brawling, inefficient enterprise; now it was organized. Jean, a man of the world, who could be violent or suave as the occasion asked, inspired confidence among his helpers and also among businessmen with whom he dealt. Practically all merchants were his customers; those who were not, found their competitors outselling them. Finally, he was a lusty fellow; about him many a woman, French or American, high-born or low, sighed and asked questions. South Louisiana, it seemed, was his.

On Grand Terre, across from Grand Isle to the east, was Jean's headquarters. Here he set up a storehouse of impressive dimensions, a well-stocked slave barracoon, a set of heavy fortifications. Sometimes one island was too small, and supplies spread over to Grand Isle. Between the two places was a deep and dependable natural pass. It permitted easy entrance for a vessel in flight, but the shallow winding ways inside the bay made pursuit impossible for men who did not know the labyrinths. The bay now filled with small and large ships, red-sailed luggers, feluccas, schooners, captured vessels awaiting remodeling. The years ahead were golden ones. The population multiplied. Some of the Lafitte men married French and Spanish girls, or brought their own women to the area. To them came Louisianians who heard that there were opportunities, and men of other states and countries, reckless, or hungry, or impelled by any of several motives which might suggest that this was a good place for them at the moment. The mass was polyglot—Portuguese, Malays, Slovaks, Santo Domingans, Cubans, Orientals, French, English, Germans, Americans; eyeless, armless men who had grown old in the trade; silent young men who had deserted navies and armies for any of a number of reasons, in other quarters of the world. Occasionally, too, men walked the beaches who bore names that were good ones in Louisiana.

The pirates operated over most of the coast of Louisiana. Toward the west they set up a base at Isle Dernière, a larger place than the others, twenty miles long, in some places a mile wide. It was an isolated, secure spot, and some of the band eventually settled there. Up many of the bayous moved the Lafitte vessels, in convoys, heavily stocked and heavily guarded.

Many tales, impossible to verify, have come down: knife fights among drunken men on the shores; unruly assistants strung up by their thumbs or placed upon the gibbet while the throng watched; quick deaths in the Gulf for crews which might otherwise, sometime and somewhere, have told embarrassing tales. Through it all, the silent lesser folk watched from their palmetto huts, in the glare of the burning ships, and thanked le bon Dieu that they had no part in such affairs.

Jean Lafitte moved about Louisiana with aplomb, on fine terms with everybody—or almost everybody—on the streets of New Orleans, despite a price that was on his head. Up near-by Bayou Lafourche he jaunted, to country dances, at which fascinated Acadian boys learned of the ways in which they, too, might join the crew. And sometimes—but not often —he was a guest at a great home for dinner. Handbills, circulated openly, told of fine wares for sale, and public auctions were held on or near the islands, and at "The Temple," a former Indian burial mound on the way to New Orleans— the location chosen for the convenience of city customers. A number of men of position who had special dealings with the chief, went to his headquarters on Grand Terre for visits. They were served superbly prepared dishes—fish, fowl of the marshlands, fine liquors; and, they reported, their host was a man of impeccable manners.

About Lafitte were lieutenants: Dominique You, once an artilleryman in Napoleon's service; Louis Chighizola, "Nez Coupé" (Split Nose), who supposedly received his name when he fought a duel with a knife for a prize of war, a handsome woman, chained to a post; and Johnny Gambi, sometimes described as the most bloodthirsty of the band.

(Jean, the islanders told me, was once forced to dismiss Johnny for his annoying sadism.) Meanwhile, old Jacques Rigaud stayed on. Some described him as a partner or ally of the band; the present generation of Rigauds denies this vigorously, maintaining that he was merely a friend of Jean's and that the pirate visited him from time to time. No enemy of the Lafittes could, of course, have survived in the territory he and his band dominated.

As the critical year of 1814 approached, matters took an unpleasant turn for the Baratarians. They had become a bit too bold, and the government was arming strongly against them. The Battle of New Orleans was in the offing. The British advanced about the Gulf. Emissaries called on Lafitte to offer him $30,000 and a naval captain's post if he would join them and guide them up the mysterious water approaches to the city. Lafitte put them off, communicated with men in power in the state and offered his assistance in the defense. But the Louisiana officials were not willing to accept it. An American fleet reached Grand Terre, destroyed the fortifications, and brought back a heavy catch in goods and vessels. Lafitte, in hiding, was still ready to join the Americans, and Andrew Jackson, his forces badly outnumbered, accepted him and his men.

The bayous almost brought about the undoing of the American forces at that. Although Jackson plugged up several of these waterways above the city, to prevent the British from entering the Mississippi and moving down upon New Orleans, the enemy enlisted the aid of Spanish fishermen of the marshes, who led them to a point within a few miles of the capital. But the defending forces, including the pirates, did the impossible, and won. For their part in the battle Lafitte and his corsairs were praised and pardoned. They found themselves legal heroes. They were gratified and appreciative of their changed status, it appears. But this new glory, unfortunately, was not profitable, and so the tinsel wore off. Jean slipped off to devious ventures in other places, and some of his men went with him. Dominique You followed his chief, then returned to New Orleans to become a politician and a popular spokesman among French-Italian elements of downtown New Orleans. "Nez Coupé" Chighizola lived respectably in his own house on Grand Isle and owned a stand in the French Market of the city. Gambi, by reputation the cruelest of them all, moved to Chênière Caminada, where he engaged in assorted enterprises and also raised a sizable family. The lesser men moved in and out of the islands, and some scattered west to the old base at Isle Dernière. An unknown number of the corsairs also migrated up into the mainland bayous, where their descendants are occasionally found in curious places. For a time the Federal government remembered its difficulties with the Baratarians and obtained land on the tip of Grand Terre, site of the former Lafitte fortification. It began the construction of a fort. Then interest lagged, work halted, and Barataria faded from attention.

The earlier islanders went back to their less ambitious ways, to fishing and trapping and, sometimes, to a little haphazard smuggling on the side. With money no longer flowing so easily, others turned to experiments in agriculture, seeking to find crops that would best fit their peculiar soil. Orange groves were planted, and long rows of rich, shining fruit covered the islands here and there. Again, sugar cane was attempted, this time on Grand Terre. A court placed the value of one plantation at $38,000 in 1831. On Chênière Caminada a considerable group of the former pirate followers congregated. Little houses, with large families about them, spread over the flat expanse, and in addition to the other crops, wide vineyards were set out, carefully tended by the French and Spanish and Italians and those others who mingled there.

For years the island people had their small world to themselves, as before. Then, during this more placid day, men and women from the rest of Louisiana began to come to the area. The coast was now "discovered" as a place of vacation diversion for the merchants and planters of the state. Each of these four islands received callers, and colonies grew with each year. Great hotels and lesser ones went up on the sands. Families appeared with their servants, to occupy suites or to set up their ménages in cottages built for this purpose. The days were light-hearted—fishing trips into the deep water with the natives as guides, picnics beneath the oaks, explorations for pirate relics. Was it true, M'sieu, all that they said of Lafitte? You know, Jacques, Grand'mère met him once, and she said that he looked more haut monde than all of the haut monde about him. And did you notice the way that young fellow looked yesterday when we asked him if he were related to Nez Coupé?

Isle Dernière became the most celebrated of the resorts. The Louisianians called it the "Little Deauville" of the South. Barouches rolled on the beach. Families brought their full staffs. Leading Creoles remained there from late spring to fall. A drawing survives of the hotel that arose—an expansive undertaking by any standard, with two deep galleries over a raised basement, ornamented pillars, three exterior stairways, not one but three towers in the center, others to the side. Like the island, it was all length—1250 feet, only 37 feet in depth, except for two enormous rooms, the dining hall and dance wing. "The Trade Wind"—the owners bestowed the name with pride, and were later to wonder at the irony of their choice.

In early August of 1856 the season was at its high point. Hotels and cottages on the island were filled; bathhouses and other establishments could not provide for all of the crowds. The vacationers danced, promenaded, admired costumes, exclaimed at the surf. The weather was a procession of rich and shining days. Then arrived one with a slight sharpness in the air. The waves put on additional height, additional magnificence, as if to amuse the visitors. The Reverend Mr. R. S. McAllister of Thibodaux, a guest at a cottage, has written of what he saw.

Great breakers extended almost from horizon to horizon. The billows "grew from day to day larger and higher, ran more and more swiftly and assumed continually a greater variety of form. Retaining an erect posture, and riding forward impetuously upon the surface of the apparently solid main, they looked like things of life . . . We stood upon the shore nearly all the time, loath to be called . . . We did not know then as we did afterward that the voice of those many waters was solemnly saying to us, Escape for Thy Life."

Soon came a morning with ominous clouds in the sky, and a "roaring noise" somewhere in the distance. The cattle, frightened, lowed and tried to break out of their enclosures. Still, few of the visitors were alarmed; a slight blow, that was all. Who had not seen worse in his day? Twenty-four hours later the wind was intensified and the rain beat heavily. By noon the air had darkened until it was hardly possible to see ahead; the wind was now a "furious tempest," and the waves, higher and higher by the hour, seemed to be fighting each other. For the minister and his group, and for others as well, luncheon was a silent meal. About three in the afternoon the wind suddenly reached a new pitch. "It seemed that all the aerial currents in creation had been turned upon us . . . Fiery lightning almost constantly illuminated the heavens, and deafening thunders, peal upon peal, shook our circumscribed islet to its center . . . We were shut up with no possibility of flight, on a narrow neck of land twixt two unbounded seas. In a strife of the elements like this there would have been disaster even in midland; here on this seagirt sandbank it would be tame to say that we were in extreme jeopardy."

Through the raging forces came a small steamer, beaten, buffeted, almost overturned many times on her way from the inland bayous. At the island edge she was soon fighting again for her life. It was evening. In the dark, ordering his men to strip away the upper structure as a last resort, the captain paused for a moment. Through the blast came a dim sound of music from "The Trade Wind." On its polished floors, the dancers were moving unknowingly to their own dirges.

A girl near the windows, gay with champagne or with forced courage, looked down and dropped her fan. The water . . . it had come in, at their feet. And the hall—so high above the ground! Simultaneously a roar outside. Good God, was it thunder? She needed no answer. It was the rumble of water and wind. The waves must be covering the whole island now! A door burst open—then another—waves swept in. Chandeliers danced, furniture rolled about in the advancing water. From the other side came a blow, and now from two directions the sea rolled upon them. Women fell and children screamed as they lost their grasp upon their fathers' coats. The heavy building shook, groaned, seemed to lurch. Men and women grabbed tables, hanging doors, bits of broken timber. Waves that were a story or two high flipped off pieces of galleries, cornices, whole sections. The hotel cracked apart.

The minister at his cottage had gathered his friends, a party of twelve, in the central hall. In any other part of the house they would have perished. The roof was pulled off with a crash; the southern wall blew away, then the other three. The force of the winds superseded gravity's rules; "everything that was in motion went horizontally." Now the hazard became suddenly greater. The wind was driving the waters in upon them, the Gulf on one side, the bay on the other. For a time they lay on the floor, but it was apparent that if they remained there, they would soon be swept away. A short distance off, a small levee had been erected. At its head, a hundred yards from them, was the wooden frame of a children's whirligig; the shaft had been sunk deep, and it held. Getting on their knees, the group crawled along the almost submerged levee top, knowing that a momentary slip would carry them under. They reached the frame. Each felt with his hands for the bar above, and there they clung, arms high in the air, feet as firmly on the water-swept ground as they could hold them. The waves rushed logs and other debris past, missing them by finger lengths. Eventually the wind made the whirligig spin, and the terrified men and women found themselves revolving through the air, in the manner of children at play. If their grip on the boarding should loosen, they would be flung into the water. They held. And gradually the wind slowed, and the waters retreated. Before light came, the sea no longer covered the earth beneath them and they could allow themselves to drop, exhausted, to the ground. From the north came a blast of ice-cold air. Drenched, weakened, they feared now that they would freeze. In the debris they found a large quilt, soggy with sea water, but under it the party huddled for hours. At least it kept off the wind.

When they were able to move about, they found scenes of dread and dismay. "The jeweled and lily hand of a woman was seen protruding from the sand, and pointing toward heaven; farther, peered out of the ground, as if looking up to us, the regular features of a beautiful girl . . . and again, the dead bodies of husband and wife, so relatively placed as to show that constant until death did them part, the one had struggled to save the other . . ."

The island had been scoured almost clean of vegetation, of buildings, of protection for these and other survivors. More than two hundred died; of about one hundred structures, none remained; most of the foundations were pulled away. Men and women wandered about dazed. One would find an aged mother, and fall in a faint over the cold body. A father stumbled upon a child, then led his wife away before she could look. Most of the bodies had been washed far into the Gulf, but now they were brought back by the tide.

Others were hunting for the dead, at the edges. Some of the dark-skinned islanders found irresistible temptation about them. They raced to prostrate Isle Dernière and foraged for furnishings, money in pockets, ornaments at the throat, rich clothing to be stripped if necessary from the bodies, rings to be cut from swollen fingers. The dead were uprooted, their possessions forced from them: earrings, brooches, perhaps the gold of teeth. They were of no value to the lifeless ones, were they? For years the families of the victims were to feel cold horror as they remembered the defiled remains.

Those who lived were uncertain of their own fates for a time. The seas were still furious, the cold did not end, and heavy rains beat down. No vessel could approach for a time. They had little food. The bits of edible stuff that they could salvage were soon gone. One animal was left, a young cow.

How she escaped the hurricane, no one knew. The survivors chased her down with difficulty. As Mr. McAllister observed, she seemed to know that it was their life or hers. Meanwhile they huddled about the wreckage of the little steamer, which had not quitted the island and served now, for the last time, as a shelter. At last came a vessel from the mainland. The arriving men and women rushed along the shore, peering into the faces of those who had survived, and asked a few questions, and then stood there, crying, as they realized that their sons or daughters or husbands, sometimes their whole families, had been wiped out. Men swore, as they stood on the tragic sands, that they would never risk their lives again at any one of those cursed spots. Isle Dernière was the first of the four islands to go; it was not to be the last.

§ 3. *Oleanders and Twisted Oaks*

WE STOOD together at dusk, the old Grand Islander and I, among the lines of oaks that surrounded his house. He slapped his palm against the heavy bark of the nearest tree: "Yes, there's law here agains' cutting them down—law in the heart of everybody. They have save' us, and some day they save us again."

The oaks were like the speaker, worn and—the word is somehow the right one—earnest. They huddled low—stunted and harassed. Against the darkening sky their outlines were things to be carried in the mind for years. They turned toward the north, away from the Gulf. There was compulsion in every line, for they were in retreat from the sea and the wind. Trees struggle here for existence. Trunks curve from the beach, twisted arms reach before them, all in one direction, and limbs are gaunt, or they are covered with scant, discouraged foliage. The few leaves at the top are frizzled by the brine spray, or, sometimes, cut sharply as if with shears. (One wit has declared that such oaks look as if they had been given a military haircut.) As the salt water reaches inland, the trees die where they stand, bleached and desolate for a time, then falling before the waves. At some points about the marsh, on mounds, oaks can be seen that have clung precariously through the years. Earth and sand has been taken away from them by the encroaching brine; the roots, all exposed, rest upon mere shells.

Inland on Grand Isle, in firmer soil, the trees are in less danger, at least for the time. My friend the islander pointed to a tree belonging to his neighbor, that had been struck by lightning a few years earlier. It lay on its side, two thirds of its root system in the air, lifeless and gray. But the other third still dug below the surface, and still sent its life upward, so that a series of new green shoots grew from one side. "That one will last for years," said the old man with pride. Any islander is proud of any tree on the island, and grateful for it.

For Grand Isle did not forget the lesson of Isle Dernière, and of other storms; their neighbors did. Therein lies much of the modern history of these Gulf people. My friend looked happily at the trees: "They are anchor for our soil. They hol' it so that it don' slip off away; and they break the wind when it come on us." He pointed: about him each house had its careful, mathematical rows. Men and women and children had died at Isle Dernière because there was no protection of this kind; the old people of Grand Isle repeated the warning many times, and set to work each year to plant additional green barriers. And as we sat among the oaks in that long twilight and watched the shifting clouds through the crooked branches, I heard again the story that many told me, of the decades that followed that catastrophe of '56.

Slow days, days of abandonment by the rest of the world, came for the Gulf islands. The natives had less money than before: no more vacationers, no more tips and fees. But there were worse difficulties—the dangers of war. During the first part of the Civil War the earlier history of Barataria repeated itself on a minor scale. Supplies of Confederate cotton were loaded aboard small steamers and sent southward through the bayous to the coast. The Federals were unable to blockade every irregular point, and numerous vessels escaped to Havana. The Gulf people cooperated in these enterprises, and were rewarded. But in time the cotton-running stopped. Then, after more days of decline, the pendulum swung again. The strangers came back, not to ill-remembered Isle Dernière, but to the other islands, and to Grand Isle in particular. Men with new money and new projects arrived. Hotels went up in the 1880's and '90's where there had been none before. On the site of one of the abandoned plantations at Grand Isle an operator remodeled the slave quarters into cottages for visitors. A set of train cars ran from the Gulf edge to the northern limit of the island, and the enterprise prospered. Like the first men who had ventured into the area, promoters decided that they had found a rich source of profit in these specks upon the Gulf. A great seaport was planned along the protected waters of the bay, with wharves more modern than those of New Orleans; near it, sea-food processing centers of wide proportions were forecast, and a vacation place for the nation was envisioned. A major problem was that of access. Everybody was talking railroads at that time, and a venture was born—the New Orleans, Fort Jackson, and Grand Isle line. Louisianians eventually boasted of it as the only railroad in the world that never reached one of the three places for which it was named. A track was started not far from Harvey Canal, opposite New Orleans, and extended sixty miles south, at a cost of a million dollars. And that was all. Other events intervened. It was Flo Field who once said that something big was always on the fire for Grand Isle but it was never anything but a slow fire, that finally went out.

Over at Chênière Caminada life was crowded and content. The village, with its four hundred small houses, grew rapidly. The French and French-Italian-Portuguese residents tended their vineyards and their orange groves, fished, shot birds, and enjoyed amiable days. Their special pride came to be an enormous church bell, of a peculiarly piercing ring, standing high and shining in its setting of palmettoes. It weighed seven hundred pounds, and ten men were needed to lift it. A former pastor had contributed his silver plate for its making, and when he appealed to the good Catholics about him, they brought forward their own bits of gold and silver, some of it pirate booty that had been long concealed. Young Father Grimeaux took over the church and he came to like his smiling, easy-mannered parishioners. They worried only when causes for worry were upon them; they were less solemn than the Grand Islanders across the way.

The year was 1893, and the annual period when the Gulf people peer anxiously at the skies. September was nearly over, and the islanders reflected happily that there had been few bad winds this time. On the Chênière they looked forward to the week-end dances. Many people were in good mood; the big grapes had produced bountifully, and the sea catch was heavy. A slight chill was in the air, and some went into their yards to cut down trees that they had planned to save for winter firewood. Over on Grand Isle, those timid ones, talking of their precious oaks! The Chênière had always had fewer growths and, see, nothing had happened to it! Men went singing to their work, and good wishes floated over the water. Bonne chance, Auguste. Bonne chance. . . . ("They were fools," mused the Grand Islander. "We told them. They would not listen.")

A few of the older ones noticed things that they did not like—the behavior of the birds, the peculiar colors at dawn. Friday, September 30, brought a black morning. The lightning illuminated the cottages, thunder was unending. The wind picked up and a blast blew without letup, hour after hour. From their fragile homes the families looked forth, their alarm growing slowly. The sea was beating and pouring toward them, then sucking outward again. The women called their children to the home shrines, lit their candles, and remained on their knees, trying to drown out with their words the howl of the winds and the sea. Some burned the blessed green fronds received on Palm Sunday, as they always did in times such as these. Before the Virgin Mary women offered promises, and Father Grimeaux made visits in the rain. For forty-eight hours the air roared.

On Sunday, a letup. The wind slackened—almost ceased— and there came a hush. Many prayed again, in thanksgiving. (According to some, the Chênière people went to their dance that night to celebrate their deliverance. Those whom I have seen deny this.) Suddenly, in the dark hours of the evening, when men and women were sleeping easily again for the first time in days, the wind changed. Its speed has been placed at 100 to 125 miles an hour, a malevolent blast that turned itself upon the Chênière. Tidal waves poured one mound of hostile green-white foam, then another, and another. Within less than twenty minutes, five feet of water had risen over the sand, over everything; shortly after that, the cover was eight feet deep. The little houses were tossed about, broken apart; boats were washed away before men and women could reach them. The island was almost a flat table top; there was little to cling to, little that was rooted. Many reached out that night for branches and treetops that were not there.

Old women saw their sons and daughters try to reach them, then disappear under a wave. A few moments later they themselves were gone. Other women held tight to their babies, screeching as they carried them under the water with them. Some families ran or swam from one shelter to another, to have each in turn collapse on them. Those buildings that were thought to be sturdiest were packed with scores of neighbors. In one instance sixty terrified persons crowded into a home, saw the water rush in higher and higher, and climbed to the top of the house. Then the place was washed from its moorings, and they clung to the roof as to a raft. The house struck an obstruction and fell apart; all were lost.

The Chênière church was smashed to pieces before the eyes of Father Grimeaux. Only the rectory held, precariously. From there he heard the cries of the drowning, and now and then he caught a glimpse of women and children gesturing vainly as they floated away in the dark on bobbing wreckage. He lit a lamp and hurried to the window. It might illuminate a way if some could fight through the water. A few did so, but most were lost; and the priest raised his hands again and again in prayer for those who were dying before him, granting the final absolution of his church. Through the night he stood at his window; through the night, as remnants of the broken church lurched outside about the waters, the bell of the peculiar ring pealed in its tower. The great silver pride of the Chênière was tolling for its dead and dying.

Of one clan of ninety, a small boy survived. Another child, a boy of eight, caught the roots of a lone floating tree, clung to them until he was about to collapse, then used the string of his scapular to lash his hands to his support. The next day he was found, unconscious but alive. A youth of fourteen, naked, without food or water, for eight days held to a raft until he was rescued. The few trees that were on the Chênière served well. Women, floating, half-dead, were caught by their long hair in the leaves and limbs. One man, his strength ebbing, his wife heavy in his arms, tied her hair about one of the branches. She lived; he died. Another woman grasped a tree: "I was there for hours, the waves rubbing my body against the bark. All of the skin was torn away. And the air and the salt water, how they stung!" It was weeks before she could walk about again. In time she learned that she had lost all her family. Another woman, pregnant, was abandoned in the terror of the night. She floated for hours, then discovered herself in low water in which she could walk. She dragged herself for miles through unknown country, delirious, crossing fences in her way, slipping, creeping along ridges in the marsh. At the edge of the water she gave birth to her child, a son. They were found, both dead, the bodies still warm.

Elsewhere along or near the Gulf, the winds forced the waters to greater heights. Waves of thirty feet or more were reported. Up every bayou moved a surge of water, trapping many in their homes, drowning them in a few minutes. In all, more than 1500 were lost. It was a worse catastrophe than the Isle Dernière storm. For weeks bodies were washed back by the waves, bloated, partly eaten by sea creatures; some of the men and women went mad at the sights. The Chênière joined the other island as a dead place of the Gulf. Today men speak of it in fear; pass it, but seldom stop. The only ones who want to go there are the old people on their deathbeds, who ask to be taken back so that they can rest with their fathers.

Grand Isle lived through the hurricane of 1893. Houses were blown down in some places, on the fringes a few died, and all was thoroughly wet; otherwise it was intact. But when the islanders arose the next morning and looked at the tip of adjacent Grand Terre, they found a disconcerting evidence of the winds. Fort Livingston, successor to the Lafitte stronghold, had fallen to a foe against which it had no defense. For years the waves had been pulling at the soil leading to it. Once, on a pleasant plain between the red-brown structure and the Gulf, herds of cows had grazed. Slowly the space had contracted until it became a narrow, unsafe ledge. But few had thought that so firmly anchored a battlement would fail. Now, after the storm, the two outer bastions and all the massive fourth wall had been torn off, their broken corners projecting jaggedly above the waters. Wide stairways, up which men had once marched, were open to the gulls and the pelicans. It was a fort from which no gun was ever fired. Work had dawdled until shortly before the Civil War; the Confederates then took it over. But the Union Admiral Farragut went up the Mississippi between two other forts, captured New Orleans, and Livingston then gave way. In time, it seems, the rest of Livingston must slip into the waiting palm of the sea. After the storm, the last men who made a living on Grand Terre went away. Today there are only the remains of the fort, a lighthouse, and a crumbling sugar chimney on a deserted plantation.

Of the four islands, only one remained intact. But if Grand Isle had escaped the furies of '56 and '93, it suffered at once from something that was almost as bad: a matter of mistaken identity. Erroneous reports spread that it, too, had been wiped out. About this time America was reading *Chita*, Lafcadio Hearn's evocative re-enactment of the end of Isle Dernière. The Greek-Irish romanticist, impressed with the rich beauties of the islands, almost killed the one remaining, with a book. Many mistook Grand Isle for Dernière, and for years few would approach the area. In vain did the island's friends insist that its protected location, out of the line of the worst winds, saves it from the hazards of the elements. It has been said that the isle has survived hell, high water, and Hearn, and not the least of the hazards was the last.

Grand Isle had, with the passing of years, come to depend more and more on its trade and traffic with the rest of the state and country, tourist and otherwise; now it approached bankruptcy. In the hard years that followed, a savior appeared, of whom much is still heard on the island. He was John Ludwig, whose name the people pronounced Jean Ludvig and contracted to "Vic." An islander, son of an islander, he was French despite his name. He inherited from his father a philosophy of the good life. Out of necessity he acquired a knowledge of many things, from farm sales to finance. It was he who devised a way to make island agriculture pay—a planned eccentricity. Sugar, cotton, large-scale orange growing—each had failed. For years the individual islanders had quietly cultivated a few green things of their own, and had learned ways to make them grow despite their handicaps. John Ludwig improved these methods and, at the same time, turned to the problem of marketing.

It was vegetable gardening—with differences. The light earth-and-sand did not seem ideally suitable to his purpose. A heavy rain, a strong wind, might take off most of the top soil. The ground had to be fitted to the new need. First it was nursed and pampered; in Ludwig's words, the crops were "fed by hand." Uniform hillocks were built for the rows, two feet or higher, four feet or wider. Tons of "shrimp bran" —rich refuse after shelling the crustacea at the factories—were dropped inside the mounds long in advance of growing time. Later came a second dosage with similar plant tonics. Windbreaks in the form of heavy straw "hutches" added a final protection against wind and cold. The crops multiplied as in a hothouse. Let rain and wind come, enough soil was left to produce a good growth. Planting began before that of other sections. The intensive cultivation had an end—to beat Florida, California, and other warm sections to the market. For years the speed-up crop came forth on schedule.

"Vic" Ludwig had another idea, and another Gulf peculiarity was put to work. Twice I have gone with the natives on hunts for diamondback terrapin, the small black turtle whose rich meat is among the most delectable known to Louisiana man. The prairie tremblante is rich terrapin ground. We went out in pirogues, and in hip boots, assisted by "terrapin dogs." Reaching a likely place, we put out our dogs and watched while they sniffed about the deceptive terrain. Eventually they set up a barking and pawing of the earth; they had cornered their prey on a dry stretch. They knew well how to stay just out of reach of the steel-like jaws, while they prevented escape to wetter spots. We worked our way to them, used our nets with care, then moved on. Such was the old marsh method. "Vic" Ludwig elaborated upon it. He built what was called the world's biggest terrapin farm, producing 50,000 or more of the turtles for the annual market. All along the Gulf men who went terrapin hunting knew that the Ludwig pens were always ready to pay for a likely snapper. Inside long enclosures bull and cow terrapins were kept, producing heavy volumes of young. (Some maintained production for decades.) Shipped alive, in barrels filled with grass to keep them cool, and sold by the inch, the terrapin brought a price that seemed fabulous to the trapper and sometimes, perhaps, to the man who ordered it in the restaurant.

But few city chefs can evolve from the black turtle what the bayou housewife achieves: simple terrapin stew—fine hunks of the meat, onion, a bit of peppers, bay leaf, flour and, if you can get it, some wine for further flavoring, and all the crisp French bread that is needed to wipe the dish dry of gravy. It is worth going hungry for a day or two in the marsh to come home to such a meal.

John Ludwig became unofficial manager of the island—creditor, arbitrator, "bos," a meaningful word once applied to Jean Lafitte. A boat was needed for a start in shrimping; "Vic" would make a loan. A new house was to go up; it was done according to his recommendations—sturdier foundations, stronger protections than the old ones, and extra trees against the winds. He was hotel operator, storekeeper, postmaster, middleman. It was a genial amalgam of paternalism and absolutism, none the less definite because the stout and smiling "bos" sat in his chair and let others come to him. He saw Grand Isle win back much of its former prosperity during the first three decades or so of the twentieth century. Visitors and business returned, and eventually even the silver bell of Chênière Caminada.

That treasure had been found after the storm of '93, overturned on the beach. Many of the Chênière people had moved to a small settlement near New Orleans, now Westwego. With them they had taken their bell, to keep it in storage. In time another church requested it, and authorities agreed to the proposed transfer. The 700 pounds of beloved silver were placed on a float and started away, the former Chênière folk watching in sullen silence. During the night the vehicle halted and the attendants left it for a moment; or perhaps it was stopped. What happened was never told fully to outsiders; but the bell disappeared. None at Westwego could provide information. It was a complete mystery, yes, m'sieu. Long afterward, a new church was erected at Grand Isle, and the pastor thought that this might be the proper place for the relic. A friendly sheriff made inquiries, discreet but insistent, of a delegation of Westwego men. No one from another section should have their bell, but to place it on the island, just across from the Chênière—that looked right. As Meigs O. Frost told the story, they led the way to a cemetery, and pointed. Negro prisoners dug. They found nothing. Had someone taken it already? The former Chênière natives looked at each other and went to another spot. This time the shovels hit something hard, and the crusted outlines of silver were disclosed.

Father Grimeaux, he who had gone through the terror of the Dernière storm, was serving elsewhere. On a day twenty-five years later he was invited to return to Grand Isle for the blessing of a new church. The invitation carried no mention of the discovery in the cemetery. The priest had never been able to wipe from his memory the horror he had watched from his window on that night long ago. Whenever he heard the unexpected sound of ringing in the dark, his eyes filled. Now, on a boat from New Orleans, with other dignitaries, he approached the scene again. A peal rang out. He caught at his throat: "La cloche! Le même son!" The bell! The same sound! He fell to his knees on the deck, weeping. And again he prayed, as he had on that other occasion, for the men and women who had died about him, in the night, to the tolling of his silver bell.

Grand Isle of today hangs uneasily between boom and depression. At last a road and bridge lead to it. But in wartime it is blacked out, for it is only a short distance from the mouth of the Mississippi, along the Gulf path of the tankers to America's Allies. The area, to which violence has been no stranger, is again close to a fringe of fury. One night I stood on the beach with a group of others, all helpless to do anything, and watched a circle of red out in the Gulf. Until dawn, the water before us was colored by the glow. Few could sleep that night; no one, I think, wanted to sleep. But soon the island returned to its brooding calm in the midst of forces of destruction.

John Ludwig has been dead for five years, and the island has felt the effect. Crops have suffered, the island no longer anticipates the market, and part of the fields have turned to weeds and reeds. Here and there wet, swamp-like stretches reclaim their own. The canals and back levees that John Ludwig supervised, to improve the drainage, are no longer so well cared for. Some of the rear areas are boglike. The terrapin pens have been abandoned. The islanders say that the older generation, which had the taste for such elegancies, is dying away. (But men still catch the turtles around the marshes, and still find customers.) A descendant of that first Jacques Rigaud told me regretfully that the boys of today are turning away from the fields. "They want things easy—they prefer fishing, because it's over, like that."

The island, only a few feet above sea level, seems to be slowly dissolving into the sea. It is not pleasant for the natives to see the hungry waters beat closer. One patriarch stood at the beach: "Look, that's where I used to play ball. It's come half a mile in, already. They used to have a bathhouse on dry land in that direction; now you have to be a swimmer to go there." The beach moves inward, and green and trees retreat at the front. At the back, along placid Bayou Rigaud, the oysters are coming in upon the islanders. As the land washes into silt, the wild beds advance. Near-by are the remains of a small cemetery, on wet ground, about which thousands of small fiddler crabs, each with his large claw doubled neatly over him, scurry with a crackling noise. The tombs are broken; some have sunk, and all are empty. Nez Coupé and other reformed corsairs were buried there. Some say that vandals, hunting gold, once broke into them. The last time I was there an island youth was methodically digging oysters. Sitting on one of the abandoned resting places, we shared some of them, chill and salt from the brackish water; I have seldom tasted better.

In the heart of Grand Isle, the tropics remain: ferns and creepers, wild orchids, tall trees of "angel's trumpets," vegetation of splashing yellows and scarlets, banana plants with elephant-sized leaves and plump, unripened fruit. Everything has added brilliance in this hot, white glare of sand and sky. Transplanted aristocrats, lowering palms, extend in stately aisles. They scorn the spray and the winds; they sway and come back to their upright position. And everywhere that the natives can encourage them to grow are the oleanders, chief ornament of the island: crimson blooms, blazing in the sun, cool whites, and many shadings. The bushes, tough and determined, are evergreen; they may bear color eight months of the year. It is not a cloying odor, or an overpowering one.

The smell that identifies the island longest for me is a combination of the wind, with its reminder of Southern seas, and the warm, light fragrance of this flower.

Bushes reach high and curl over; spear-shaped green leaves meet across pathways to form covered alleys of cool shadow in the sunlight. Under the moon they are still tunnels, open to the lighter sand at the end, spotted with specks of white light. At such times, near one of the aged houses, there are no signs to indicate that this is a tamer night than that in which a freebooter might have wandered under the sky with a dark-haired girl.

It is a salty-rustic existence in some respects. During the day, herds of cows move about the grass; with night, they wander to the surf and there spend the evening, sleeping on the beach or moving silently about in the tide. It is a novel experience, this, bathing in the moonlit, phosphorescent waters with a set of bovine companions. On a darker night, especially for one who takes a final dip after a visit at one of the several near-by bars, it may be more than novel to bump suddenly against a mysterious wet hide.

Small houses and small paths conceal themselves among the palmettoes and oleanders. A trip on foot is a pleasant lesson in informality. Probably a hundred lanes curve and branch about the low ground, covering it in much the fashion that the bayous spread over the rest of Louisiana. The ground plots and houses sit next to each other in hodgepodge fashion, with few lines of separation; paths cut along sides of houses, through front yards and back, across fences with steps. I have never mastered the trick of telling such a half-seen community roadway from a lesser footpath in an islander's own yard; but I have made a number of good island friends by these mistakes. Olive-skinned children, with straw hats far back on their heads, hold open the gates, but they are not inclined to talk. Neither they nor their fathers, in most cases, have been off the island. Their names? Reluctantly they tell: Azalie Bourgeois, Lindbergh Boisblanc, Don Ameche Naquin. (There is obviously a movie pavilion.)

Most of the older houses have the indispensable porch, where men can sleep and women can fan. The curtains, flying back from the heavy batten windows, reveal large beds with the important mosquito bars in place. Few places, I will warrant, provide so many wind markers, thermometers, and barometers to the square yard. In many houses there is one of each; to lack them might mean death in September. Almost every place has a small bird-home, elevated high in the air on a pole. Propped against both walls of many houses, old and new, are long boards or poles, sunk in the ground and braced firmly against the woodwork. Such buttresses are an added protection against the wind. A family without them might feel insecure. Around their trees, some stack upright the loose wood that they find on the beach. When they have completely circled the trunk of one, they go to the next. A man who has surrounded three in this fashion feels equipped for the winter.

The present island and its surroundings do not seem less conglomerate than in other years. Many languages, many shadings are here, most of them with French combinations. The place is less predominantly Gallic, however, than it was in the past, for new overtones and new accents have followed the addition of elements. A general South European air and appearance hangs about the scene, a shrugged acceptance of a life that may be hard or easy, according to the viewpoint— and a hot Latin violence of temperament that breaks forth from time to time. An untamed look flares in a pair of dark eyes; then the face is blank. A week before my last visit, a dispute arose between a Chinese from a near-by settlement and a Portuguese. The former started after his gun; the other stopped him and killed him with large bare hands. "It took five minutes," said an observer. At one of the dance places on stilts, our party sat for a time with a striking couple, a man who was part Malay, part Spanish, and a slim, attractive girl who seemed largely French. They said they were engaged; they were also, it appeared, sensitive in matters of racial definition. Before the night was over the man was in a fist fight with a drunken broker from New Orleans.

A quiet Englishwoman knits in a house whose interior seems, except for the frame of landscape through the window, little different from a small apartment in London. A New Englander, married to a Frenchman, sighs for her Maine hills which she has not visited in forty years. There are a number of men and women here who have seen much of the outside world and like to talk of it, and of the island, too. Among others—those who spend their time on lonely waters—there is a darker mien, an unspoken distrust of the intruder. Such natives look on silently when they pass to the front and see outsiders in bathing trunks or suits with bare midriffs; and they spit into the water. They will guide these aliens on fishing trips, and some are ready to amuse those who hire them, with quips and jokes. But that is all. The islander wants to be left to himself. He does not like to leave the island, whether he is young or old. One of the teachers told me of unsuccessful efforts to persuade honor pupils to take scholarships that would mean a stay elsewhere; other pupils rejected jobs in New Orleans.

The war and the draft of the early 1940's brought their changes, and some of the youth of Grand Isle learned of many parts of the world much farther off than New Orleans. Among those left on the island, however, there continues a diffidence bred of their isolation. Social workers and others speak of lethargy, of a grim fatalism that cannot be penetrated.

I suspect, too, that the priests sometimes find their work difficult. For many years visits to the island by pastors were rare. Several told me, "We got out of the habit." Today the islanders are civil to their priests but they like them, I gathered, to "keep to their own affairs." If the men and women are not inclined to attend services, for instance, they do not want to be pressed.

In some cases, in the back part, the sharp pain of poverty has been felt. One family, it was discovered last summer, had been living for about ten days on the left-over fish that neighbors gave them—three meals of it a day, and that was all. Malnutrition is a new name for an old ailment here as in other places seemingly less well endowed by nature.

For years I had heard vague tales of buried doubloons along the blue waters. No new stories had come out recently, and so I presumed that public schools and the war had made men forget their fantasies. I am now better informed. Over all the modern Gulf there still hangs the uneasy shadow of the pirates and their treasure chests. A century and a quarter after Lafitte, the section is still obsessed with visions of buccaneer gold. In every third family, by my unofficial estimate, there is a story: Two trees, with the top limb of each one pointing to the west; if a man can only find them now . . . Or— They took a knife, the bearded fellows, and made a cut just like this . . . Or— Go eight steps left and then eight more south; there, in a little depression . . .

Through the years men dig into countless mounds and ridges on the islands and in the marshes. John Plaisance took me to several of these, at a certain point on a high ridge through the wet land, reached after some damage to shoes and trousers. We inspected water-filled holes where men had worked furtively in the night, certain that they were "on the right track," at last, and anxious that no one find out what they were doing. One elderly islander who had "drowned a family" in the Chênière storm, as the local terminology has it, labored hard for two decades afterward, then decided to use all his money to find hidden jewels. A relative on his deathbed had whispered a word or two of direction. (The message originally had come straight from a son of a pirate, who had in turn given it on *his* deathbed. There has, of course, always been an affinity between deathbeds and treasure hunts.) The old man since then has used hickory rods, electrical apparatus, and the services of a hypnotist. He digs always in the same area. He knows that the treasure lies somewhere within the triangle there. If he can only work long enough . . . To friends he tells of the way he almost reached it once. Just as the shovel sounded on the box, it disappeared, "went right into the earth." The next year— Mon Dieu, how can he say the horrible thing that happened! A spirit, it must have been . . . something rose up and all of his men ran away, and what could he do but run too!

An island man who does well in a business is frequently the subject of whispers among others. John Plaisance, a successful trapper, guide, and farmer, has been discussed on many occasions among his friends. A man of hard sense but also of humor, he chuckles about the matter. He told me what to expect when I asked about him. I was well repaid for my inquiries. This one knew that one night at dusk, Johnny heard the sound of metal against his hoe, and bent over, and there was a pot of Spanish gold. Another said that it was on a ridge, and he knew a man who saw Johnny come out, all excited.

At the time of the Chênière storm, bits of gold and silver were found for weeks on the sand. This is the source of many of today's yarns. The explanation was simple: Many of the families used a common method of concealing their money, thrusting it into the mud walls; and when the houses fell apart, the metal washed out. But wise ones of today assert that it is more than mere bits of family cash that have been hidden hereabouts. One woman, looking over her shoulder to be certain that no others were listening, explained how her grandmother told her of Johnny Gambi and his wife, and the way they buried a great container of things before the winds struck. She claims that it was in their fireplace. Another tells me that it was some distance off. But nobody has ever discovered it.

On three occasions during the past year men of the bayous have asked me if I had a little money to "get a part" in a treasure search that they were almost ready to begin. I regretfully declined the offers but promised to pass on the word to anyone whom I found interested. (I will ask no cut, but the first doubloon.) One had a map; another had been practicing with a rod that he invented. The third had the services of an assistant with second sight. ("That man predick the fines' thing!") The whole Louisiana coast is Lafitte treasure territory. The buccaneers were everywhere; modern men pry everywhere for their leavings. Owners in many places still threaten to shoot the next person whom they catch prospecting for gold near their good oyster beds. They plan to do some investigating there themselves some day, when the oysters play out! The pirate appears often in the daily conversation of the Gulf people. When a man sees a friend who has taken on some weight since they last met, he gibes at him, "What you got there, Estève?" He taps Estève's big belly. "Lafitte's treasure, ahn?"

The island is at its best, I think, at dawn. The salt water rolls in and out; double and triple lines of parallel logs and leaves are thrown upon the sands. Small crabs, the color of the beach, with sharp periscopes of black eyes thrust into the air, move noiselessly—"ghost crabs," say the islanders. Ahead, a group of men, only the outlines of their figures discernible in the half-light, are seining, tossing their long nets, then drawing them in, as they will be doing for hours. They talk and they gesture, but their words cannot be understood from the distance. A native woman, shoeless, bulging in pale pink gingham, wide straw piece on her head, passes with two small boys. On her hat she wears an oleander flower. Without a word they walk into the water. The mother gives each a line, and the three stand together to cast for their breakfast.

Far out, a bobbing point of black is their father's boat, or so I gather from their conversation. The mother makes a good catch, and the excited cries of one of the boys sound over the water. The sky, which has been a deep blue, slowly changes to purple, then to crimson, and the waves seem to stain the sand as they move in with their weeds and broken flowers. Overhead the laughing gulls swing downward, their half-maniacal shrieks sounding over the slow push of the waters. An awkward file of brown pelicans flies low over the water, their wings beating in unison. They sail on for a time, then resume their flapping. Eventually they head for a small island in the water, a mere spit that is covered thick with terns and gulls and other birds, and they search the slow waters like the men and women about them.

To the rear stands the island, lightening gradually. Outlined against the sky, black against the red, are the salt-driven oaks, scant leaves fluttering slightly. I feel a quick chill. It may be the wind—or only the sight of those sad trees. How long will they remain and fight? That, perhaps, is the key to Grand Isle's future.

§ 4. *Reapers of the Water*

"DEUS, qui dividens aquas ab arida . . ."

The words echoed on this August morning over the softly agitated waves where the two bayous converged. God, who had separated sea from land, was being asked once again to grant favor to those who follow the water. Two thousand years earlier, the first Christians sought by ceremonial to invoke safety and good fortune for the ships that they sent across the Mediterranean. Centuries later, off the Normandy and Brittany coasts, French peasant-fishermen knelt while their priests intoned the same words. In coastal Louisiana, with rites that have changed little through the years, the Church of Rome was bestowing its blessing on the shrimp fleet.

We had risen before dawn, the Boudreaux and I, and everybody had helped stow things into the family lugger, the *Jeune Fille*. Yesterday Papa Boudreaux and the boys had put the last touches on the shining vessel, after days of scouring and painting it with white and green. Like all the Boudreaux neighbors, we had our line of small colored flags flying in the breeze, nets newly tarred, and all the family arranged on deck, in chairs from the kitchen, or otherwise disposed beneath the canvas, so that we would not be boiled red as crawfish in the sun. The girls were in crisp blue taffeta, Papa had on his best starched khaki pants, and Maman and Grand'mère wore their stiff black bonnets. For an hour now we had moved along lakes and inlets and other waters, crowding among hundreds of others on the same route, waving bonjour as we went.

"Comment ça va?"

"Pas much. . . ." Maman shrugged to her friend.

"Allo, Allo! . . ." All the Héberts were calling to us from an adjoining boat.

"A goo-ood year, you say, Martin? . . . Aye, the baby!"

Jean-Jacques, starting to roll toward the edge of the deck, was caught before he went far, and Maman turned to lecture the two sisters. But by this time we were at the landing, and Maman had to store up her feeling. Others, four thousand or so of them, had arrived, and Mass had started. From the place we chose we could see and hear everything. Under the oak at the edge of the shore the mothers' society of the congregation had set up a white altar, with flowers from the woods. Dwarfed by the girth of the great tree was a miniature organ, connected to a sound truck. On other days the oak-lined spread of green was a picnic ground; now it became a cathedral, the arched branches forming the groins. The crowd, seated on the grounds, half in shadow, half in sunlight, turned to the Archbishop in his golden cope and tall miter, a resplendent figure against an unwonted background, the darting silver of the water, the green and lavender of the hyacinths, the slow movement of an occasional boat.

Incense floated up about the dripping gray moss, and the sound of the altar bell rang out. Automatically all who had stayed on their boats dropped to their knees with the others on shore. The prelate, next taking up his sermon, recalled that the disciples of Christ were drawn from the fishermen of Galilee. Through the night, at the Lake, they cast in vain. Then He told them to try once more, and lo! the nets came heavily loaded. . . . Now there would be days when you, too, would cast your nets without success. . . . Be not discouraged; His all-seeing eye will be on you. And in the storm, when your boat tosses like a thin leaf, hold firm. . . .

Papa Boudreaux was a solemn man that day. From the beginning of my visit with the family, a week earlier, he had told me of the hard and perilous days ahead. This and that man, as careful as he, had never been seen after a trip. A slip off a wet deck, a sudden sickness so far out . . . Maman, perspiring in a dress that was too tight, had also lost her usual jollity; she held firmly to the baby in her arms and her lips moved. Who knew whose man would be next? Grand'mère, who had described how three of hers—her husband and those two boys—had not returned, now looked toward her son. On how many more occasions would she herself be on the lugger? Seventy-eight years is a long time.

The organ notes reached a climax; the Mass ended. The greatest moments were to come. A rush to the boats. Those who had stayed on the water gesticulated to the others to row back in a hurry, while some stepped, not without permission, across the closely packed vessels that stretched far out. Chanting the Litany of the Saints, the Archbishop, his assistants, and the altar boys were moving across the grass to the bank and to the vessel that awaited there. For the rest of the year this was an oyster barge; today, newly whitened, a small cross at its top, it was transformed. Slowly it moved toward a central position, and on the two hundred or so luggers, hearts began to beat faster.

Most of the others looked toward us, and nudged and pointed. For Papa Boudreaux had been chosen this year for the supreme honor; his hull would be the first to be touched by the sanctified water. (Two men had a fist fight the previous week before the selection was made.) My friend Boudreaux, at the wheel, was peering now for the signal. It came, and the murmur of the crowd grew louder for a moment, and then ended. Mon Dieu! Maman put her hand to her mouth; the motor would not start. We sat frozen. The eldest boy, the forthright Jules, said "Jesus! . . . what a time—" and Maman hushed him. Everybody prayed. Ah, there it was; the lugger slipped forward. As we approached the Archbishop, all dropped to their knees, heads lowered. The prelate dipped his gold aspergillum into the container of holy water and lifted it high. As the boat passed, the drops fell on the scrubbed deck, on the nets, on the shoulders of the nearest ones. The baby was intrigued by the sparkling spots, and dipped her finger wonderingly into one of them. Maman pulled her back; and we were on our way.

Ours was also the first boat in the procession that formed. The others took place behind us as each was blessed, and we moved up the long waterway, crowds watching and waving: the *Sea Dream*, the *Normandie*, the *Barbara Coast*, the *Little Hot Dog*, the *God Bless America*, the *Madame of Q.* . . . The water march over, we returned to the oak grove, where the proprietor had the party ready.

Today was more than a religious occasion; it was the great social day of the bayous. On both sides were long boards resting on wooden supports, with newspapers covering the tables thus formed. Men hobbled out of the kitchen with tall buckets, pungent, steaming, early shrimp by the unlimited pounds. "Shrimp for all," read the sign, and that was literally true. Enough shrimp were emptied over the newspapers, to be shelled and eaten at the participants' will, for the rest of the day and for the night as well. Shrimp for lunch, shrimp for dinner; and for many, including the Boudreaux and me, there had been shrimp for breakfast, too. (Fried with potatoes, they start a day surprisingly well, though I wonder what the dietitians would say about it.)

During a lull in the day's events, the dancing and the games, I was taken to the cooking room by the proprietor. It was a lesson in mass production—and an introduction to the inferno. In the center was a former sugar-house kettle, supported by a brick base into which piles of wood were being thrust. The holder was filled to the brim with the shellfish, coral-hued in their cooked state. From them rose billows of smoke, peppery and aromatic. Five helpers stirred, dumped, removed, and kept the fire going, and they seemed entirely unaffected by the heat; but I had to leave after a moment of it. The owner told of the day's schedule in figures that sounded astronomical: gallons, hampers, pounds of red and green pepper, salt, onions, lemons, bay leaf, cloves. He did not tell everything; he had to keep the secret of his mixture. People came from all around on Saturday for his sea food, he explained. They got all they wanted, as many plates as each could consume, and free, to go with what they bought for drinks. Above my sneezing, the effect of the condiments, I heard him say, as he smiled: "It is not an expenditure. It is an investment."

At half-past three the next morning, Jules Boudreaux woke me and we dressed by oil lamp in the kitchen. An hour later, in a chill fog, Papa, Jules, and I were with the others at the fleet's assembly point below Houma. Fifteen other luggers made up the party; all except one or two had been working together for years. All went by prearrangement; and as we started down the narrow bayou, the suction of our passage making the low reeds dance at the edges, I learned more of the system. The fleet would be out for two weeks or so, in the Gulf or about the coastal inlets and channels. Our only connection with the rest of the world would be through "the company"; and there was "the company," moving behind us—a big vessel, twice the size of any of ours. In the old days, a man would get the hold of his boat filled, then turn around and lose many fishing hours on the way to the factory and on his return to the grounds. Today the firm sent along the "buy boat," which would remain near the luggers and pick up the shrimp as the boats filled. This company boat was high-powered, and carried a large supply of ice. The fleet boats would remain at the scene; the "buy boat" would move about from one fleet to another in this vicinity and would shuttle back and forth between the fleet and the factory. That was why each of the luggers flew a large flag of green and white. It was the company's banner, the same as that of the "buy boat." The "buy" pilot had no trouble finding us across the broad waters; we had no trouble identifying and signaling to him.

As we went south, everybody had something to yell to his friend on the next boat. "Come on over tonight, Alcée, for cards, and bring that brother of yours so we can trim him. . . ." "For Chrissake turn that radio lower; it will be wore out when we need it next week. . . ." What did Papa Boudreaux want to bet he wouldn't turn in half as much as last season? "You're getting older, Papa." Papa let it be known that he had been shrimping before the speaker was born, and could eat them and digest them faster than that one could catch them. (This is a somewhat expurgated version, but it will do.) As a tenderfoot, along mainly for the ride, I took my share of guying—advice as to what to do when I felt myself slipping off the wet deck, suggestions of strange animals to seek in the catch—the equivalent of the "type lice" that the fledgling newspaper copy boy is told to hunt on his first day. In company, I gathered, there is relief from the tedium of the long stay on the waters. When the clouds lowered and a heavy rain and wind hit us, I found another reason for the fleet. The luggers drew close together for the safety that there is in any numbers.

The weather cleared, and we spread apart. For hours we moved slowly, aimlessly I thought, about the water. Then Papa Boudreaux gave a signal and we halted. The others slowed up at the same time. Over went our "try trawl," a bag-shaped net that was to tell us whether it was worth while to drop the large one. It came up. Papa frowned. We moved on for a few minutes, and then we repeated. Nothing again. It was a highly uncertain procedure at any time, Papa pointed out. "Sometime you see the swimp on the water, flicking-like, on the top, if you got good eyes and know how to look. Most time, you don't. Sometime you can guess, the way the water is muddy, that they might be plenty—plenty of them down there. Most time you can't. Gull on the water—that might tell you swimp there; or they mightn't."

I gathered later from others that Papa was not letting out everything he knew. Some said that he had a sense of shrimp, that he could almost smell them through the water. Be that as it may, several hours later our test trawl came up filled with small, neutral-colored bits of flesh, flipping, leaping, hopping. We had hit water in which the shrimp were running. Behind us we dropped a heavy trawl, thirty feet wide, and we started to scrape through the water. Anything that was in our way was taken in. We dragged carefully along. After an hour or so, Papa was satisfied, and the trawl was drawn up.

Out of it poured the life of the sea, in conglomeration: scurrying crabs, sea horses, flounders, catfish, small squid, jellyfish, blobs of fleshlike, gray-colored, unidentifiable stuff, seaweed, tiny things by the thousands—wiggling, twisting, gasping; dangerous, some of it, beautiful or useless, much of it. And, of course, among and about it all, there were shrimp by the heavy poundfuls. We got to work with hoes, bits of wood, and our hands, to sort and clear, throwing out this one, helping that one to slip off the deck. Warned too late, I touched an interesting-looking object and then learned that it was a sting ray. (I burned for hours.) A great deal of what we discarded was good fish, and I thought of the Boudreaux and the other families around them; they could eat for a week on what we were so blithely tossing out. But, the others asked me, what good would it be after that long trip home, without ice—even if we were leaving soon, as we were not? Only a few large and splendid items and two turtles were saved. We used one for our supper; the rest would bring a good price from the company boat.

The gulls had been enjoying our "throwback," swerving back and forth, shrieking, plunging low to snap for the quivering bits. They were not alone in their liking for our catch, we suddenly found. Jules Boudreaux yelled; simultaneonsly a man on the next boat pulled up his trawl, but too late. I caught sight of a vague, heavy underwater shadow. A porpoise—bitter enemy of the shrimpers—had bitten into the filled bag. One of the others took out a rifle and fired. Apparently he frightened away the menace; but it had done its work. A gaping hole was left, the neighbor's net ruined. For the next few hours all of us peered anxiously about. If we had drawn a school of porpoises, Jules pointed out, our trip might be a complete loss. Luckily, we were bothered no more. We were in rich shrimp waters for the time and we worked the trawl for hours, until finally, when the last catch was thin, Papa Boudreaux decreed a stop. The company boat took our full loads, and though everybody was tired, we celebrated with wine, the radio, fish, and "cache," a kind of poker game.

Long before light hit—approximately a moment after I dropped into the bunk, it seemed—I was routed out. Dawn shrimping can be the most profitable of all. But this day looked like a bad one. We cruised and tested, cruised and tested, and a dull discouragement settled on the fleet. "Sometime it go on like this for days." Papa Boudreaux was philosophic, but Jules fretted. I slept on deck and developed sunburn. By noon, somebody near us yelled. Even Papa was excited when he saw the supply at hand, and we worked without letup until far after dark. This time I went to sleep at the supper table.

So it went for the next ten days—several rich days, a dull one, another of nothing at all. Finally, shortly after dawn one morning, we hit luck. Through the day almost every trawl that was lowered came up overflowing. When the company boat made the rounds, the fleet members decided to stay on as long as the shrimp held out. I was due somewhere else and so, not too reluctantly, considering my sore palms, legs, back, and skinless nose, I shook hands and made the return trip on the company boat.

It was a race against heat. The rich catch had delayed our departure. The sun had beaten relentlessly on us that day, and the ice was low. We roared up bayous, skirted bays, took a short cut. A spoiled cargo, the worried man at the wheel made it clear, would mean hell to pay; nothing, not even a prayer, could keep ice from melting. As we approached the town, he pulled heavily on the whistle, then again, then again and again. Everybody knew his signal. At once, though it was almost midnight, an answering siren came from somewhere, high-pitched, nervous. As we approached the factory it was in full blast. Men and women, waked in the night, were converging, some throwing on their coats as they approached.[1] A whole floor lit up as we stepped ashore. Everything was ready, and the girls already sitting in long rows began work almost at once, their fingers moving quickly and skillfully.

The process is a methodical one: head torn off with left hand, shell broken with thumb of the right, a quick pressure to force out the meat intact. In the next department the shrimp are dropped into heavy containers of brine, from which they emerge toughened and coral-pink. Some are "wet packed" in brine, some are dry packed; others are put up with green and red peppers. In recent years the industry has seen a near-revolution with the introduction of quick-freezing methods. These are new ways. A day later I saw still another method, a survival of another day and continent.

About seventy-five years ago Lee Yim, merchant of Canton, came to Louisiana. He saw the great volume of sea food and he could conceive of no reason why the Chinese delicacy of dried shrimp could not be produced from the Louisiana article. Today "shrimp villages" spread about the ends of the bayous near the Eastern Gulf. They are settlements on stilts, a series of huts, warehouses, and other quarters centering upon wide drying tables. Chinese, Filipinos, Malays, Span-

---

[1] At some points a truck races up the road, sounding a special siren. When it gets to the end of the line, it turns about, and those who want work must be on the roadway, to be picked up without delay.

iards, an occasional Mexican or part-Mexican, part-Indians—
it is a mixture that is motley, more Oriental than Occidental
but possessing some of the characteristics of each. One platform is Manila Village, which Catholic Filipino immigrants
named for their natal city. For years another, Bassa-Bassa, was
an all-Chinese center. In some instances single Chinese families
have been in control of such establishments for decades. I
found one not unattractive girl with olive skin, highly Oriental eyes, blond hair, and a good command of French. She
smiled over her copy of a confession magazine.

The platforms rise over small shell islands, approached only
by water. No trees, no vegetation grow in any direction;
everything is still water, gleaming white shells, unpainted
wood, and shrimp. On my visit I was greeted with a handclasp
from a vaguely affable manager of undetermined nationality,
by wide grins from a few assistants, and dull stares from the
rest. Men lounged about in pajama-like attire, some wearing
Chinese-type straw hats of broad brims; inside small gloomy
buildings others shuffled silently. After a moment, a cackle
of voices broke out. At least five languages were being spoken,
and English was not among them. The excitement dwindled;
in this atmosphere, tension soon wears. The cause of the excitement, a trawler, was arriving, filled with shrimp—the
smaller ones which the factories reject, which the platforms
welcome for their purpose. Payment was by an old unit,
the "Chinee basket." The rest of the process was largely
non-scientific. Iron pots had been set up; into them was
dumped the catch—head, shells, and all. A man stood at each
container with a paddle, and stirred. After a time, when the
shrimp had changed color, they were lifted to wheelbarrows,
then dumped over wide areas of the platform. Workmen,
using rakes, spread them in thin layers. For the first time I

observed that the wooden expanse was not entirely flat, but shaped in a series of slight rises, to permit better draining of the liquid. Regularly, the shrimp are re-raked so that the heat from above will reach all of them. A layer of coral thickness shines in the sun, its shade varying from place to place with the extent of the drying process; and it is frequently over-powering. From a distance the sight, and the odor as well, is more impressive.

In the old days, I knew, the shrimp were "danced"—arranged in wide circles on which the men, women, and children, with wooden shoes or burlap bags on their feet, walked or jumped in slow single file, while one of their number chanted an ancient song. Their movement beat off the heads and shells. Today a revolving drum does the same work, and at the end of the process each shrimp is neat, separate, hard as a metal pellet. They will last indefinitely. Those who buy them will soak them and like the flavor.

Nearly three-quarters of the nation's shrimp catch comes from Louisiana. Sea food is big business here, and the shrimp is the biggest item. Until comparatively recently the industry was small and placid, the Acadian fishermen seining quietly inside the shores, with scant knowledge of the habits and movements of the shellfish. Then Federal investigators discovered an untapped source of rich shrimp life—"jumbo" creatures out in the Gulf. The finding brought new methods and new men. Heavy ocean-going trawlers transferred their base of operations from Florida and the South Atlantic to compete against the Louisiana "mosquito fleets." Going as far as forty or more miles out in the Gulf, they brought offshore shrimping from nothing to a normal catch of twenty million pounds. The Louisianians gradually have acquired vessels of larger size and power, but the greatest portion of the supply is still caught inshore or near it. The Federal investigations disclosed curious things about the mysterious shrimp. They mate fifty miles or so offshore; the young must drift in to shore or die. At the mercy of the currents, they eventually reach brackish water that permits them to grow, and now they go through a series of fourteen molts, changing into fantastic shapes until they begin to look like the shrimp that the fisherman knows. Then, as young shrimp, they begin another progression, this time out to sea again. After a year out in the deep they are dead; but meanwhile they work to insure their own continuance. The female drops an estimated 300,000 or so eggs.

The crab provides also a seasonal business for the lowlander, but one that is largely the concern of the individual man—no company boats, no expensive trawls. The pursuit calls only for a boat, patience, and a good set of back muscles. There are uncounted thousands of crabs in the coastal waters, buried in the sea bottom or wandering about for food; the problem is to gain access to him when he is at his best. Jules Boudreaux, who was an expert on the subject at the age of eleven, taught me about it that same spring. (The best crabbing is in spring and summer, just before shrimping, which comes just before trapping, in a convenient schedule.) Near the Boudreaux home, reached by their own bayou, is a shallow, brackish lake, or lagoon, and here Jules and I followed his trot lines about the water.

A stake was fixed at each end, a series of baited nets between, wooden "floats" as markers on the water surface—and we were ready. Then ensued as remarkable a demonstration of balance and control as I have witnessed. Jules stood up in our flat-bottomed boat and poled us along the line. The pole was about eight feet long, with a hook at the end. Leaving one net, he sank the pole into the soft base of the lake and gave us a push forward toward the next marker. Just before we reached it, he used the pole hook to reach downward, catch the net, lift it quickly, and dump its contents, neatly and with dispatch, into the boat's bottom. In a moment he had replaced the net and we were on our way forward, as before. He managed it all in one process, without a slip, from one net to the next, ten yards away, the hand never touching the net.

Dropped carefully into the boat, the crabs tried hard to escape; and my assignment at this phase was to keep them within bounds, using a wooden tongs. One nip by those powerful claws, and a man develops respect both for them and for the tongs. As we made the rounds, we exchanged reports with neighbors who were crabbing from vantage points—short, single-plank wharves extended for the purpose into the lake. On the end of the wharves stood or sat grandpères and youths of the surrounding areas, working for the market or for their own tables. Sometimes they used nets like ours; again they had only strings with bits of bait attached. A nibble, and they pulled up slowly until they had the crab almost to the surface; then they used a dip net to scoop him up before the wily victim saw light and slipped away. But often, Jules observed, the crabs use those claws to clip away bait, end of the string and all. "The crab, he is not a fool."

Back home with our catch, we got to work. Into the bottom of a big hamper went a covering of moss, well moistened, then a layer of crabs, then moss again, and so on. The crabs were never tossed in, but deposited lightly; and never on the upper shell. Jules shook his head at my first efforts: "Do you want them fellow' to fight and kill each other?" Once, with an air of triumphant vindication, he showed me the result of a battle brought on by my heavy hand: eight claws in the basket bottom, three broken shells. At the top of the basket was always a covering of moss; then came a judicious dropping of water over the top. "Ah-ah," Jules told me. "Not that much. You wan' to drown 'em?" At the market a new lesson in mathematics offered itself, in which a dozen was not always a dozen. The count was by size. For "jumboes" and "counters," the two largest types, the usual twelve is the unit; for "three for fours," middle-sized, eighteen is a dozen; "three for ones," thirty-six; and for the smallest, forty-eight to a dozen.

Jules was as ruggedly individualistic as some of his barnacle-covered crabs. He would have nothing to do with a poor man's "crab fleet" that I watched as it left our vicinity every day. This dozen or so of crabbers arranged with a friend who owned a lugger to tow their skiffs, one tied to the other, to a larger, better-endowed lake some distance away. There they worked most of the day, and eventually the lugger came for them. The operation cost them only a few cents a day. But when a good blow came, Jules pointed out, they had to row like hell to safety. They told me that it was worth it, and the last I heard they were still working on the young conservative to persuade him to·join.

Meanwhile, all of us had been seeking the crab de luxe, the soft-shell. Until he is completely grown, the crustacean must shed his outer armor again and again. He can increase his size only by breaking through his shell, growing a new and larger one, then breaking through that one. For the first year or so he sheds almost every month. Under his outer covering he grows fat and heavy and pushes hard. The tightened frame cracks and he backs out of it. Now he has only a soft, shriveled outer layer; it will take him some time—a day or so—to "work out" the wrinkles, filling his new enlarged covering and gradually hardening it in the water. During his soft stage he is at his most delicious, his most defenseless, and, for the consumer, his most expensive. He recognizes his own natural deficiencies, and shortly before he reaches this stage and while he is still hard-shelled, he creeps to whatever cover he can find in the shadows, under grasses, under ledges. Every bayou boy or girl knows all about this process, and describes it graphically. When hard-shelled, the crab is "green." Ready to shed or "bust through," he is a "buster." When the shell is just breaking, he is "cracked." Next he is soft and vulnerable. Waiting for the new covering to gain thickness, he is a "paper shell." Hardened again, he is a "clear" one.

Some of the waters, especially the coastal lakes, are known to be favorite retreats of crabs that feel the soft stage approaching them. They provide much grass at the edges, many dark places for the hiding. Men, too, have learned of this natural protective area, and have penetrated it. For many years the soft-shell crab was caught only in the "old way," by men who trudged through the water, barefoot, seeking him out with seines or individual nets. But an accident of the past decade brought a great change. The usual way to get small shrimp for bait has been to sink green branches into the lake waters. The women, between household tasks, would immerse the bush in the water; up climbed the shrimp, and when the shrimp-seekers returned a bit later, there was the bait. One day, as the natives tell the story on many occasions, a bonne femme forgot the branch, and it remained under water longer than usual. When she picked it up, she blinked. It was packed with soft crabs. Seeking protection, they had moved into the waving green stuff. The bayou people profited by this new knowledge of crab tendencies; today hundreds make a living for the season by following long lines with branches at intervals—"bush fishing."

The crabber helps nature and his own pocketbook by speeding up the softening process. When he has his catch, he sorts the members. They are before him in several stages, "greens," "busters," and the rest. A quick inspection usually tells him into which class each falls; if he is not certain, he will press the shell lightly or feel one of the claws. Many are between their phases, and here the professional crabber gets to work. Sometimes his experienced finger finds that the shell has already begun to crack. Then he peels the "buster" into a "soft," comme ça. It is no small trick; Jules was always proud of himself afterward.

Usually the process is longer. A crab out of water stays at his current stage, hard or soft; put him back and, if he does not die, the normal progression starts again. Jules and his friends have ready a series of small, shallow boxes with open slats. Into each goes a crab of a particular phase. These fellows over here are "busters"; the others are getting soft, and doing it fast; these on this side may or may not be soft in a day or two. Jules shrugs and takes a chance on the last ones. The boxes go into water, and the crab resumes development. Along many of the bayous, the passer-by sees small mats of leaves, moss, and other cool stuff attached close to shore. These are the tops of the water boxes; inside, the crabs are at work, obediently softening for the eventual frying pan. Every few hours Jules and his friends come back and check, and here is more than mere interest or love of work. The crab is a cannibal. The hard-shelled one is delighted at an opportunity to chew upon his helpless softer brother. If one of the softs becomes harder because he is left too long with the other softs, he turns on them. The "busters" are getting softer by the hour, and approaching the status of possible victims of their brothers. Jules showed me a box in which, a few hours earlier, he had carefully deposited two near-"busters." One had become soft more quickly than the other. We found only one there, in the middle of a heterogeneous collection of claws, flippers, and shells. "It is a prob-lem'," said Jules.

The oyster, too, is farmed here, planted, transplanted, and harvested. It grows best in water that is neither fresh nor salt, but a mixture. Louisiana's coastal combinations of the two elements provide what some have called the best of "soil" for the wet crop. In these warm waters the oyster, like many other things, matures more quickly than in other places. The weather permits the oysterman to remain in the field throughout the year. Like Achille Delaune, who has been at his work for forty years, many along these indented stretches do nothing else; and like Achille, grizzled, the possessor of impressive handle-bar mustache and gruff-friendly disposition to match, they grumble that they still have insufficient time to give the oyster his proper attention. When I asked Achille the best time to go along with him on his rounds, he snorted. Let me come any day except Christmas and All Saints', and I'd find him at work. I will not vouch for his efforts on all these other 363 days, but every time I called, I found him at one of his highly involved tasks.

The oyster, he made clear as he guided his lugger to work, is a strange case. Male and female do not meet; each sends a milky substance into the water and sperm joins egg.[2] The

---

[2] The oyster often does somersaults in sex, from male to female to male again. The process is less whimsical than might appear; apparently it is a device of nature to make certain that there will be sufficient mollusks of both sexes in close proximity to insure continuation of the species. The productivity of the oyster puts even the shrimp to shame: one lays sixty million eggs.

young mollusk is free-swimming. He grows a pair of minute shells, and he must find a hard base to which to connect them or he will eventually slip into the soft mud and "smother." Once contact is made, the oyster is attached for life. Here Achille entered the situation. We stopped at a restaurant near the wharf and he bought a large pile of left-over oyster shells from the kitchen. Shoveling them aboard, we moved out into the center of the brackish lake which Achille had good reason to believe would produce a good oyster. Then he transferred the shells to his skiff and we went to a shallow place, marked by short wooden poles projecting a foot or so above water. Here, with a skill that came with years of practice, he "sowed" the shells by tossing them out over the water—not close upon each other, but well scattered. On them, the young oysters would "set." That done, we moved to another near-by bed. There the young oysters that had been "planted" eighteen months or so ago had become "seed" ones, and required attention. Achille took out the oyster tongs, a set of two long rakes attached at the center. Grasping each with one hand, at the top, he grappled for the oysters and lifted them into the boat. It was, he grunted, as he had expected. Clusters of the shells had grown together. Using a sharp-edged hatchet, he broke them apart, then sowed most of them again on the water bottom. With most of these Achille was contemptuous; they were too small, not ready yet. Some of them, however, he kept. They could be taken on to the last step. He broke open one of them. It tasted good enough. But, he pointed out—and I agreed—it lacked that final briny flavor that was to be provided for a Louisiana oyster.

We moved now to another oyster bed, miles away, closer to the Gulf, and re-sowed the large ones. For a time they would imbibe the rich salt of these selected waters. We left.

When, a few weeks later, we came back, Achille dug down again, and again we sampled. This time we looked at each other, and reached over for more. These oysters had "arrived." So they were piled high into the skiff, moved to the lugger, and taken to the cluster of buildings on poles that is Achille's home. Here, to the side, was Achille's "boarding" place in which the oysters were dropped in brackish water, to be kept safe and fresh before the trip to New Orleans started. There the counters and tables were awaiting them.

Probably every Louisiana lowlander over ten years of age is a connoisseur of oysters. He looks with unimpressed eye on those who repeat the pale joke about the first brave man who ate one. Children taste them before they know meat; and why not? Achille asked. What is better for anybody than a juicy fellow, flipped right out of the shell into the mouth? The oyster bar in the town of this area is an institution before which men and women wait their turn. Thousands know the oyster shucker like the bartender, as a purveyor of delight and philosophy, a handservant to good living. Some openers are proud of half centuries or more in service, often at one spot, and "never a bad one to a customer." The Louisianian consumes his raw oysters in quantity; the man who calls a halt at a half-dozen or a dozen is a weak-gilled Yankee or some other foreigner. All of this applies, of course, to the elite oyster.

The state has also "wild reefs," where the mollusks grow without attention and are gathered in quantities for canning or steaming, to be sold to cooks who will add them to stews and stuffings. But the oyster gourmet knows only the counter or bar variety. Over much of South Louisiana tradesmen move regularly along bayous in boats, or on bayou roads in wagons or trucks, calling out their wares in the shell. A neighborhood feast on oysters is a common thing, with the best-qualified man of the environs shucking them for everybody in the kitchen. But don't try to emulate him, if you are a stranger to this art. As Achille told me after one bloody attempt, you will want to save those hands and fingers for other things.

Through the months, the fishermen of the bayou cast their nets and set their lines for other products of the deep water and the shallows: the sweet-fleshed pompano, the redfish, flounder, Spanish mackerel, bluefish, drum, white trout, sheepshead, sea bass. Thousands of pounds are pulled out of the water, iced, and sent to New Orleans or other points, and thence to the world. The waters hold rare fish, monsters, fish that are spectacular fighters. Sportsmen battle with the silver tarpon, holding breathlessly as he leaps in and out of the water, his scales reflecting the sun like countless fragments of mirrors. Scientists inspect and record the marine life, a subtropical fauna that is of heavy richness. There are creatures of grotesque shape and coloration—giant manta, "the bats of the Gulf," of a beauty that makes the beholder uneasy, their blanket-like bodies floating at the surface, upward points of their "wings" leaving lines behind them. There are floating boxes of bone, sharp-eyed, horned against their enemies; "lemon fish," recognizable by their large yellow lips, seen clearly as they turn; great green-and-milk-white sea turtles, four or five hundred pounds in weight; mammoths that may go up in bulk to three tons.

Outsiders, seeking curiosities, come and leave; natives work on from the hours before dawn to those of the dusk. They can live because these water gardens are theirs.

§ 5. M'sieu Mus'rat and His People

ONE FALL DAY a corduroy-capped, high-booted Louisiana lowlander, who had four dollars in cash resources, turned a canal and waved au revoir to his friends. Within three months he was back from the marshes, and in his pockets were seven thousand dollars. His muskrat traps had earned it for him. In all his life he had never seen so much money—"all in one hand!" He has never seen that much again. His case was not unprecedented. Others received windfalls of this size, and also somewhat larger, perhaps.

These records of the flush 1920's are only memories. Today the marsh man could not duplicate such feats. But with luck he can still do well, for trapping remains the Louisiana small man's most lucrative part-time business—and by turn, his most bitterly disappointing. In no other enterprise does he start out with less certainty of his status. He may end up sufficiently well off to need to do nothing the rest of the year (a thousand dollars can maintain his family with ease); or he may find himself approaching want.

The state's marshes are a sub-tropical fur empire, the greatest in the world, and the muskrat is King. Over hundreds of thousands of acres of rustling green he has meant prosperity to men who had previously owned little. He has also, in recent years, brought turmoil and warm violence. Few subjects have been a cause of more spectacular changes; on few other matters have many South Louisianians so furious a set of opinions.

Albert (Al-bair') Alidore took one end of the trunk and I took the other, and each of the other six Alidores filled his or her arms with objects ranging from blankets to a small, worn medicine cabinet. It was our twentieth trip from the house to the lugger, which was now filled inside, outside, front, and back. When a family is to live away from home, without neighbors, for seventy days, it needs things, as Albert said; everything that had come to mind had been gathered up. The trapping grounds on which Albert had a lease were many miles off; there would be no jaunts back and forth. For several days I had watched Madame Alidore at work, repairing shirts, pressing pants, sewing dresses, and going over a list of supplies with the town grocer, who was the owner of the trapping grounds. Now the cat was handed up; Madame gave a final, nervous look around the house, and we started.

Several days were ahead before the season opened. Like everybody else, the Alidores were going down in advance, to clear up all details for a quick start when the day came. For then they would have to use every available minute of the day and part of the night in concentration on one purpose—the garnering and processing of the last available pelt. Every member of the family had a part in the work, learned from past years' experiences. As we approached our destination, the feeling of excitement seemed to grow, and with it a half-holiday mood among the children. It was, after all, a vacation in one sense for them. In the middle of the school year they would be away from classes for more than two months.

The camp on the bayou edge, whose appearance was hailed by the younger Alidores, was three-roomed (one more than usual), with a large iron stove of all purposes, four beds, a table, and an assortment of chairs. It was as crowded a place as any in which I have stayed; but the days ahead were also to be crowded. The trapper's life leaves little time for wondering how much better others are managing. While Madame and the girls set the rooms in order, Albert and the two oldest boys took me to the edge of the clearing along the waterway and showed me the general scene of operations. At that point began a shallow ditch, only two feet or so wide, about a foot deep, extending far back through the grasses. It was the traînasse. Albert and the boys had previously spent a day or two in constructing it—a somewhat simpler task than it seemed. All they had done was rake the soft earth lightly to either side; the moisture had seeped in from the sides by the time they returned, and thus they had their own canal through the grounds. But the traînasse was little wider than the pirogues themselves; I could hardly see room for the use of a paddle. One of the boys pointed out a tall pole thrust into the earth. I got into the first boat and, standing in it, Albert push-poled his way through the shallow water, sending us floating at a quick rate. No paddle could have served so well; we could not have walked so rapidly across this soggy ground.

A short time later Albert halted, and we started on foot. In a moment we came to the first of many small hills, about three feet high, about six feet wide, of tightly packed grass and mud. They were muskrat houses. I could find no entrances and, from outside inspection, no marks of habitation (the law forbids tampering with the homes). Albert said that the surrounding area probably concealed seven or eight "dive holes," into which M'sieu Mus'rat swam, through tunnels, until he reached his living quarters over the water level. Aboveground I could make out a series of tiny, curving roadways through the wet grass. Albert was especially interested in these, for they were the indicators of his season's success or failure. They told him the volume of muskrats that were on the grounds.

We went on from one house to the next, and Albert checked over "the signs" and grew happier. The land had plenty of "three-cornered grass," the kind the muskrats want. The water was brackish but not salty, and there seemed no danger of any sudden inundation that would drown the rats. "A good year, yes, I think," he told the family over our gumbo that night. Everybody was in good humor, and after the dishes were cleared, Albert and the rest of us helped the women with the traps, scraping, cleaning, testing. That was our schedule for the next few days—inspecting, preparing, talking about muskrat futures and pasts. The little animal has a lore of his own among the marsh men, tales of trickiness, of prowess in concealment, and of many feats. A small animal he is, a foot or so long, and he has no perceptible neck. His tail he sometimes uses as an oar in the water and as a help in sitting up on land. Children occasionally make a pet of him. He is a marvel of self-reproduction; his brides—and there are many of them—can produce as many as five litters a year, and breeding apparently can go on during all but two months of the year. Had Papa told me about the one that just got by him for three years, the one that twitched his nose like Grand-père?

The day, November 20, approached. Over the marshlands families went to bed early the night before; and many, like me, woke several times in the dark to see if the time to start had arrived. Long before dawn everybody was up. Albert, the oldest boys, and I felt our way through the dark to the traînasse and the pirogues, carrying the traps carefully behind us. The previous day had been rainy; now I learned how wet a marsh could really be. With the first step or two from the traînasse, the youngest Alidore and I sank to our knees, while the others clicked their tongues and gave directions. Albert foraged in the dawn about the first muskrat house until he had found likely "runs" through the wet greenstuff, and here he carefully deposited several traps. The law bars the use of bait. From these he "followed the trap line," setting the course that we would follow during the days to come, from trap to trap. Slowly we disposed of the 250 instruments that the rules permit. We worked, poled, slipped chest-deep, rested for food—and it was dusk by the time we finished. In the meantime the oldest boy left us, to set a smaller line of his own; he had worked with Albert long enough to know the methods. The other boys stayed and watched. When the time came, they would have their own lines as well.

The next morning we found our first trap with the first light of dawn, and it was filled with a good-sized animal. M'sieu Mus'rat is a night prowler, and he is caught as he advances along his runs (though he may be one of the smart ones and step or swim neatly around the pitfall). We tossed him in the pirogue and paddled on. By noon the vessel was so well packed that Albert and the boys took out their knives and quickly skinned most of them. Into the boat went the pelt, into the water the discarded flesh. We wasted little time; all knew that if we moved only a little faster, things would be easier for the family for the rest of the year. Toward the end we had to race to reach the last trap while we could still see.

Madame and the girls were at the door when we arrived home, and supper was on the table. They had already eaten, and they got to work at once to finish the skinning. Madame had a clothes wringer ready, and into it she slipped each pelt, to take off any remaining bits of skin. She and the girls worked also at a high pile of metal stretchers, and one by one the skins were transferred for drying. Outside, a tall rack received the rows of stretchers. Before the women were finished, Albert, the boys, and I were asleep. That was the routine during the days following. We worked as long as the light allowed, while the women finished the care of yesterday's pelts and awaited our arrival with the new ones.

Days came when traps were light, and we speculated as to how other families were doing. When a trap went empty for too many days, it was changed to another run. Sometimes we found "kits," the half-grown muskrats, and "mice," the very young, caught while out on their first forays. That was not good; everybody would have preferred to catch them later, when their pelts were larger; but the small skins would bring some return. Once a bad stretch of weather made our work practically useless. Again, Albert got up one morning so feverish that Madame kept him home. The oldest boy took charge, and all day we talked of the trouble in store if Albert stayed sick. He was up the next day; it is hard for a trapper to stay in bed under such circumstances.

At intervals the owner-grocer came in his cabin cruiser, took the skins, and left an assortment of food. We found another connection with the outside. Near us, on a high rise, were two houseboats, a wood-and-tar-paper shack and another of palmetto and boards—the homes of other trappers. We visited them several times, after light days, and found them hearty companions. The radio, card games, and guitar playing by one of the men were our diversions; the children popped tac-tac (popcorn), and we joked about Alphonse's and Gustave's beards. For most men there is no time to shave while in the marsh, and what does it matter? Whenever I have visited a trappers' camp, someone has been pushed forward for inspection of his phenomenal chin ornamentation. In confident mood after a good period, the older ones talked sometimes of what they would do with their money, and their ambitions were always similar—clearing off the mortgage at home, trapping lands of their own, a new lugger; and two of the women said quietly that they wanted better education for their children, no matter what else was done.

One evening on this trip I was served a pungent dish accompanied by well-seasoned gravy. I had three helpings, one above par for me. At first I decided that it was chicken, then that it must be squirrel. At the end I was informed that it was muskrat. Like many others who have been introduced to this delicacy under similar circumstances, I was momentarily taken aback; but I have eaten it several times since, and enjoyed it the more on each occasion. Many marsh men, like others, have a violent feeling against the muskrat as food, and have never tasted him. One trapper told me that he liked rattlesnake meat and alligator tail but would never touch the mus'rat. Yet he is a clean animal, and flavorsome. It is largely the last part of his name that is against him. For years he has been sold in Northern markets as "marsh hare" and, sometimes, disguised as terrapin. In 1943, with meat shortage upon the country, state officials pointed out that muskrat flesh to the equivalent of 16,000 dressed steers a year was being thrown away.

After two weeks and a half I left the Alidores, with my thanks and with most of the season ahead of them. A few months later I met Albert again. How had they come out? About $550, he figured; it could have been much better. But then, the way the landowners worked things, he frowned. . . . He had had a fight with that one of his, and now he would have to find new grounds for next year. Over the

Alidores as over most of the other trappers hangs the shadow of a discontent. Much of it is the grievance of tenancy, for these muskrat hunters are Southern sharecroppers of a sort, as shall be seen.

For many years a steady, quiet flow of the pelts took place from the reedy stretches. A man went to the marshes when he decided that it was a proper time for the animals, and he worked his lines as he wished. The land was "free"; no one questioned his right to use whatever seemed good. The pelts brought only a few cents each, but they were plentiful, and the work filled in a gap in the year. Comparatively few Americans were as yet wearers of fur. Most of the Louisiana skins were sent to Europe, where they had a place, but not a large one. The dealers preferred the silver foxes and seals and the other more spectacular pelts. Then, as the present century approached, the Far-Northern centers of these luxury products saw an impending depletion. About the same time the average American woman learned more of furs; mass production made available many things that previously had been confined to the wealthy. The smaller, less costly pelts found a place, and the market realized that Louisiana was a widespread fur farm. Workers trimmed the muskrat pelt, dyed it and matched it—sometimes several thousand pieces for color and quality in a single coat—so that, disguised, it became "Hudson Bay seal" or "Southern mink" or other variations of magic words. From the muskrat back came sections of dark brown; from the stomach, the white or "silver"; from the sides, portions of red-gold.

The price to the trapper jumped. At one time he had received as little as eight cents a skin; now it reached $1.50, $2, $2.50, higher. The marsh men thrived, bought handsome automobiles, new boats. Some are still prosperous merchants and dealers as a result of good investment of their returns; most are small trappers again. Others saw how the muskrat trade was booming, and here and there new men appeared, to serve notice that they were owners, or holders of leases from the state, of rich sections that no one had claimed before. Some who had been known only by names on assessment rolls, and had never been seen by the natives, came forward; middlemen moved in, with fur corporations whose officers were local politicians or merchants. The trappers, who knew nothing of sub-leases and lawyers' documents, protested; they defied those who tried to take "their" trapping land; and blood was spilled. Men were ousted in the "trappers' wars"; others were imported to take their places, and there followed shootings of "scabs" from ambush, riddling of boats along the bayous. The courts were invoked, and they ruled against the trappers. The fur corporations reign over most of the yellow-green salt marshes. The trapper is the tenant for the season, and he can keep only part of what he takes.

Today the marsh man does the best he can in a situation that shifts, and in dealings with men who may do the same. I have watched gradings of furs that were cynically unfair, and yet the trapper was usually afraid to protest. The man doing the grading had provided him with his "furnish" for the season, and he was in debt to him, and he hoped to be back on the same land next year. Sometimes the trapper can sell his furs at open auction, but generally it must be to the owner only, and the sale must take place when the owner says. This means that the trapper cannot take advantage of changing market prices, but is prey to the other man. Diseases have struck the muskrat, adding further to the uncertainties of the annual catch; and nature's hazards are ever present. The trapper is therefore not impressed when someone reminds him that in this area an acre of land may bring a yield greater than that of sugar or cotton in other parts of the state. Like Albert Alidore, he "does what he can, and hopes maybe for better." [1]

The richest fur corner of the world, according to some, centers about a stretch of land near the Gulf in St. Bernard Parish, less than twenty miles from New Orleans. Here is the last remaining remnant of Spain in Louisiana, the only spot, in fact, that ever became or remained truly Iberian during that nation's forty years of rule. It demonstrates better than most others the uncertainties of those who depend on M'sieu Mus'-rat for their living.

About 1778 Governor Galvez received a group of Canary Islanders, brought over at government expense to populate this one of several Spanish specks in the Gallic sea of Louisiana. Each family was given land, cattle, and funds for four years. They settled below the capital city in this general section, called Terre-aux-Boeufs, for the great number of oxen that lived there. At one time it was a thriving plantation area on which rose estates dating back to the French seigneurs and the stately summer homes of the Spanish officialdom. A few years after the islanders came, it saw experiments which led to the successful granulation of sugar and the transformation of the state's agricultural economy. The Canary Islanders were simple tillers of the soil, men whose forefathers had long been peasants, and it might have been expected that they

[1] The Roosevelt New Deal brought long-needed improvement for many trappers. Public auctions were provided; loans enabled them to acquire their own lands, and delinquency of less than three per cent was reported, despite high waters. More than a quarter of those assisted have paid back their loans in full, and the rest are making rapid progress to ownership of their lands. Trappers on land owned by the state also get the benefit of public auctions.

would thrive here as farmers. But chance arranged things in another fashion. The islanders had been glad to leave their home soil because of tragic drought; in Louisiana they were to suffer because there was too much water. They found themselves along Bayou Terre-aux-Boeufs, in a country of mixed qualities, with limited land susceptible to cultivation. Their small span of dry earth, though not a true island, became known to the settlers as La Isla. Eventually it had a patroness, the Countess Livaudais de Suan de la Croix; she is remembered today in its name, Delacroix Island.

The Isleños did not complain, and they did not ask questions. They turned from farm work to the water and the marsh, to trapping and the taking of sea things. On La Isla they erected their houses of split wood and palm roofs, lifted above the threat of water. Swarthy, inarticulate, they stayed to themselves, a people apart in their home area and in their infrequent forays to the outside world. New Orleans came to know a few of them when they transferred their catch to the city markets by vessels with high sails, or by great wooden carts pulled by oxen yoked by the horn in the Spanish style. On their way back and forth they passed the great palaces, and they may have admired them and wondered about the strange life inside such places; but they were a humble folk, and when they found themselves near the high ones, they bowed and went on quickly. About them, through the generations, moved others—Acadians, Anglo-Saxons, Italians. The Isleños held tightly to themselves, keeping intact their language, their customs, and their identity. Gradually they came to depend more and more for their subsistence upon the fur animals of the marshes. When the present century began and the muskrat assumed new importance, the Isleños realized for a time the advantage of their position in the heart of a superbly stocked territory. Some of their people became well off; the test of a man's status was his ability to take a vacation, and it was rather frequently to one spot—Cuba. Many of the Louisiana French had gone regularly to Paris; Havana served for the Isleños—a place where they could speak happy Spanish and play card games and be with friends who understood their ways.

With the years, however, came a series of blows. The islanders found themselves victims of many forces. Their location put them in jeopardy of two elements. A few miles off was the Gulf; closer was the Mississippi, widening as it approached the blue water. The hurricane of 1915 struck with bitter fury, wiping out all but one or two of the frail houses, sending the Isleños fleeing with their small possessions. The scant church records and other documents that they possessed were washed away; today they have few written links with their past. Afterward, stoic as ever, resigned to what Diós ordained, they returned and began over again. Seven years later, the Mississippi levee gave way a short distance from Delacroix Island, and their settlement was flooded deeply. The waters seeped away slowly; they had to wait nearly two months before they could return. In the interim they struck a hard blow at their own well-being. The frightened muskrats fled to the highest elevations and waited, helpless, for some deliverance. Taking their hunting guns, the islanders shot them for their fur, killing old and young indiscriminately, and further depleting their supply for years to come.

Then, only five years later, in 1927, the river water's rage was once more turned upon them, in this case by man himself. New Orleans was threatened. Some other area must be sacrificed to preserve the Queen City. The levee adjacent to the Island was blasted open, and the Isleños stood by help-lessly as the silt-laden stream surged over their homes. This time more than their settlement was endangered. All the sur-rounding marshes, holding their main source of livelihood, were inundated. Some of the muskrats managed to escape ahead of the waters; others were drowned, or trapped on raised spots. Unless something were done quickly, the rats faced extermination.

The Isleños had learned since their last flood. Assisted by conservation officials, they worked now to save their animals. They built "life rafts," covered them with moss and grass, and anchored them among trees and bushes, to provide food and a place of rest for thousands of the animals during their long swim to higher grounds. Some set out wooden packing crates, similarly covered. Snakes, rabbits, turtles, and musk-rats rode together on some of these floats. Abandoned build-ings were opened to the animals, and colonies thrived on beds and in armoires. Some of the "kits" could be rescued and were fed by bottles. Through it all, men stood guard with guns against those who would try to kill the tormented animals as they sought refuge.

For some months the Isleños were the subject of friendly concern; then they were forgotten by the rest of the world. They received compensation for their losses, and officials said that it was adequate. Within a year or two they came to attention again, uncomfortably and unhappily. Charges were made that many among them were suffering from want, some close to starvation. The Isleños insisted that they had received payment for only part of their losses; that in some cases they had been tricked. Worse, the marshes were far below their usual production of the rats; and for a time, due to the dam-aging overflow, their fishing and their oyster digging were also in sharp decline. If they waited several years before trapping, some suggested, the rats would multiply again, and all would be well. But meanwhile they had to eat, señors.

Authorities spluttered. Some help was given, and the Isleños slipped into the background again. Gradually the marshes regained much of their former prodigality. The trappers' wars and more storms broke over the area from year to year—and politics, not the smallest factor in some of their troubles. Spanish tempers, heated by the efforts of rival forces, have repeatedly exploded. St. Bernard Parish, in which Delacroix Island is an important center, is as bitterly torn by factionalism as any in Louisiana—a state in which partisanship wears gaudy colors. When the storms hit in 1940, as Father Edward J. Kammer has pointed out, refugees of one group declined to accept emergency housing in the same courthouse halls with those of another group. Officials, as a matter of fact, were afraid of "trouble" between the two, and a second place was found. On occasion, separate blessings of St. Bernard shrimp fleets have been required. One faction will not kneel down for prayer in the neighborhood of the other.

But I found general conditions somewhat improved on my last visit among the Isleños. Like others, the men of the marshes have benefited by war economy. With sons on the battlefront together, the elders have agreed to a rationing of internal bickering. Federal loans of recent years, too, brought rehabilitation in many cases. Curiously, some of the women of La Isla are learning how to turn to the agriculture of their mothers. Farm agencies are instructing the housewives in the value of fresh foods and mixed diets, and have persuaded them to devote their small scraps of land to crops, hogs, and chickens. When one agency brought brooders, it had some difficulty in locating a place for demonstrations. It finally found a room—at the back of a barroom, of which the area has a good quota; and this served as a community gathering place.

The Island is changing, but slowly. The Spanish language has relaxed its grip only to a limited extent. It has an odd flavor, like the settlement itself, with archaic expressions seldom heard in other places. The small cottages, which have succeeded the lost palmetto-thatched ones, are splashed with rich reds and greens and yellows; nothing is drab or subdued. To the outsider, the Isleño is reserved; but when he has satisfied himself that the visitor is not trying to cheat him, the situation changes. The minimum demonstration of regard is a trip to one of the bars, and as many rounds as the caller can take and several more, while he is introduced all around and everybody talks pungent Spanish-English.

The house at which I visited most recently was as humble as any in the lowlands, but the friendship was capacious and rich. While the husband and I talked in the combination living-and-dining room, well-peppered dinner was quickly prepared; and as always, no matter what else there is in the house, a little wine was on the table. The old grandmother, who could not speak a word of English, smiled and smiled. The grandfather, white-bearded, thinner than his jovial son, and wearing the paleness of age, watched and ate in polite silence. He cannot read or write in Spanish or in English, but his manner is as ever that of restrained dignity; the stranger might take him for an elderly grandee, sojourning among simpler folk. After the meal, he lay on the cool floor, with several of the children, for the siesta.

Miles to the west, in the middle of the marshes about Terrebonne Bay, is another island whose livelihood has largely been by the skin of the rat. It is the Isle à Jean Charles, a ridge that appears on few maps. Most of the names among the 180 residents are French, and French is spoken more often than any other tongue. But there is a copper color to the skin of its men and women, a sharpness of nose and cheekbone, that tell of another race. Most of them are descendants of the Houma Indians, who have mixed with others to such an extent that the government has declined to grant reservation rights. And Lafitte, who appears in many unexpected places, bobs up here. A well-entrenched tradition declares that one reason for the "strangeness" of these people is a connection with the pirates. More than a century ago, it is said, when trouble came for the corsairs, some of them slipped into this place and merged with others. Be that as it may, the people of Jean Charles seem like other Indians of the state, a shattered people, mild and submissive in most things. In their dark eyes there is usually humility; but now and then an anger can burn, when they feel that they have been victims of a particular piece of unfairness. They are at a racial fringe, and it is not often possible for them to forget it.

Some unflattering items about this group were passed on to me in the thriving French town of Houma. I was warned that they were "not representative"; and I hereby declare that they are not so. Why, I was asked, did I want to visit that sort—"undependable" or worse? It has been only in recent years that outsiders, some of Houma and elsewhere, have wondered about the people of Jean Charles and concerned themselves; others, it was clear, disapproved of such goings-on. But I went; and I went with a number of good recommendations, and well accompanied. The islanders have confidence and trust in Marie Louise Duval and Marie Louise Lacasse, who taught them and helped them with such things as pressure cookers and milk.

We rode by winding path to Pointe-au-Chien, last mainland settlement, and then by motorboat along a meandering passage that narrowed and shallowed, until we could go no farther, and then stepped off upon land that was more or less dry. A single file of houses stood on a slight ridge, with footpaths in the mud along a sluggish central stream. In the doorways of the aged and tired houses sat stout women with children at their breasts, with older ones wearing palmetto-leaf hats. At the end of the small waterway men and boys were preparing to leave, with fishing tackle and traps. (No one is needed to tell these men how to follow the rats; their fathers were skilled in the art when the first whites arrived.) All peered at us, a few waved, and one called out: "He at home now." Nobody asked a question; our procedure was taken for granted. Those who go to Isle à Jean Charles call first on the Chief, Victor Naquin, in his "maison blanche." Freshly painted, built not of logs and palmetto but of split boards, it is the grande maison of the island.

The Chief was in his front room. He was a tall man, heavily built, impressive in his strength and in his calm command, as he sat bolt upright in his chair and solemnly fanned himself. Nearing seventy-five, white-haired, with ruddy face, beetling brows, and gold spectacles, he dominated the island whether seen or unseen. Standing behind him was the smiling Madame Naquin, gaunt, sharp-nosed, gold-earringed, and gold-spectacled, like her husband. Neither spoke English; we managed in French.

Again I heard a story of agriculture that declined under the blows of nature. In the older days, when the Chief was young, his people raised good crops—"fine fields of rice, and corn and greens." The year 1909 was their tragedy; a tidal wave washed upon them and when it was gone, much of their soil had slipped away. The Chief and others whom I met talked sadly of the thinness of their ground. One or two showed small patches, bordered with sticks, which were held in place with strips of palmetto. Today there is another problem for the island people; white men from the mainland pasture their cattle there and the cows trample and eat the crops. The owners say that they permit the islanders to milk their cows; but that would still seem a somewhat inequitable arrangement.

We walked about, and men and women came forward, shyly at first, then with less diffidence. Trapping—that is the thing, said the men. Their fathers, they did well with it. For years the area was theirs to use as they wanted; it had always been trapped by the island people. Then the state leased it, "and now we are shut out." When they raised questions, they were told that they had had the same right as others to bid for the leases. It was all advertised in the paper, wasn't it? Today they are confined to the less desirable grounds; and their living is harder to get.

More and more they depend on fish, crabs, and shrimp. Most of them have no motorboats; they must use their pirogues. Accordingly, they are limited in the territory they can cover. To Pointe-au-Chien trucks come from New Orleans in the evening, to take their catch. But when seafood is not so plentiful . . . they shrugged. I heard of children who cried because, after many days of repetition, a diet of fried-potato sandwiches became unpalatable. Two families whom I met were those of artisans, making boat paddles, hide-bottomed chairs, and other furnishings. Their work was of fine design and workmanship, graceful and French. Most of the homes of Jean Charles are provided from these sources; armoires are large and impressive, beds high and well-carved four-posters. Yet when I was invited into the houses of several others who had possessed a little money in other years, I found store furniture, badly made, its cheap veneer cracked. The family in each case was proud. The stuff "came from the mainland."

I edged about, carefully I thought, to the question of origins. The Chief flared. "Lafitte! It is not so. No! People from outside invent that." His mouth snapped shut. Then he softened and spoke of his great-grandfather, Monsieur Jean Charles Naquin, who came here from France and gave the island his name. Two others, men whose names were Chaisson and Dardar, followed. Almost every islander of today can trace his ancestry back to one of the three; the families have intermingled their blood many times in the subsequent years. There are others, Vardins, and Billiots, and a few more, but mainly the names are of the other group. Who were the first mothers of the island? The Chief and others were less voluble on that point. The islanders, I learned, tell different stories at different times. Generally it is assumed that they were native women of the Houma tribe. On this day the Chief said only: "Our people are French and German."

Willie Naquin, son of the Chief, sharp-eyed and sharp-witted, is one who has talked more freely than the others. Now gone from the island, he was formerly known as one of the best guides in the parish. Through his contacts with outsiders, he acquired a sophistication in advance of the rest. He told my friend Jim Calvert: "I have listened to the old people since I am as big as a raccoon. All the time, it was of the great Lafitte that they speak. They say it was some of Lafitte's big men that came here. The great Jean would sail his ships into hiding around the island and slip away from those that were on his tail." Willie obviously was not impressed with that phase of the subject. He chuckled: "One time, our people search from one end of the island to the other for gold. All they find was prairie water, that seeped into the holes."

Through several generations a file of somewhat shadowy men has moved to the island, men who chose this far-off spot for reasons that were not clear. The Chief said that one was a deserter from the French army; of the others, he was not sure. Each taught French to the islanders. Some of the men of Jean Charles have learned well; their speech is more than a patois. In recent years school has reached the children, largely through missions at the nearest mainland point. Daily, children have crowded into slim pirogues and paddled the long distance back and forth. The demand has often been greater than the number of boats, and some have been left behind, crying. The teachers reported that they do well. After two years, several had advanced to the third grade.

This anxiety to reach the outside schools is, perhaps, significant. Other forces besides the war have taken youths from Jean Charles. Their fathers were willing to stay and take what others were willing to give them. The younger ones, I sensed, will try for themselves. Isolation may not be their answer. Some are offering to the market the things that their island life has given them. I saw a number of the people before their open fireplaces, seasoning food in heavy iron pots; and their gumbos of shrimp and crabs and game combine the cooking arts of France with those of the Indians. Several of the boys have used this knowledge to become professional cooks.

As we started to go, someone suggested a song. The Chief's brother, white-haired and sturdy, like him, was pushed forward. Reluctantly, he agreed, if he could have a drink first. We had neglected to bring anything with us; he settled on a swallow of coffee from a near-by house. He stood on the bank, clasped his hands, and sang a "chanson de guerre," of a soldier and his love. The soldier asked leave to see his girl. His captain granted it. Ah, but the girl, dear Prospère, she died. The soldier was disconsolate; his life was ruined. His friends worried. And then his dead sweetheart, Prospère, came to him in a vision. She told him—shades of romantic frustration!—to be sensible and get himself another sweetheart. And he did. French realism still lives here.

§ 6. *The Wart That Became a Paradise*

AVERY ISLAND is a bump, six miles round, on the smooth cheek of the Louisiana earth. It is a caprice of natural forces, a sudden elevation of several irregular peaks, its highest point 195 feet above the reed marsh and bayous. In other parts of America it would be a small hill. Here it is a Himalaya of the wet grounds.

For most of the half-hour trip out of the city of New Iberia this "island" over the land rose slowly before me. I had heard many things about it and its master, some of which I was not inclined to believe. Then, with Edward Avery McIlhenny, I stood upon that highest spot, the greatest natural elevation along the Gulf coast from Florida to Texas, and the tales suddenly seemed likely ones. Beneath us, visible for miles, stretched the world of these lowlands, in concentration: thick marsh, cypress swamp, dry forest in which bear and deer can be found; hills and ravines, wide pastures for grazing, a bayou threading its way. On all sides were birds by the tens of thousands, great black ones, many-colored ones, and delicate white herons, resting on the mixed surfaces, flying toward the Gulf below, or circling higher. For centuries this has been a kind of conjured place to Louisianians, a separate kingdom, from which peculiar, inexplicable phenomena have often come. That summer day I walked about it with its owner, listening to him and thinking of those things that I had been told, and the farther we advanced, the more remarkable it all seemed.

The first white man to come here found the mound a thing of deserted beauty. Richly thicketed, bountiful in its wealth of that which grows and moves, it had become a place that was hated and feared. In 1790, long before others had ventured so far, an odd youth, John Hays of Pennsylvania, age fifteen, arrived at the mount. He was the first modern man to be captivated by its fabulous combinations; he never left it. He remained on, eventually as "old John Hays," until he died, in his nineties. He was a friendly fellow, and the Indians liked him and helped him. But when he invited them to join him in hunts on the hills, they declined. They averted their eyes from the place; some grim disaster had occurred there long ago. That was all that he could learn. One day in 1791, he came upon a ravine in the middle of the island, with a spring, an unusual thing in these flatlands. He bent over the water; it was so briny that he could not swallow it. Boiling it, he obtained a large handful of salt, and thereafter his supply of the mineral came from this source.

A few years later John Marsh of New Jersey appeared on the scene, with a grant of all the island from the Spanish governor. For a century and a half the place has remained, like the d'Estréhan-Harvey Canal, in the hands of a single clan. The new owner heard young Hays talk happily of the fine salt spring, and for a time limited quantities of the commodity were taken. But John Marsh, like other propertied Louisianians of the day, saw his future in sugar rather than salt. He placed a spreading plantation about the slopes and plains, and shipped out his crop by the Bayou Petite Anse that wound about the island. He prospered; the spring was largely forgotten. America was then obtaining most of her salt from Europe, where rock deposits were available. Only brine springs were at hand in this country, and it was easier and cheaper to obtain the stuff in bulk.

With the War of 1812 and England's blockade, the new nation found itself suddenly in need of the mineral. John Marsh established a saltworks, and thousands of pounds were obtained by crude methods, with wooden implements sunk into the water, and mule power pumping it out for boiling and evaporation. But with peace, the European rock supplies took the market again. The island supplied only the local needs. Another conflict, the Civil War, was required to bring the commodity forward again.

New Orleans and surrounding areas fell into Federal hands; this part of the state, to the west, remained Confederate territory for a time. The South was cut off from this vital necessity, salt, and in 1862 John Avery, grandson of the first owner, decided to deepen the old spring. One of his Negro men dug for sixteen feet, and called up: "Struck a log." Told to dig around it, he reported that he could find no sides. It went on and on. Avery followed him down, felt the object and put his fingers to his lips. It was the first important deposit of rock salt to be discovered in America.[1]

Here was the explanation of the great rising over the marsh. Below the rich top layer of soil was an enormous bulk of the

[1] The existence of a large rock salt deposit at the island had previously been suspected. The matter was a subject of controversy and derision at the time of the Louisiana Purchase. Jefferson, badgered by Congressional critics, once said that he understood the territory possessed a solid salt

mineral, six feet in circumference at the top, widening many times below, extending for miles, perhaps, into the ground. Ages earlier, when this part of Louisiana was water, the sea had deposited deep masses of the mineral. Later came covers of other matter, silt and vegetation, burying the saline spread far below the surface. Then a crack developed in the upper layers, and the pressure from below forced up this mighty pile. Now as men dug they found fragments of three prehistoric animals—the ground sloth, the mastodon, and the horse. Here they had taken refuge, probably, when sheets of water swept down from the melting glaciers; here they had perished. Below these remains and in conjunction with some of the salt, excavators came upon pottery and other evidences of Indian life. Men apparently had used this mineral many years earlier; they had known the secret of the island. Then tragedy had struck; and the Indians had forgotten the reason.

Meanwhile, the discovery of the rock salt during the Civil War was an important matter for both sides. The Confederates placed heavy guards about the operations. As many as 500 teams of mules were found at one time on the island, seeking salt supplies for every part of the South. The Federals dispatched a gunboat up the bayou, but the pilot knew nothing of this terrain, and the boat was stuck in the bottom. A year later, after more careful preparation, the Federals captured the works and destroyed them. Then the Averys had to leave. Returning in Reconstruction days, they beheld the desolate waste of their estate. With the help of some of their

mound 180 miles long. His figure was off, but he was more nearly correct than many realized. His opponents gibed at him:

Jefferson lately of Bonaparte bought
To pickle his fame a mountain of salt.

From *Mountains of Salt,* by Mary Willis Shuey

former slaves, they began a slow upbuilding. A new shaft was sunk, men learned slowly the full extent of the rich deposit, and salt replaced sugar as the foundation of the family fortune. Since the beginning of the present century, drilling has been going on at a single level, 518 feet; the exact lower limit of the salt has never been determined. Some have expressed belief that the plug will provide the commodity for hundreds of years to come. Since its discovery, four similar but smaller deposits have been found in the area, all apparently extrusions from a great "mother" body of salt six miles or so deep. I found the Avery mine impressive, with caverns sixty feet high, walls supported by thick pillars of crystal. Essentially it was like other salt mines; the difference lay in the realization that far above was the low, moist, rockless terrain.

It required another chance incident, and again war—two wars, in fact—to bring forth the next major product of the island earth. During the years preceding the Civil War, a man known to the Avery family went with the Army in the Mexican War. Returning, he brought with him a pack of red-pepper seeds from the state of Tabasco, with the suggestion that they would make handsome trimmings for the flower beds. The plants thrived. The family cook was an adventurous soul, and from the fiery seeds developed several sauces which met with quick approval. One was particularly pleasing, and guests requested it whenever they came again to visit.

Years later, home again after the Civil War had ended, a member of the family came upon a few shining red plants in the wastes, and thought of the condiment. Intensive cultivation was started, the sauce was made, and it was sold. Among the visiting friends of the family was the Federal administrator of Reconstruction days. He sampled the sauce, liked it, and took several bottles North to a brother, who headed a wholesale grocery house. Response was rapid. The mixture was sold throughout the world, and when Lord Kitchener went to Khartoum, he reported that he had found it farther in the desert than any other manufactured food. Official tribute has been paid it—the word "tabasco" has been taken into the language to signify the ultimate in burning seasoning. Today the name is patented; an Avery Island factory issues the product in great quantities, and wide acres here and in adjoining sections are covered with scarlet pepper pods.

A few years after tabasco sauce appeared, a new son was born on Avery Island, and the history of the place now becomes that of Edward Avery McIlhenny. Part of his story I heard from him during my visit; part came from others; and some of it is derived from my observation of this man who fits into few grooves.

The only place Ned McIlhenny knew during his formative years was this richly endowed area of jungle-like thickets, hills, and woods. Before he could walk with ease, he was taken on trips about the bayous and marshes. Soon he was asking many questions. His mother and father told him what they knew, and added that the way to gain some of the other answers was to watch closely for himself. He did, and this he has been doing ever since.

Young Ned accompanied Acadian helpers along the waterways, inspected muskrat houses, peered at the bears in the swamp, and crouched in the pirogue to watch while birds flew about the trees. From the beginning, the birds interested him in particular. The island and its surroundings are in the center of one of the greatest feeding grounds of wild birds of the continent, a place about which move great lines of migrants on wing. His land was filled with awkward pelicans, the brilliant roseate spoonbills, thousands of circling herons of blues and pinks and startling white plumage, and many others. He spent much of his time among them. A tall, powerful, blond youth, Ned seemed more at home in the woods than under any roof. Today, more than a half-century later, he still walks loose-hipped, with the woodsman's easy stride. Despite great bulk, he can move so silently in the woods that most birds do not sense his presence.

In time he went to Northern schools, but between terms he was always at Avery. He was a young man with ideas of his own and, it developed, they were sometimes large ones. He accompanied Peary's Arctic expedition in the '90's, studying a favorite subject, migratory birds. He liked that so well that he organized an expedition of his own a few years later. He had done tall things at home; he knew no reason why he should not do them when away. He has told many times of how he and his force saved 105 whalers wrecked in the Arctic ocean. Lacking food for these additional men, the nearest settlement 700 miles far south across impassable territory, they made their way to a lake where they, killed enough caribou to keep them alive. One of the mixed crew, as he described it, was the man who is known as Jack London. McIlhenny remembers him as "the laziest man that ever crossed my path," one who had to be forced from his bunk to take exercise, but who was a favorite of them all.

By this time "M'sieu Ned" had decided that the place in which he was born was the interest of his life. Other brothers went to law, medicine, business; he went to Avery Island, and he changed it more than had any other man in its history. For some years he had been watching a gradual depletion of the bird life of South Louisiana. Many species that he had known as a boy were no longer to be found; and even the thickly-packed Avery Island itself was beginning to suffer. In particular he had seen the practical disappearance of the snowy egret—a slim, long-necked migrant of delicate white beauty, that had once filled the marshes. Female vanity and male greed were responsible. The creature at mating time sprouts long, thread-like, curling feathers; Paris ordered this plumage for women's hats, and regiments of hunters moved toward the Gulf coast. Dealers paid a dollar a plume. The adults, male and female, have twenty on each shoulder. Forty dollars a single bird! Many eyes brightened at the thought, and guns blasted over the lowlands.

The plumage appears only at mating time. The egret will not desert its young when its mate is taken. When one was killed, the hunter took a position near by and waited a short time. The other came back, and profit went up to $80, while the young were left to die. Skilled plume seekers used spy-glasses to locate the birds and traced their lines of flight to their colonies. Days might be needed for pursuit, but when a single colony was located and wiped out, all agreed that the time was well spent.

One day a British visitor called at Avery Island, a former official of India. During the evening he told of a rajah who amused a bored concubine by building a great cage of bamboo and filling it with many birds. The rajah died, and his successors were not interested; the wood rotted and broke apart. But the birds did not fly away; their lives had been fitted within the narrow range. "M'sieu Ned" nodded and thought about the story several times. Then he called together two Negro helpers. In a slight depression on the island they built a dam to form a lake. From the marshes they brought buttonwoods and other trees on which egrets perched in the water, and they planted them in the new lake. With lumber and mesh they raised a small cage of their own. Now they set out to find a few last egrets in the wet lands. They crawled through thickets and liquid mud; after several days it seemed that they had failed. But they traced a few faint cries, and eventually they returned with eight small birds.

Placed in a cage, these newcomers to the island were treated like incubator products; hovered over, protected from all hazards, hand-fed by the master with tadpoles, shrimp, and other foods. Ned McIlhenny gave part of each day to the birds. They no longer started in fright at his approach; they flew about his head, rubbed bills against his ear, and "talked" to him. From time to time he let them follow him as he rode about, and they came back with him to their cages.

Early fall arrived, and the egrets shivered slightly. A vague urge told them to go away; but there were no elders to guide or direct them. Perhaps, after all, this was the best place to stay? McIlhenny was not training house-pets, he said; he expected them to leave with the season as did the other birds, then remember and return to this protected place with the next year. Also, they might freeze if they stayed here. So one night he left the cage open and bade them good-by. When he called again, the door was still open, and they were still there. He locked them out; they perched on the cage top, quivering. He destroyed the cages, and they took places on near-by bushes. At last instinct won. One November dawn they were on their long journey across the Gulf.

Through all that winter Ned McIlhenny wondered about that small band of confused egrets. As spring approached he watched the skies. Other seasonal birds were back, joining the year-round residents of the area; his white herons were over-

due. Would they join the few remaining others in unpro-
tected places in the marshes, and be killed? Were they dead
already? One morning he caught sight of several dots of nervous white on the trees that he had planted in the water. The
birds had not forgotten. He had won, thus far anyway. Six
of the eight returned. And now in mating season the males
grew their plumage and danced and shook out their ruffles of
soft white. The females preened themselves and accepted the
tadpoles and other courting gifts which were held forth to
them. The eggs appeared, and Ned McIlhenny embarked on
a policy of robbery and deception of the birds in their own
interest. He removed the contents of the nests. Not far off
were those of the commoner Louisiana heron; these he cleared
out, replacing their eggs with the egret eggs. The Louisiana
herons noticed no change, and soon were raising all-white
aristocrats as theirs. Then the egrets, disturbed but not incon-
solable, produced more eggs of their own. The speed-up
doubled production. With fall, thirteen egrets flew away;
with spring, all thirteen returned.

Other birds learned of this place of safety, and each season
brought an increase in population. The pool had to be expanded, and then expanded again, and more trees planted.
When I visited the sanctuary, McIlhenny estimated that about
115,000 birds come every year. Other types of birds drop out
of the sky and, no objection being raised, take up quarters.
There are five heron varieties and numerous others. He smiled
as he explained: "Our old boarders are always bringing strangers home with them. You can tell the new ones—they're shy
at first, and don't come down so easily. They learn, and then
they tell others." The project at times has become too successful, developing problems of housing and priorities. Nest-
ing material became insufficient some years ago; the birds

were denuding the near-by trees and threatening prized growths in other parts of the island. Workmen today spend part of each spring preparing wagonloads of twigs and branches, partly processed, for the birds. The master took me to a series of floating platforms in the lake. The men row out each morning during the early part of the season and pile them high. "It's all empty before night," he chuckled. "We give the birds about forty wagonloads a season."

We looked at Bird City's apartment projects, and therein lay the record of another puzzle, and another solution. Years ago, all the tree space was used up. Nests had to be built so close together that one seemed almost on top of the other. Birds began to fight. The best place for new quarters seemed to be the lake, and upon it the McIlhenny forces got to work. Poles were sunk into the bottom and platforms erected, with first and second story homes. The birds liked it; but eventually nature interfered, when water rotted the wooden foundations. To build expensive new ones every few years was out of the question. In other places in Louisiana, creosoting has protected underwater timbers. What was good enough for people was good enough for McIlhenny birds. Bigger, safeguarded boarding houses were set up, and all sat back to watch the residents take them. They reckoned without their guests. The herons circled about, sniffed the aromatic matter, and wheeled away. They did not like it. They spurned even the near-by bushes on which they had nested for some time. Would the whole venture fall? There was nothing for the management to do but wait and see which would conquer— creosote or sex. "We were very much worried," the owner admitted.

Sex pouted and held off as long as it could. Then one or two pairs of herons fluttered reluctantly to a bush as distant from the creosote as they could find. Others followed, warily, until the line of birds approached the new apartments. For a time none of them would cross the line. Many hours later, one bird swept over and sat down. Nothing happened. He inspected the twigs and began to build. Others joined him, and Bird City was safe.

The island has become more than a summer watering place for birds. It is now an all-year-round institution. When the herons leave for the South, in fly ducks and geese from the North—the blue-winged teal, the gray duck, spoonbill mallard, lesser scaup, and others. For them, as for the herons, the natural scene has been changed here and there. Some birds like to dive for their meals; the management plants deep-growing food. Others want to stand and sink their heads; for them, shallow-water plants. A third group do not want wet heads; floating supplies are theirs. The proprietor told me how he sometimes takes hunting friends, who leave guns behind, to his ponds. Here are the most elusive types of birds, swimming about, paying no attention to the intruders. An hour later, if the same hunters are only a mile from the island, the same birds will scatter from them in anxious flight.

Life at Bird City is partly self-regulated. Wise and compassionate rules have been adopted by the birds for the welfare of the young and elderly—a social security program for the lake. The pond is packed with food, but the able-bodied adults do not touch it. They will make long trips back and forth for their food and that of the newly hatched ones. The tempting stuff in the water is for the young birds who have left the nest but are as yet unable to negotiate long distances, and for the old, who are too weak. "We have some who are our pensioners for life," explained "M'sieu Ned."

To go at dawn is to see Bird City under the happiest auspices. It is possible to take a stand within a few feet of the trees and apartments; a highway and a train track run close by, and the birds seldom stir on that account. In the uncertain light all that can be seen are small white rolls of feathers, some restless, others quiet. On the tall trees the birds seem clustered only about the lower branches, none at the top. As the day brightens, the caller finds what he had missed at first; there are thousands of other birds, darker ones of other classification, in the top branches. This division has taken place naturally, according to the tastes of the birds. Now it is evident that almost every foot of available space is crowded with birds of many kinds: Louisiana herons of many shading hues, gray-black, rose, white; the drab-blue herons, slate-colored with red-brown head; the small, short-necked green herons; the shiny black ibis; the curious anhinga or "snake bird," of serpentine neck that darts back and forth. The snowy egrets, with their darker bills and legs in contrast to their delicate bodies, merely stand out the most clearly.

The first close view of the egret nest brings a surprise. Such a bird might be expected to build a home of fine artistry. It is, instead, a haphazard bit of construction, of jagged ends thrust in all directions, apparently the work of an amateur. It seems precariously balanced, too, with little attention paid to selection of site. But it holds, and holds well.

The mothers, alone for the night in the nest with the young, are slowly rising, standing on their gangling legs, yawning, stretching their great white wings, combing their feathers with sharp beaks, then dropping down, wings partly extended to protect the young. Small chatter, soft gurgling and chuckling are to be heard; suddenly here and there the noise grows. From the distance a few dark forms can be seen in the sky;

as they approach, their tone lightens. It is the heron fathers, coming with breakfast, their long beaks far ahead, their wings beating slowly, legs hanging loosely. The young open their bills wide and jump up and down; they are the usual bird young, ugly, awkward, bad-tempered. Father and mother first give each other a warmly affectionate greeting, spreading plumes, placing bills together, making soft noises. The mother leaves the nest to get her own food and pick up more for the young, while the father stays to feed them. From his gullet he brings forth tender bits of food which the children pick from his beak.

An enterprising young bird often buries his head far down his father's throat, exploring. Another, impatient, will take hold of the parent's bill with his own and shake it with such determination that the father is sometimes annoyed. He may fly off a short distance and, from a neighboring limb, give a well-peppered lecture. This goes on all day, mother and father alternating in finding the food and bringing it home; and each time they meet, they show their love and their joy at the reunion. Some of the children seem large-sized, and from time to time the parents work hard to draw them into tentative flight from one branch to another. A number are already making short flights about the pond with the elders; and some who are alone, below, learning to live off the food in the shallows, seem little larger than brothers who have remained behind.

Through the day the dialogue continues among the birds: liquid murmurs or sharper notes, reprovals, chuckles of merriment or encouragement. The visitor, well advised, comes back in time for the events at dusk. The islander finally points a finger. At first the outsider sees nothing; then in the far distance he makes out a file of dark things, moving toward him.

From another part of the horizon, another line, then another, and a fourth. They come at different levels. Soon a few are directly overhead, and everything seems frantic confusion. But each bird knows precisely where he is going. Above his tree or apartment, he closes his wings, his beak points downward, and he drops into place. The families are in loud communion, with questioning notes, gurgles, and mild bickerings, each moment another crescendo of joyous babble. Slowly the cackle dies down, and then the soft notes subside. By the time it is dark, only vague and intermittent noises of unsettlement are to be heard. Bird City is asleep.

Edward Avery McIlhenny gave the nation its first bird sanctuary; at one time the egret could be found in only a few places outside the island. Others have followed his example. He joined men in other parts of the country in agitating for improved conservation laws, and eventually states and the Federal government made egret killing a criminal offense. The birds are no longer slaughtered, though he told me that plume hunters occasionally engage in bootlegging. He described how he "re-established the egrets" in Florida, sending two carloads of birds from Avery Island to create a similar colony there; and he has told many others how to imitate his project. Through the years he has also worked upon private individuals and persuaded them to donate grounds for refuges. With another wealthy man he was the first to present land to a public agency for a wild-life center. Again, others followed, and the Louisiana marshes provide a series of state and Federal game shelters that have set patterns in the conservation movement.

Near the bird center is the second major work of Edward Avery McIlhenny, and to some it is the more phenomenal—

his Jungle Gardens. The result of forty years of effort, it is a fantastic three hundred acres of trees, bushes, and flowers, an encyclopedia of exotica multiplied, proof that a man in love with the Louisiana soil can produce almost anything out of it. His listings include scarlet daisies from the "Mountain of the Moon" along the African equator; soap trees from India; papaya plants from the tropics. Purple Chinese finger bananas. From Tibet, an evergreen that hangs over the centuries, almost alone as a survivor of the Age of Coal. Dwarf wisteria and orchids of Japan. A hedge of wormwood. Water gardens of pink and cream Egyptian lotus. A Chinese orange of near-black fruit, said to be the tiniest in the world. His own seedless orange, produced after experimentation, almost the size of a grapefruit. Cactus in a desert garden, with twenty-seven kinds of palm. Eighty varieties of fern. Brazilian rubber plants. Jujube trees. Crêpe myrtles from India. Ginger lilies from the Philippines. A winter-blooming Oriental plum. Ten thousand bushes of camellias, in five hundred or so varieties, including one which, strange to say for a camellia, has a fragrance. (By some this has been called the world's greatest collection of these flowers.) Iris gardens with seventeen hundred varieties, some twelve inches across the petals. Thirty thousand azalea bushes.

Here you will find a Chinese garden with a line of mirror pools, surmounted by a glass-enclosed temple containing a six-foot-high Buddha, covered with gold leaf. We walked about the pool and the owner told me of the Buddha's history and his connection with it. It dates back to the twelfth century. It was taken from a ruined temple by a bandit general and sent to America for a museum purchase, he declared. But while negotiations were proceeding, the Chinese government captured the general and disposed of him; and a friend acquired the prize for McIlhenny. It does not seem out of place here. Nothing does. As he outlined the story, there seemed little that was unusual or remarkable about it. Conical bits of lapis lazuli cover the Buddha's head; and McIlhenny told of the Chinese legend that friendly snails crawled upon the Gautama's crown to keep off the rays of the sun as he sat and thought, and in time turned blue under the exudations of his mind. The temple is in a cleared grove of live oaks. An artificial lagoon, six hundred feet long, curves at its base; fringing the waters are "seven sacred hills of Buddha," built to a height of twenty feet, each planted with Chinese azaleas of a different variety.

Forests of bamboo rear sixty feet into the air, some titan cane, others light and delicate. The owner believes that imported bamboo will become the pulpwood of the South. He had the foresight, he said, to begin his plantings in 1902, and he has added and enlarged from year to year and agitated for its wider use. "It grows fast, a lot faster than anything else; once it reaches maturity, a cutting can be made every three years. It keeps coming up." He quoted impressive figures of his shipments, and said that much of the Louisiana sugar lands would be well fitted for bamboo. Emphasizing its speed of growth, he told how he clocked one variety and saw it increase an inch and a half in an hour.

The visual effect of the gardens lies partly in a half-hidden artistry. Craftsmen with the world, literally, to choose from have shifted and merged the growths, uprooted, transplanted, and re-transplanted; experimented, broken rules, and made new ones. At some points flowers shade in a pattern with each few feet of earth, white to red to blue to purple. Bushes form arches; growths are planned so that vines join in the sky high above the water. Curtains of bamboo frame long vistas of sunken gardens. A delicate cream blossom stands alone in an almost luminous setting of leathery, near-black growths; many a stage scene is not planned with a greater eye to dramatic impact. Chrysanthemums cover long stretches. At some points, "M'sieu Ned" was not impressed with the effect of live oaks, hundreds of years old, so he blasted them out and planted wild flowers.

Presiding over most of the island is a lord in restraint. In his seventies, he is powerful, active, possessor of a hearty disposition, a full head of hair, and, as ever, his own mind and will. His sovereignty includes, besides the birds, animals, and plants, six hundred or so men, women, and children, largely French, who live here much as did their fathers and grandfathers before them. In some families every member except Maman is employed by M'sieu Ned, in the factory or as caretaker or laborer.

This Great White Father is oracle, philosopher, unofficial judge, and at times amateur doctor for his people. His families bring him their problems—monetary, marital, and digestive. He built the school on the island; the state now provides the teachers. To him, regularly, the children bring their monthly report cards; he chides when marks are bad, and gives nickels or dimes when they are good. James Marlow has told how a hysterical French mother once cried to him that her child had just drunk half a bottle of dog medicine. He tried to sooth her. If the stuff would not kill a dog, it would not kill a child. She still wept. He swallowed the rest of it to prove that he was right.

The island has its French village. Some call it Tango. One street is named LeBlanc, with a reason. Alpha LeBlanc, retired trapper, lives in the first house; the others are those of his seven sons. The last time I was there, wood was free for the village people, and vegetables from a community garden were placed daily on each doorstep. Meat and dairy products, raised on the island, were sold at a commissary. The boys tip their hats as M'sieu Ned passes. The pretty Acadian girls go to their dances on Saturday night, with Avery Island flowers in their hair. Nobody to whom I talked could remember a case of burglary. M'sieu Ned wouldn't like it.

There are other branches of the Avery-McIlhenny family on the island, with their estates, like his. The mine is now leased to an outside company; the pepper factory is still in the family. But Ned McIlhenny seems monarch of it all. I tried to think of the place without him, as I sat talking with him, and I failed. He is—and he has done—many things. He wrote his own book of the island's birds, and also an "autobiography of an egret." In other spare moments he has turned out works on the wild turkey, on the life of the alligator, and on Negro spirituals. He was a photographer before the century's turn, and he still makes many pictures. Not satisfied to be an amateur zoologist and botanist, he embarked in his sixties on a study of insects. He is proud that on that last expedition to the Arctic he taught men of the North to play football. At college he was a leading amateur boxer, and talks of a workout or two with Jim Corbett. He has experimented in the crossing of water buffaloes with African zebus for work in the state's rice fields. He mated a greenhead mallard and a local mallard and produced a bird heavy with rich meat, combining the habits of both types; because it can't go two ways at once, following the habits of each half, he says, it remains in Louisiana all year. From Argentina he imported nutrias, large-sized water rodents that he believes may eventually become popular Louisiana fur-bearers. He has dug canals to duplicate their natural environment; he feels that the

Louisiana marshes are not entirely dissimilar to their native pampas. "And think of the pelt," he urged—"the size of a coon's!"

Interested in bears, he caught a baby black one, brought him home, and called for a wet nurse from the women on the estate. One served until the animal was placed on a bottle. For three years the bear played with the children; the master wrestled with it, and chuckled when some of his guests cried out in a state approaching panic, at seeing a 350-pound animal padding its way toward them. He raised an alligator fourteen feet long, to which he fed forty pounds of meat to the meal. He has his own terrapin crawl and his own heavily stocked fishing pond, so that one has only to drop a hook and pull it up again. (A friend of mine felt guilty: "It was like going to French Market and picking them off the racks, and getting credit for it.")

Despite his compassion toward some things, he is a happy hunter and has led parties in several countries with avidity. He inaugurated one of the earliest of bird-banding stations; and he has engaged in a controversy or two with conservationists and others. One who knows him called him, all in all, "a romantic reaching toward the scientific."

"M'sieu Ned" has the fixed habit of certainty, and the manner of command. One small Frenchman of the area, whom I met about the same time, said, "He's a *big* duck, that one"; and in his voice there was something of envy, but also of grudging admiration. It is probable that few have contradicted him to his face in anything. He is a man of large conversation; but also, it seems, of some large deeds. At times he employs the wide gesture. But these are a master's privileges. Of him it may be said that, born to privilege in a paradise, he has not rested. That, I think, is a compliment.

Part II: *The Longest Village Street*

TILDEN LANDRY

§ 7. *Small Man's Bayou*

BAYOU LAFOURCHE, say Louisianians, is the longest village street in the world; and I don't know of any place that has attempted to refute that claim. It covers 120 curling miles, and along practically all that length it is impossible to ride or walk and be out of sight or hearing of a house or houseboat, both filled with people. For mile on mile, a single line of homes hugs the waterway on one bank, and sometimes on the other as well. Here and there towns appear, but often it cannot be determined when a town ends and mere residences on the bayou begin. The string becomes double for a time, the second following the curve of the stream like the first; and then it thins again. How many houses stand in this file, nobody knows. Some have declared that not even Holland of the old days had a greater multiplicity of rural people per linear mile.

Lafourche may also be defined as an attitude. Other Louisianians see or hear a thing, smile and say: "That's Lafourche for you." It is as contented a place as I have ever found—good-natured, quick-talking, never pretending to be anything other than what it is; and pre-eminently it ranks as the bayou of the small man, a man who is busy enough at his duties but seldom too busy to enjoy a pleasant time with his friends.

The Lafourchais describes his manner of elbow-to-elbow existence by saying that the boys can toss a baseball along the bayou from one front yard to the next without losing it between the beginning and the end. (I made no personal test, but if the boys have moderately good pitching arms, I suspect that it can be done.) And one day a farmer told me the story of the day the news of the First World War armistice reached Lafourche, back in 1918. Octave, up at the northern end, received a telegram. He had a cousin, way down at the other limit, who would want to hear this news, yes. Octave started toward his car, when Arsène, his neighbor, stuck his head out of the window to ask what was the matter. Octave told him: "La guerre est finie!" Arsène ran to his other window and called the word to Gustave, next door. Gustave gulped and ran to his other window. Before the hour was past the news had gone from house to house; and when Octave, chugging as fast as he could, reached his destination at the lower line, his cousin came out and cried: "Octave, you have heard? La guerre est finie!" And *that's* Lafourche for you.

The Federal government, back in 1866, recognized that the peculiar nature of this bayou would make mail delivery simple. Marcellus Lejeune won a contract to carry letters from its source to a point near the end of dry land. Thirty years later, the area received a pioneer American rural free delivery route, one month after the first in American history, in West

The yard is watery, and the cows are welcome.

Bird and 'gator—good neighbors, or merely neighbors?

Madewood Plantation—the little people had some big neighbors.

Guy Bernard

This mud-and-moss chimney is as old as the family.

Levees have been put to crops along the world's longest village street.

The bayou won't ever give up the merchant-on-wheels.

For All Saints, the graves are lighted along the water.

Eugene Delcroix

E. M. Morgan

An amiable angel keeps watch.

Virginia. It is a simple business, say the bayou people; a man just rides in a straight line, and then rides back again, comme ça.

Lafourche and its ways grew out of two factors: isolation and concentration. The first is gone; the second remains and continues to make the place distinct and to itself. The bayou opens at a point only eighty miles or so to the west of New Orleans and it reaches the Gulf about twenty-five miles to the west of Grand Isle. Today, as I write, in New Orleans, I can reach its heart in an hour. Yet Lafourche is still largely rural in its own fashion, and willing to remain so. I set out last year to cover it from its start to its finish, part by steamboat, other parts by motor launch, pirogue, or the road that stays always with it. The trip began with old Donaldsonville, a pleasant, settled town with a past; it concluded near the blue waters with new Golden Meadow, a loud fish-and-oil village. Between this town and village are the houses of the Lafourchais, with their farms behind them, for the most part like beads on a necklace, one little different from the other. There is uniformity and there is continuity along all this route. A man can stop at almost any point and know that he is on Lafourche. It could be no other place in the world. I have stayed with several families through one pleasant season and another; and these, too, seem little different from each other. The handsome Rose Abadie, brunette and twenty, to whom I made that observation, wasn't sure at first that it was any tribute; then, after a while, she agreed with me. After all, she nodded, it was one big-big neighborhood—the most stretched-out neighborhood that le bon Dieu ever made.

It is a small stream by most standards, to some a trench, and very shallow at its topmost point, widening until it reaches across 125 yards or so at the southern end. One observer in the last century thought that it looked like a "magnificent artificial canal," and others have agreed with him. It runs southeastward, roughly parallel to the Mississippi, to which it is a kin. Many centuries ago it was a mighty body of swift water. The geologists are certain that the prehistoric Mississippi itself once washed heavily through this course to the Gulf. Then the master stream shifted toward the east and its present line of flow. A lesser waterway remained, beginning at a juncture with the Mississippi and taking some of its excess waters on occasion. Today Lafourche is a restricted trickle inside a great trough, with smaller levees of its own built up within the ancient larger ones deposited by the Mississippi.

The overflow of the waters has created natural embankments spreading two to three miles in each direction, narrowing as they go southward. To east and west is an uncertain twilight region—swamp-marsh, lakes, other bayous. Along these levees, with their bursting wealth of green, lived the Indians of the 1700's, moving upward and downward with seasonal changes in the bayou. The whites found the region a place in rich disarray, moss-hung trees pushing their way into the water, thick reeds and flowers trailing along it, the flow often choked by an overabundance of such growths. Everywhere were ducks, wild geese, pigeons, snipe, raccoons, muskrats, rabbits, deer, and lumbering bears. On one of their first trips along the Mississippi the French settlers halted at the point where the bayou met the river, and saw the red men living there, the Chitimacha tribe. They were sufficiently impressed to give the spot a name: La Fourche—"The Fork." But few of the French went down the bayou; their interests were elsewhere, on the immense Mississippi itself. The line of plantations moved up the river, and as early as 1719 a large one was in operation near the meeting place of the two streams.

But Indian troubles for a time kept any white men away from the bayou reaches. The Chitimacha made difficulties; they killed a missionary, then retreated down the territory now known as Lafourche, and into the swampy ground, where, from low, hidden spots they conducted forays against the colonists who had settled near the Fork. The French enlisted the help of other Indians against the Chitimacha, and after some years peace came. The Chitimacha agreed to leave their vantage points, and moved up the bayou. Slowly, a few French settlers moved into the vicinity; for the most part the colonists stayed near the Mississippi. For more than a half century the bayou country had to wait for an event that was to change many things about Louisiana—the arrival of the Acadians.

During a hundred years or more before Louisiana was colonized, men and women of France had lived in Acadie, the present Nova Scotia of Canada. Many settlers before them had died on the chill and rugged shores, but when a new trading company was formed, it pledged itself to fill the land with sturdy settlers who would hold where others had failed. They were chosen, with discernment, from Normandy, Picardy, Brittany, Saintonge, and other areas largely of the north and west of France, and for the most part of stout rural stock. In the old country they had been farmers and fishermen; their new life was little different in its essentials from that of their home provinces. The place they came to was on the coast, low-lying, part of it marsh-covered, and one of the first tasks of the newcomers was that of building dikes and reclaiming the land. They were given a start by the company and then left to themselves, to die, or to thrive by their own efforts.

They thrived. All labored; a private edict that was never questioned held idleness to be a curse. The men and the boys at work in the field or on the water; the women and children at work in maintenance of the small cottages and yards— that was the only way. The system was patriarchal, the word of the père unquestioned. In arguments between families, the elders decided; as a last resort, they called in that other père, the priest, who knew all things. Marriages came early; when a girl could weave and a boy could make a pair of wheels, they were of proper age. By necessity and by custom all helped each other; and their days were not short ones.

But they were not a dour folk, for they were French, and they liked laughter. The Reverend Mr. Andrew Brown, who lived near them, described them as "fond of black and red Colours with Leg Bandages, Belts, etc., hanging in Knots and Bows." In the evenings they gathered for "Entertainments and Frolicking. . . . And seldom any of them remained long silent in Compagny, never seeming to be a loss for a Subject of Discourse."

From their first years in America, however, a threat hung over the Acadians. The British, citing early exploration, claimed the soil, and for years men met in scattered skirmishes. Land was taken and retaken, and diplomats conferred over the faraway ground. World politics and clashes of religions were involved; the wars of England and France had their Acadian phases. From this strategic point the British feared a spur might one day be driven into their colonies along the Atlantic coast. The French felt concern lest the British were plotting against them. In 1713, a few years before the founding of New Orleans, far to the south, Acadie was taken by the British and it passed forever out of French hands. The treaty provided that those who wished to remain as British subjects, but also as Catholics, might do so; others were to depart within a year. The subject is confused by many recriminations. Few Acadians left. The majority of them continued on for years, technically citizens of one nation, yet intensely sympathetic to another. In time they asserted a status that has an ironic ring to the modern ear. "Neutrals," they asked peace when there was no peace.

After years of uncertainties, war approached again between the two nations. The year was 1755. The British were alarmed over this large group of suspect persons gathered not far from other French forces in Canada. The majority of the Acadians insisted that they would never do anything unfriendly to Britain; but they would not take an unconditional oath of loyalty. The officials decided to take no chances, and inaugurated one of the bitterest episodes of American colonial history. Mass deportation per se was not then considered quite the cruel thing that the Axis powers have made it; yet the Acadian removal was accomplished with a cold ruthlessness that has never been forgotten. Companies of red-coated soldiers collected thousands of men, women, and children, hunted down others, packed them tightly into vessels. Families were sometimes separated at the shore, children shrieking as their mothers were pulled into boats without them; old women were held back as their sons were taken on other vessels. The Acadians were to understand that there was nothing left behind to which to return. From the water they could see the outlines of their homes, in flames; the dikes that their fathers and grandfathers had raised were being broken, and the sea was slipping back over the fields. For it, the Acadians have a term—Le Grand Dérangement.

Worse days were ahead. Each of the American colonies was ordered to take a certain portion of the expelled people. Yet no advance preparations were made, no funds were set aside for their care; at best they were unwelcome guests; more often they were hated and despised. The two countries were soon at war, and the Acadians became alien enemies, Papists in Protestant settlements which regarded the Catholic as a dangerous pagan, indulging in who knew what practices. Some colonial governments declined to receive them, and many were sent to England, to remain prisoners for as long as eight years. Others, in America, were less fortunate; they died of cold, of disease, and of terror. Of those who lived, many became public charges, beaten in the streets when rumors spread of "plots," made to work in various places as bondsmen. Yet in other cases the attitude inclined toward kindness, that of one set of human beings toward another in sorrow. For years the Acadians moved about when they could, hunting lost relatives, or seeking small settlements of their people or mere refuge for the moment. They had many different fates, but not the one that was decreed. Liquidation as a people would not be forced upon them.

Thousands of miles of hazardous land and water barriers separated the Atlantic settlements from Louisiana. Yet some of the Acadians knew of this French outpost to the south, and often during the years of their wandering they thought of it, wondered about it, and asked each other, Could a family hope to live through such a trip? If they reached there, what would happen? In God's name, were they wanted anywhere? Within the first decade after their expulsion from Canada several bands managed to make their way along the Mississippi to

New Orleans. They arrived, gaunt and tattered, at the levee; and because they received, at last, a smiling, friendly welcome, they cried in quiet happiness.

No places were available for them in the city itself; the riverbank sites were already taken up for long distances. But a few small stretches were empty between other settlements on the Mississippi. Some of the band were escorted to the vicinity of the "Coast of the Germans," a place of small farms, occupied by the children of men brought to Louisiana when John Law floated his Mississippi Bubble over all the continent of Europe. Others were directed to Pointe Coupée, a place of expansive plantations, into whose background they fitted themselves. Then, too, there was that sparsely settled land of the bayous to the west; in particular, the nearest site, Lafourche. Many went there, and eventually others moved over with them from the Mississippi area. The Acadians found other points of settlement, but for years Lafourche was a particular objective. Other families had preceded them, and others, of different nationalities and different ranks of life, were to follow; but the Acadians stamped their name on this waterway.

All received seeds, tools, and provisions. Soon they were writing to friends wherever they thought they might be. Many miles to the east and north, men and women received messages, long delayed; or an emissary brought a whispered word to those in bonds. Clans gathered secretly, and decisions were made. About this time the war between England and France had ended, and conditions had improved in the colonies for the Acadians. Some stayed where they were and merged with the other inhabitants; but most of the Acadians knew now where they wished to go.

Louisiana had sudden new problems of her own. In the

international trading that accompanied the peace in 1762, the colony was slipped under the table from His Majesty of France to His Majesty of Spain. (Oddly, this deal remained more or less secret for several years, and then Spain delayed assumption of control.) The Louisianians could sympathize more than ever with the Acadians; they knew the uncertainty of men with a new ruler. Would they, too, eventually be suffering much as these sad ones? Still the bands of settlers came —some from the eastern colonies, and some from Santo Domingo, where they had found life hard in the extreme heat. The Louisiana officials, French and Spanish, wrote home in something like concern: Louisiana is "going to become a new Acadie. . . . They no longer are spoken of in hundreds, but in thousands. They say that there are about 4000 coming. . . ." Provisions in the colony were scanty, but, as one authority wrote, the Acadians "will actually die of want if they do not receive succor. I believed that humanity and the honor of the nation (France) obliged me to do something in favor of these poor families, who have been wandering for ten years and are unfortunate only because of their inviolable attachment to their fatherland and their religion." Another declared, with unconscious prophecy: "They are reborn in Louisiana, and they will perform marvels if they are given a little assistance. Thus, at a time when least expected, this country will flourish."

The "marvels" were soon under way, and the Acadians flourished so well that word reached others in France. For years the Acadians had been almost heroic figures in the home country, regarded with a mixture of admiration and friendly affection. Hundreds had made their way back to the Continent, and the government welcomed them with doles and promises of settlement in pleasant surroundings. Many found themselves in Normandy, Brittany, and other provinces from which their great-grandfathers had originally come. Most of them were sent, however, not to the rural areas but to towns and cities, and it soon became apparent that they were little fitted for such places. A number who went to the country sections seemed poorly adjusted to them as well. The Acadian had become a different man from his fathers; the isolated scene had made its changes. New problems arose; the repatriated Acadians had no work to do, and found none. Dependent on their government payments, they began to lead aimless, fretful lives.

Officials planned projects on which they would be placed—colonies on islands and outlying stretches. Red tape and graft held up some of these efforts; but the Acadians themselves became problems. Suspicious, perhaps because of their past difficulties, they asked questions in advance, or accepted such offers and then returned disillusioned. They quarreled with officers and they quarreled among themselves. They became involved in local politics. The French public slowly revised its idyllic conceptions, and concern for the Acadians gave way to apathy and resentment. Dole payments lapsed, and agitations increased. Eventually word came from Louisiana, and the Acadians in France decided that they wanted to join their people in this other place. They were, however, largely penniless. Would the government help? The government was bored. Furthermore, why should it spend French money to help Frenchmen go to a country held by Spain? (Some smelled Spanish machinations, designed to lure simple Acadians to half-empty Louisiana.) At last the Acadians found a way; they solicited certain influential Spanish officials. The home government, thus approached, relented, and the two courts agreed on expenses of transportation. And so it was that in 1785—thirty years after the dérangement—1500 or more Acadians left France for Louisiana. They formed one of the largest groups of Acadians to reach the colony.[1]

In Canada, the Acadians had been used to locations along or near the water. In Louisiana, these same conditions were provided. The Acadians were eager to be together; that, too, was possible. The officials used a scheme of settlement that had been followed in the old country, in Canada, and in parts of Louisiana. Along the Mississippi the grants began at the riverbank and extended back toward the swamps and low places. Plantations, several miles apart, formed an uninterrupted line along the stream. The Acadian concessions followed the same general design, but with an important difference. Frontage was much more narrow—only two or three arpents.[2] The usual American farm pattern is the "checkerboard"; one family takes whatever available land it thinks best, and it may be behind, before, or next to another. In Louisiana the first Acadian farmer took his location on the bayou; the next moved close beside him, the third one directly beside the second. Louisiana topography made such arrange-

[1] Considerable confusion has existed regarding the number of Acadians who came to Louisiana. Standard authorities frequently contradict each other. Wilton P. Ledet, a Louisianian who studied this phase of the subject at exhaustive length under a Rosenwald Fellowship, has concluded that not more than 2750 Acadians actually arrived in Louisiana between 1764 and 1785—from the Atlantic colonies, France, the West Indies, from Nova Scotia after the peace between France and England, and from other countries. Today's estimates are that from 300,000 to 500,000 Louisianians have Acadian blood!

[2] This old French unit is somewhat less than the acre. Today throughout the Acadian areas, residents talk and think of land in arpents. Last summer I was talking with a student official of Southwestern Louisiana Institute, and he was directing me to a house: "You go down the road, and two arpents on . . ." His friends snickered, and he grinned: "That's the Cajun in me." One friend quoted: "You can take the Cajun out of the country, but . . ."

ments advisable. Thus each man had a range of land: the best at the front, for home and garden; that directly behind it, for crops; at the rear, wood in the swamp or forest.

The result was a chain of farms, held together by the thread of the bayou. Where the waterway curved, the farm curved; where it formed a half-moon, the farm followed. So it is over most of the bayou area; nowhere is the situation better exemplified than on Bayou Lafourche, past and present. Through the years there has come an accentuation of the picture. When a man knew that death was near, he called his sons and divided his property. Would he break it into squares, one heir to receive a section near the bayou, the next another a short distance away, and so on? Mais, non, that would be unfair; the one at the front would be better off than the next, and that one would have an advantage over the next. So, logically, Papa cut the narrow land lengthwise, from bayou to back. Each son received the same: part of the best, part of the next best, part of the rest. When the sons died, they made the same kind of division, and the tracts further narrowed. I once passed about fifteen houses set tightly together in a row along Lafourche. I asked if it were a small town or settlement. It was merely the family's collection of farms. Behind each house was its strip of ground, leading to its strip of wood or swamp.

This was much the scene that the plantation man saw when he ventured beyond the Mississippi during the last century. He had a name for the bayou people—"les petits habitants"; and if there was occasionally a note of patronage in its use, there was also an element of appropriateness. The bayous, with their smaller natural levees, were unsuited in many places for the plantation system, but they fitted admirably into the needs of the bayou man. The means of subsistence were close at hand, and they did not require large capital or many helpers. A small cash crop, hogs, chickens, and a cow or two were easily raised; in the marsh or swamps was game on foot or on wing; the bayou had fish, perhaps shrimp or crabs, or led to waters that offered them. There was only slight exaggeration in the statement of many of the bayou men that they could hook breakfast from their front yard, shoot down their dinner from their back steps, and trap supper by stepping outside their fields.

Sometimes the Lafourchais might feel homesick for the shores to the north. What had happened to the old church, and the graves, and those Héberts who had been their neighbors? Who had the acres that he had plowed? But there were advantages. Here were a friendly climate, a soil and a warm sun such as he had never known in the North. He could be outdoors all the year; he had no rocks to fight in planting his crop. No snow fell; his younger children asked what such things were like. Most important, he had the thing he wanted most, the precious privilege of remaining to himself. When Louisiana became a part of the United States, the Anglo-Saxons usually had as little contact with the Acadians as did the other French. In addition to the other obstructions, new ones of language and national differences presented themselves. Let those smart Yankees stay to themselves, if they pleased. Let them keep their new ways. The Acadian saw no merit in novelties; the old methods were always the best. "Je fais comme mon père"—"I do like my Papa"—he knew no better rule for his life. Inevitably, he came to develop a tinge of suspicion toward outsiders. He saw so few of them; the old folks warned so fervently against "les autres." "What did the strange one want here? You know it is not well to tell everything, Jacques. . . ." It was for these reasons that

H. W. Gilmore termed the rural Acadians of today "the largest unassimilated national group in America . . . the best example of large-scale community isolation to be found in this country." T. Lynn Smith called their life "probably the purest example of a seventeenth-century peasant culture in the United States." [3]

During the nineteenth century many visitors inspected the peculiar Lafourche country; from their descriptions a picture of the residents slowly emerges. Berquin-Duvallon early in the century found that the connection with the Mississippi at the bayou's head was badly obstructed by successive deposits of wood and mud, so that for seven or eight months of the year, except at high water, the people were "cooped up." During the other period, some took their produce to New Orleans, selling farm produce, woven goods, and animal skins; but opportunities for exchange were so ignored that this observer concluded that the district might have been placed in the "mountains of Asturias," for the good it did the colony. Then, to make things worse, when Andy Jackson prepared for the battle in which Lafitte's men joined him, he placed obstructions in the way of bayou entry.

To Lafourche other elements had followed the Acadians— other French, some of them Royalist refugees, and Spaniards who were brought over at the same time as the Isleños of St. Bernard. The Royalists took landholdings of their own, away from those of the Acadians; the Spaniards set up several settlements but eventually lost their separate identity. For the most

---

[3] On many occasions today on Lafourche I have felt the silent inquiry of older members of the family: "A Yankee, ahn?" To some of the Acadians, oddly, anything that speaks English, regardless of how Southern it is, is Yankee. But when I tried my sometimes halting French, the elders relaxed. Nobody could be wholly dangerous who spoke *français*.

part, Lafourche became known as a place of the Acadians. As early as 1814 the bayou settlements were assuming the appearance of a long single street, and were so described by callers. H. M. Brackenridge commented that "for nearly thirty miles on each side there appears a continual village, and it is tolerably well settled for thirty miles further." Ever since that time this settlement has been lengthening, seldom thickening.

Meanwhile the agriculture of Louisiana had revolutionized itself. The secret of sugar granulation had been discovered; the cotton gin had been invented; and the opening of the nineteenth century saw the advance of these crops into every available corner. With them went the plantation system, for these were crops best fitted to the mass-labor production of the time. The Mississippi frontage was used up, and the planter looked toward the bayous, picking spots where the soil was broadest, and expanding his holdings wherever he could. Frederick L. Olmsted has described an illuminating conversation with one who found himself among the habitants. He pointed to a "hamlet" of a dozen or so houses and farms at the end of his acreage; he was ready to pay two to three times what the property was worth, to remove them. The settlers, in his opinion, were "lazy vagabonds, doing but little work, and spending much time in shooting, fishing, and play." Some, he admitted, were good mechanics and had helped him build his sugar works; but he preferred to use slaves. The habitants, he feared, "demoralized his Negroes"— and his reasons were significant. "Seeing them living in apparent comfort, without much property and without steady labour, the slaves could not help thinking that it was unnecessary for men to work as hard as they themselves were obliged to, and that if they were free, they would not work. . . ."

It was a bayou version of the clash between two systems of economy. Some of the Acadians, impressed with payments that looked to them like great wealth, gave up their lands. When the money was gone, the family found a crisis to meet. Pioneer Americans under such circumstances would probably have moved on to Texas or other parts of the West. The Acadian, ever a gregarious man, wanted to stay in a country which he knew, near people·whom he knew. So he retreated to the smaller bayous, with their narrower levees, that connected with Lafourche and with other waterways. Before this, and after this, some found low places, usually dry, in the back lands. Cleared by burning over of the vegetation, they became known as "brûlées"; many of these still survive as back settlements. Some went to the swamp edges, and others toward the Gulf, where the land came to sudden ends. But there were others who would not sell. This was their land; they would no sooner give it up voluntarily than would their grandfathers across the sea leave their land.

The planters who went into this area, according to W. H. Sparks, felt that they were entering a "foreign land." They found the people poor and uneducated, their language incomprehensible; but the habitants were "amiable, kind, law-abiding, virtuous and honest beyond any population of similar character to be found in any country." The small settlers, too, were "content and unenvious," and toward the Americans "confiding and truthful." But once deceived, they could never be won back; they withdrew completely from contact with the deceiver. Disputes were few; the priest, the "universal arbiter," was obeyed without question. Fond of amusements, they met regularly in each other's houses; but even on such occasions everything was simplicity. On all the bayou, there was "but one pleasure carriage and not half a·

dozen ladies' bonnets." The bonnes femmes of Lafourche used handkerchiefs for headdress.

The travelers shook their heads over the lack of comforts of the Acadians, and often wondered how they could live with their restricted means. W. H. Russell went to the settlement at the head of the bayou and found a curious character, a Westerner, who had learned French, married into a native family, and become constable. This individual cogitated over a problem: "How did the friends, relatives, and tribe of his wife live? No one could say. They reared chickens, and they caught fish; when there was a pressure upon the planter, they turned out to work . . . but those were rare occasions." The colony "toiled not and spun nothing but fishing nets," yet "lived better than Solomon and were probably as well dressed." Yet the small man of Lafourche managed more adequately than many thought. At least he could say that he lived within his income—and this was something which many planters could not claim.

Cotton and sugar were now in a race for control of Louisiana. Indigo, tobacco, and the other crops were forgotten. Men looked at the market reports and shifted overnight from one of the new ones to the other. A sugar mania was soon upon Southern landowners; a planter in a Mississippi or Alabama town met a friend, listened without comment to the latest word from Louisiana, then went home to announce that they were moving into the other state to get in on the boom. The 1820's brought an Anglo-Saxon family, the Pughs of North Carolina, whose name was to become one of the great ones of the Lafourche plantation era. All Louisiana knew the wheeze: "Why is Bayou Lafourche like the aisle of a church?" "Because it has Pughs on both sides." The family acres spread along upper Lafourche; in time, Colonel Thomas

Pugh built a mansion, Madewood, requiring four years for the cutting of the timber, all of it from his own plantation grounds, and four years for the building. The smaller folk looked, and wondered.

W. W. Pugh has given his recollections of the area on his arrival as a youth. He stared in curiosity at the small French houses, each with a front porch, walls of moss-and-mud mixture, and neat picket fences. In later years, when some of these unpretentious homes were demolished, enough wood was found in one to be sawed in half for two new residences. The number of Americans was "very limited"; and the natives were "not particularly cordial" to them; but among themselves they were happy and content. "There were no aristocrats of either sex, whose superior toilets could create envy or bad feelings." To the American, it seemed a pleasant kind of life.

Other changes were in the making, for newcomers and old residents. For more than a century Louisianians had been traveling on their bayous with only slight improvement in means of transportation. "Batteaux plats" or flatboats moved by sails or with the assistance of oars and poles; and there were always the pirogues, small or large. Now came the steamboats, and another day in bayou as in river transportation. The first one negotiated the Mississippi in 1812; within a decade, others had reached Lafourche. A steamboat had to be a special kind of steamboat to fit the bayous. If its bottom had to be lifted and flattened for the river, it had to be lifted and flattened even further for a smaller stream. If a pirogue had to float on a dew, a bayou steamer had to move in the equivalent of a light rain. Beside other steamboats, the bayou variety looked like a toy, short and narrow; and it was not for nothing that the paddle wheel was at the back rather than at the sides. Every possible quarter inch of space had to be saved.

But eventually bayou steamboat days had their luster of legend and high deeds not less than those of the greater streams; and certainly, a towering palace-on-engines was a more impressive sight when it seemed to stretch from one bank to the other; when, to a man a few feet away, it appeared to be floating over the land. The Mississippi had one advantage, however: there could be no great races of steamboat against steamboat on the bayou. Such competition would have meant that one of them rode the bank; and as advanced as the art of construction became, none could meet this requirement.

Lafourche's first steamer, as Mr. Pugh remembered it, was *The Eagle*, an impressive sight to the population, but, he thought, a very puny bird. Gilded and sophisticated creatures were soon moving about her, but *The Eagle* fluttered on for many years. She became in time "old, dilapidated, sending forth an unpleasant odor and noted for an absence of fresh paint," but she was dependable, and Lafourche liked her. The Captain was Ferdinand Streck, a personage of deeds and sayings, noted for three things: "the number of his visits to the bar without producing any visible effect; his accommodating disposition in waiting for freight whilst on his way to the city; and his punctuality in starting from the city when the second bell ceased to notify late comers." In no hurry to get to New Orleans, while picking up produce, he was ever anxious to leave it when his *Eagle* was emptied. To hell with the city; he was a bayou man.

The Captain and his Lafourche schedule were friendly things. Their stops were numberless. They would wait for a friend, or for almost any man, or for a hen. In one instance, a shipment of eggs lacked the final item to make a dozen.

The fowl had walked already to her place of performance, had deposited herself. With a wave of his hand, the owner denoted the place. Monsieur le Capitaine, a man of good will, he waited, of course. And then, when a triumphant cackle came from the hen house, the owner walked in, came out in pride, with an egg; and the boat started again.

It was a sight to see, m'sieu, when that paquebot sounded her big whistle and came puffing and thumping up the bayou, scraping against the arms of the big trees and sending her smoke up in the live oaks that sometimes almost met overhead. Everybody on Lafourche jumped from his galerie or from his field, and ran out to see. The young ones came from all directions to race with her, and their pères and mères told them to watch out for those soft spots on the levee. No river boat ever looked that big!

As elsewhere, plantations and steamboating went together. But the habitant did not disappear on Lafourche. Through the years he saw trouble strike the planters. A sudden frost, and a sugar crop could be wiped out. A new tariff law, and the market had no bottom. In one season, Lafourche planters opened the taps and let the molasses flow, gallon by gallon, into the ditches. After such years the agents, hard-eyed men, came up from New Orleans and went about with little books and markers; and a silent family walked to the landing, and did not look back at the high house that had been theirs. The bayou man could tell his people, then, that their lot was not so bad. The great ones came and they left. Today there are not many plantations on Lafourche whose owners are of the same family that held them a hundred years ago. Usually, corporations have taken them over. The habitants remain.

§ 8. *La Vie Lafourchaise*

A MAN is among friends when he lives on Lafourche. Bayou good-will makes the usual American variety seem pale and self-conscious. A man who is an ami of another is an ami of his family, from bébé to grandpère to cousin secondaire. A relative is not someone whom one may not like, yet to whom an obligation is felt. He is a good friend, yes; the man of Lafourche likes him as such.

Mutual understanding flows more quickly than the bayou waters; mutual resentments sear like the July sun on the lake. If Jules has done ill to one close to Alcée, then he will have Alcée to answer to. Has Alcée's friend lost his money? Then Alcée will be sad with him and offer some or all of what he has. An illness next door will plunge a family into worry as earnest as if one of its own were sick. Has Narcisse received an A in catechism, and a special word from Father Michelet? The neighbors will boast for days. Many things besides a cold are contagious on Lafourche.

Take, for instance, the Babins and the Broussards and the Abadies; they live, respectively, along the upper, middle, and lower reaches. Of the families along Lafourche whom I have known, they are the best examples of the good companionship, Acadian style. During the past year or so I arranged to live for a time near each of them, stayed with them over week-ends, made trips and visits with them. I had never met them before; but as soon as they knew that I knew friends of theirs in other parts of the state, the gates were open. I was welcome at all times; my concerns were theirs; they were guides, advisers, teachers in bayou matters. Since then I have received letters, postcards, gifts of duck and fish, invitations to visit again. The eldest Babin daughter also forwarded to me all the neighborhood family pictures, several birth certificates, and a heavy collection of statistics. (I had indicated that an additional fact might be helpful.) From now on, as long as the Babins, the Broussards, and the Abadies are alive, I am sure, we shall be exchanging regular communications.

Relatives grow on four sides—to left and right, across the bayou, and back along the swamps and smaller streams. The Babins were spread as follows: nextdoor were P'père and M'mère (Grand-père and Grand'mère) living with their eldest son; on the other side, a married Babin girl, with her family; and in adjoining houses with their families, three other brothers, an uncle, aunt, another sister, two of the uncle's boys, and a cousin. Across the bayou were three other cousins; to the rear, four brothers and sisters. The bayou patriarch can gather all his kin about him with one or two calls from the front gate. P'père Babin told me that the family had lived here since it first came from Acadia; the width of most of the holdings had dropped to only forty feet or so, but the little farm, it was always there. Further, with only a few separate families in the area, much intermarriage had taken place. For several miles I found practically everybody related to another in some fashion. One of the Babin daughters confessed, in glum mood, that she was afraid she would "have to marry some kin. Everybody I know is connect' to me, somehow," she sighed.

Far fields look drab to the bayou youth. Between wars and other upheavals he remains on the home territory because he has been taught from birth that this is the place for him. Even those who go to the cities for higher schooling will often come back when they can. As doctors, engineers, or lawyers, they will take up practice in the nearest bayou town. One of the elder Babins, a graduate of Tulane University at New Orleans, lived in his own house along the line, with his offices in two settlements up the bayou. He and others like him know that if there is any trade in the area it will go to them. Competition from outsiders is something about which they need never worry.

A cousin (coo-zan) is a close relative in the Acadian scale. More than that, one whom you like, any special friend—he can be called a cousin, too. (The politician's great desire is to be known to his constituents as Cousin Jean, Cousin Theo, and so forth.) A godmother (nainaine) and a godfather (parrain) are warm connections. Each may remember the little one for whom they have stood at baptism until he is fifty and they are seventy, or as long beyond that as they all survive. A parrain will give his godchild money, advice, a job on his boat, or his life. The nainaine and parrain are expected, at the least, to send a birthday present every year until the child is grown, a first-communion present, and other tokens at appropriate times. I met one parrain who made a seventy-five-mile trip by boat from his new home to his old one, with all his family, to be present for the birthday of a goddaughter. If a mother or father dies and the home must be broken, the parrain may assert a strong claim for the care of the child. A nonc and tante, to be sure, seem far closer than the usual American uncle and aunt, and they may ask for the child as their right. Between the affection of a good tante and a good nainaine, it would be hard to gauge a difference. After some years the voisin (neighbor), too, becomes almost like a relative and is so treated. To be a neighbor on Lafourche, it is no small thing, I can tell you.

The visit is the supreme rite of bayou friendship and relationship—a happy habit that is partly inherited custom, partly the sheer delight of being with others. When I was with the Babins, we made calls or had callers five to six nights a week. (Any night except Monday. That is the bad luck time for a visit. "You will get enemies that way, sure.") It was not a matter of two or three persons making or receiving the visit; all went along, from the newest one at Maman's breast to Grand'mère and Grand-père. One night I counted seventeen of us as we left. All the notice that was needed were a wave and a call across the bayou, or over the shoulder in passing somebody's house: "Vernon, you tell parrain we coming tonight." Or the first thought might come when the family gathered after supper and somebody said, "Les' go spen' a piece of the night with the Badeaux's"; and we did. A family has only to make sure that the other family will be in, and not, perhaps, on its own way to see others. No question is ever raised as to the strangers who may be brought along. If you have three cousins in from the back, or two tantes from New Orleans, c'est okay, too. What you think we are, not wanting to see your relatives, ahn?

When the house was but a short way off, we all walked, in single or double file, on the road, talking, arguing, calling "Allo" to others on the way. If we found Nonc Albert or Cousin Edmond walking ahead of us, somebody caught his arm and he came along too. On one occasion our destination could be reached only by water. We went in four pirogues. Just before we pulled out, Maman Babin spied a member of the next household: "Etienne, you have not lef'? What you said? Don' wait for him; I know that one. Come with us; there is always room with the twins in the back. Dispose yourself right here. Make way, you two." I thought that the frail vessel was going to the bottom. It sank to about a half inch above the water line, but then it went no more, and I breathed again. On the way we met another pirogueful of friends, headed for the same destination. I feared the effect of this mass visitation; but the family that received us was additionally pleased. See how it had so many friends!

The home on Lafourche is always prepared for a visit. When it was built, the owner made certain that it included one thing above all, the galerie. This is no mere projection at the front, but a part of the house as important as the kitchen. The roof continues forward over a half-outdoor chamber that is deep and wide, always the width of the house. It is probably the biggest room in the house, and the coolest. During most of the year the family will spend its evenings there, and many of its mornings and afternoons as well. It is a place on which a housewife can sit and work and look, or merely sit and look. In one case, I found a sewing machine on the galerie, where the bonne femme could attend to her duties and enjoy simultaneously a view of the happenings outside.

There was little difference between one evening on one family's galerie and the next, at the Babins', perhaps, or at someone else's. After supper the family disposed itself—old, young, dogs, pet raccoon, toy pirogues, and babies; some on the steps, others in the rocking chairs; in straight chairs brought from inside the house, and on the swing. We inspected the passers-by, called out questions, answered others directed to us, and talked among ourselves. Down the road came the sound of voices that we expected; it was the famille Jeanfreau, paying its call. Everybody got up; each Babin talked to two or three Jeanfreaus; the Jeanfreaus answered back in simultaneous conversations, some taking part in several. Eventually all were settled—most of the young ones at one end; wives in the center, with younger children about them; men on the steps. The groups did not remain rigidly apart; each listened with one ear to the other, and inserted its own comment when it felt inclined. The subjects were usually the same: the crops, who would win the war or the election (the interest was equal in these matters); how cluttered up the bayou was getting again, and "When you think Clarice will make a marriage with that ugly Ledoux boy?"

Calls are of several kinds. To go in the morning is passer la journée; in the afternoon, passer l'après-midi. At night it is a causerie. There are scales of obligation generally recognized by families on all parts of the bayou. A man or woman should take his or her own household to the "old family" at least once a week. Less, and the "old family" will have cause to wonder and feel neglected. For the family of a brother and sister, at least twice a month; for nonc and tante, once a month; for a parrain, about the same. It can be seen that the relatives alone in a large family can keep a household busy on half of its calling nights. All this refers to formal or "big" visits. Others make "ti' calls," [1] brief stop-ins, during the day light hours, alone or with two or three of the children, from day to day. One town lawyer told me that since he was married, twenty-five years ago, he had failed on only a half-dozen occasions to make a trip a short way up the bayou to see his old ones in the morning. "I felt guilty every time I had to miss it," he explained.

Good neighborliness is not confined to smiles, calls, and bonjours. It takes more concrete form. A "ti' gift" is a frequent exchange from family to family. A man who makes a

---

[1] "Ti' " is a contraction of "petit."

trip of any extent comes home with presents that are edible, ornamental, or useful, for children and adults to the right and to the left—all inexpensive, but signs of thought and good heart. After a hunt, the head of the family will call his wife, gather the ducks or deer or other items, and make a division in the kitchen. I remember one evening with the Babins. It was so much for Nonc Théodule; that for the old people; a big part for Widow Cadzo, who was having such a hard time; a good five pounds for the brothers, and that for Pierre (with that new baby he needed all he could get). Once Madame Babin found when she finished her distribution that the family had the least of all. But she felt good, she told me, "to think how many I have help'."

The bayou families are not fools in this matter, of course. Turnabout is fair play here as elsewhere. No return is expected from the widow or from the poor family. But if a man no worse off than the rest becomes a taker and that is all, he soon goes off the list. Nor can he borrow any spare motors for his boat, that one. Sharp feuds may develop in such cases. Once, the west bank of the bayou was not speaking to the east bank during the time I was in the neighborhood. A friend took me aside and warned that if I wanted to remain in the graces of his side, I would do well to keep away from those "sonsabitches across." I kept away.

In the main, however, mutual assistance overflows from one bayou home to the next. If Madame Babin became ill, as she had during the previous winter, one of the women from the near-by houses came over and took full direction of the household. When a family is called to another section to be with a brother who is dying, or to attend the marriage of a relative, everybody goes. No one worries about what will happen at home. The neighbors will watch, milk the cow, take care of the hogs and dogs, and see that the ditches do not overflow. When a man is ill or his sons have been drafted, and the crop goes badly, the men around him arrange to help. One comes over one day, another the next; then, after a week or two, the round begins again. If the crop is badly retarded, all drop their own work for several days and appear together, to handle matters until they are under control. In the old days a family setting up a home on the bayou received the aid of all the neighbors in clearing and building. The spirit has not been lost. There is a favorite term for the practice—"coup de main," helping hand. No reward is expected except thanks and an occasional drink. Last summer a man pointed to a crop and told me: "See that? It was harvest' with biens mercis."

Life is an open record on Lafourche; matters which would be regarded in other places as "personal" become community topics. The concern of relatives, nainaines, parrains, cousins, and voisins is continuous, often passionate. While I was on Lafourche I was consulted on intimate family affairs and asked just what I thought of the things happening in the houses nextdoor. When I indicated that I was afraid some of these subjects were not my concern, I was gently reproved. Ah, that was not the right attitude. Everybody knew these people, had known their family for years. The matters that everybody knew about included, among others, the food supply that the Lemoines had put away for the winter, the condition of their mortgage, that old hernia of Severin's, and the baby that Josephine, the recent bride, thought that she would have, but would know about in a short time, certainement.

No bayou crop is more productive than that of children. The people of Lafourche believe in large families, and they practice what they believe. A British official in Canada once set down his wonder at the "great increase of those people" who, he said, were "like Noah's progeny, spreading themselves over the face of the Province." In Louisiana, the rate of growth did not slacken. Seven or eight children—that is a moderate blessing. Ten, and all know that God is smiling. A husband and wife with only one—a shrug. None? C'est triste. Such unfortunates will adopt others whenever they can, and they will be nainaines and parrains on every side. Adoptions, incidentally, are not confined to the childless; often they occur among families that seem rather adequately provided for in this respect. I met a couple with twelve of their own, who had taken in four more. The husband explained: "My wife, he didn' have no more in ten year. The house didn' seem right without lil' one."

Classic Acadian records tell of families of twenty-four, twenty-two, and twenty-one, "not counting those that didn't live." Households of today reach eighteen and twenty in well-celebrated instances. Before me I have birth certificates of friends who live near the town of Thibodaux. The wife is forty-three; the husband is forty-seven. They have been married twenty-five years, and their children number sixteen to date. Three of the latter have married; the original couple has eight grandchildren. The first père and mère expect to have more children as well as grandchildren. How many would they want? "Why a man should set a limit for heself?" the father asks back. A bayou family needs a lot of beds, as the Broussards—my friends of the middle Lafourche—explained. It is usually the major household problem. There was not a room in their house, including the kitchen, that did not have one or two sleeping places—upright ones, or mattresses on the floor; as a last resort, a bed was moved on the galerie, to be pulled in when it rains. Lafourche emphasizes this abundance with a saying: "Stand anywhere on the bayou, throw a brick, and you'll hit a child." But then run from his Papa and Maman! It is in the naming of the young that the Acadian heart is joyous. The task is assumed with verve and resource. I was with the Broussards when twins, a boy and a girl, arrived, and I watched the process of selection of the names. Every member of the family had a thought; after twenty minutes of collective pandemonium, Papa said everybody for Chrissake shut up, and he went to the Book of Saints. What they were reaching for, it soon became clear, was a worthy but obscure character or two with a lush combination of letters. Somehow, none in the Book seemed to do. Soon the family was canvassing Greek mythology,[2] listening impatiently, if hopefully, to the suggestions of friends, to the one the postmaster had mentioned; and I heard mention of many of the names that have spread luxuriantly over South Louisiana: Télesphore, Télémaque, Ulysses, Félicité, Alcibiade, Achille, Sylvain, Anatole, Honoré, Ursin, Lezin, Symphorion, Homère, Ovid and Ovide, Onésiphore, Onézime, Elodie, Cléophas, Artreman, Cénas, Cedonie, Sidonie, Euphémie, Pelagie, Désirée, Sosthène, Epaminonde, Aristide, Philomène, Nysida, Aspasie, L'Odias, Peigneur, Emilite, Dévince, Elia, Elias. Match them, if you can. I remembered Fortier, the historian, who found an Acadian youth who answered to the musical call of Duradon, with five sisters known as Enyoné, Méridié,

---

[2] The ranks of mythology have undergone thoroughgoing Acadian exploitation. Just why this should offer so tempting a source is a question; some have suggested the interest of the priests in the medieval revival of classic learning. Accounts of the provinces of France during the nineteenth century have told of difficulties of officials with this predilection; orders were given in some districts that no more strange designations were to be selected, and "approved" lists were issued. In any event, the modern Acadian follows a strong tradition.

Ozéina, Elfig, and Fronie; and, in another case, a father who called his son (presumably with a mixture of awe and affection) Deus; his daughter, logically, Deussa.

But the Broussards were still arguing. I was called upon for contributions; at the moment I could think only of Ametilia (so one of the men who told me of buried treasure had called his wife), and, weakly, of my own first name. I was thanked; but it was obvious that these were lacking in the proper lyric note. At last the choice was made: Cledimir for the boy, Melicert for the girl. I had to agree that both were on the superb side.

The most dazzling feats of nomenclature are those in which a family sets itself a goal in uniformity and never loses sight of it. A letter or a syllable is chosen, and names must conform, regardless of whether such names exist in any language. Down Lafourche I learned of four children: Carm, Carmel, Carmelite, Carmadelle. From Fortier came a classic case: Valmir, Valmore, Valsin, Valcour, Valérien. Others have told of the resourceful Mayards of Abbeville, in the "O" line. Their children were Odile, Odelia, Odalia, Olive, Oliver, Olivia, Ophelia, Odelin, Octave, Octavia, Ovide, Onesia, Olite, Otta, Omea, and Opta. The father was Lastie Mayard; the mother, Perpetuée. Some Louisianians look knowing and say that such eccentricities are no more. It is pleasant to report that only six months ago I came upon this procession: Rita, Reus, Rena, Rayo, Rayance, Ray John, Regile, Raybe, Rhea, Raymal, and Ramide. I saw them, me.

Despite all this effort, the grandiloquent name is soon forgotten. Practically everyone on the bayou has his "ti' name," his nickname. A man without one, he must be a cold fish. The "ti' name" is a sign of friendship, of affection, and, sometimes, of realistic description—a foible or a failing. Among the Broussards, Maman, christened Eulalie, was Chute; Papa, who was Edouard-Auguste, was Dédé; Valentin was Ba; Pierre, Ta-Tase; and others were Sa-Son, La-La, Ti-Ti, Noo-Noo, and Coe.

Two Jeans lived near the Broussards. Years ago the neighbors hit on a way to distinguish them. One went often into the trapping country, and his legs were dark and sunburned. The other was, as Papa Broussard put it, a "pink leg fellow." The dialect word for hoof is patte. The first has become Jean Patte-Noire; the second, Jean Patte-Rouge. A clumsy fellow was called Patate (potato); a towhead, Coton. Another, it was claimed, was so lazy that he would not cut lumber for himself, but pulled off loose bark; he was Bois Sec (dead wood). One accused years ago of taking a bunch of bananas, never had opportunity to forget; he was, forevermore, Felix Banane. He will have the name for life—and, I would guess, beyond. I found on a graveyard tombstone, "Here rests Albert Po-Po Thibodaux"; and friends tell me that they have seen others like it.

A nickname can extend from father to son. A Broussard cousin was known as Coo. His wife had a new baby. By the time I left, the son was Ti' Coo. Another nickname was a trade asset. One of the best-known cafés of Lafourche proclaims, in blue neon, that of its owner, "Bo-Bo's Place." Few who eat Bo-Bo's crab-burgers—bayou adaptation of the commoner article—know his true name. Under such circumstances, a man's real name can be forgotten. Mayor Delas of Thibodaux told me of an assistant who made a twenty-five-mile trip back from the bayou, seeking a man whom we may call Oscar Martin. He searched in all directions, asked questions, returned in failure. Then somebody discovered that the individual of the affidavit, Oscar Martin, was really Cojo Martin, whom both of them had known for years. They could have located him in a moment had they asked for Cojo. Who would think that little Cojo was an Oscar!

Even the bayou father—though he can tell quickly the "ti' name" of each of his children—may take long to remember the name he gave his child for baptism. One of the Broussard uncles started off well when I asked the names of his children: "Ta-Tasse, thas' Onesiphore; Crevi (écrevisse, for crawfish), thas' Théophile; Minette (kitten), that our name for Amélie. And Gaffe, here . . . now, Gaffe . . . I know his name as well as my own. . . ." He had to turn to his wife, "Tay-Yay, whas' Gaffe for-true name?" In that connection I learned that the dates of birth, when there are so many, are impossible of recollection. For records someone puts them down in a book; but for everyday purposes the family has a simple way of telling the approximate time by the season of the year. "Noo-Noon, he came in the middle of that sugar freeze; eh, but that was a night, Maman? And Boo, you were suppose to come with the cane, but you arrive with the cotton, you rascal."

Some have looked at the bayou man, early and late, and pronounced him lethargic. It has been said that the Acadian philosophy is "Digest well by day, sleep well by night." There is some point in that observation, but it is only partly true. The Acadian, like many another Frenchman, has the gift of natural leisure. He works, but his work fits the demands of his existence. Man does what he can, Papa Broussard explained to me; le bon Dieu provides the materials; those on earth, if they are wise, adapt them to a design that is pleasant. A man who forces himself into a state of collapse, he lives without pleasure; dying, he lacks even the recollection of a good time.

For himself, Papa Broussard would admit, he was one of good cheer and good appetite. The Acadian can produce a fretful, forceful executive on occasion. He will agree that Adolph is a fine, hard, driving boy—and he will let Adolph be hard and drive while he himself watches.

I observed the Broussards and their friends at work. A man, or several men, would set a task—so many arpents that they should finish, the plowing of a third of that field. They rose early, to get most of it done in the cool. If the allotted assignment was finished an hour before noon, they could knock off for the rest of the day. If by eleven o'clock there were still two or three hours' work to be done, they could leave and come back later in the afternoon. Meanwhile they could stretch out on their galeries, or visit, or walk to the store and see what was happening. Life wears no heavy overcoat here.

Yet it is not all cakes and gumbo. The true bayou man, while he does not expand his operations, keeps up his arpents and meets his obligations. As the Broussards put it, he would "fight a mortgage like the lockjaws." One sees few Acadian farms in neglect. What he has, he cares for. When there is a need for it, he can struggle with fury. I saw the Broussards and the others labor without letup, for twenty-hour stretches, when frost threatened their small sections of cane. And there are the trappers and the shrimpers. But for normal times, normal ways. . . .

Passing along Lafourche one day, I smiled at the casual, joking inquiry of my companion from the city: Were all these houses part of a single real estate development of some older generation, designed by one man? Later, I decided that there was a point in what she asked. In a sense, it is a single housing project along most of Lafourche; the architect has seen the

Acadian people themselves, evolving their own type of house through the years. The Acadian house can be spotted in a moment. That broad porch-of-all-purposes faces the water; the house goes straight back for a distance, then branches to the side, forming a "T" or an "L." The building itself always looks as if set up by a man who changed his mind at several points. As a matter of fact, the owner built small at the beginning, when the family was small. Then, as the household enlarged, he added new sections; the process of growth can be traced by him who looks carefully. The central section is sturdier, more weather-beaten; the roof is higher than the rest of the house. A slightly newer bedroom, side roof sloping to the main one, is here; in back of it, another room added more recently; then others; some put up when lumber was clearly scarce. The Acadian did not build and then produce his children to fill. He grew his family; the house followed.

Here the kitchen is practically a separate unit, often reached by a doorway of its own from the outside, or from a porch at the side or back. This makes sense in a warm climate. After supper, the kitchen is locked. One of the younger Abadies—the third family whom I visited, in an area a short distance off Lafourche—dozed after a meal on the kitchen bench in the shadow, and was incarcerated, until Maman counted and found one face missing.

The Abadies had one of the oldest houses in the country about Bayou Lafourche, with an ancient "mud front." In the first days of settlement Lafourche earth was an indispensable ingredient in home construction. A pit was dug, the spaded earth was covered with water, and moss was tossed in by the heavy handful. All who helped walked up and down barefoot until the materials were well combined. The house was constructed of split cypress, and the mud-and-moss was the filler. Over the front went an extra coat for extra protection. The mixture had further use in the construction of a chimney, made of the tough material packed between wooden frames on the outside of the house. The Abadies, like some of the others, still retain their fine, broad chimney. After some years, the wind and rain will weaken it. Then a new one is easily manufactured, the Abadies said; and they added that, modern changes or no modern changes, nothing could throw heat like that chimney, and they should go on rebuilding it.

The Abadies possess another aid to good living that is disappearing—an outdoor oven made of mud. Under the trees in the back yard was a small, squat object, rounded, built over a wooden base, and protected with a ledge above. Years ago, following directions given by his father, Papa Abadie mixed the material into a mold, baked it, and had it ready for the years. In former days it was used as often as three times a week—ten loaves or more baked at a time. Today the Abadies turn to it less often than before; the children, sad to say, prefer bread from the store that is a mile or so off. One day I tasted a homemade loaf just as it came out of the heat-packed structure in the yard. Shaped in the usual French loaf, it had all the soft delight of country bread, and more—a flavor sharp and distinct. But the younger Abadies rejected it. The whole thing, said the poised Olivia, was so much trouble: moving back and forth in the yard, getting wood, keeping the oven going, and cleaning it out. "And then, what did you have?" asked her brother Justin. He preferred the kind in wax paper. The waxed stuff impressed him: "You know it's fresh," he pointed out.[3]

• The family, too, kept its grenier, or small attic room for the

---

[3] The bayou man never asks for a "loaf of bread"—always it is "a bread." Often, too, I have heard Acadians in stores ordering "a pants."

bachelors of the family. It was reached, as in all the older houses, by a set of outdoor steps from the end of the galerie. The flight was a steep one; some offer a balustrade, but if the Abadies ever had one, it disappeared long ago. The strange young man who used it had to be sure of his tread, or of his equilibrium. But the Abadies were accustomed to it from early days. There is, of course, economy of space in this arrangement. Another method of saving was pointed out to me. In such old houses as the Abadies', doors swing out rather than in, conserving some more inches of elbow room. With fifteen children and five rooms, you too would be careful about such things.

Along the roof extended the ancient wooden gutters, that carried the rain water into a barrel at the side of the house; the roof was of split cypress shingles, and the house itself stood on old cypress stumps. It was a place built to last.

In the day hours the family threw open doors and windows at the front. But some privacy was needed, and the Abadies had the same solution as their neighbors—sets of curtains, on which the family lavished its sense of color—always pink, or bright yellow, or red, or green.

There was paint on the house, too, applied with care—but to the front only. Sides, back, everything else was worn, and wan. This was true French frugality, and a kind of insouciance. A family cannot afford everything, the Abadies pointed out; if it has several dollars left over at the end of a season, enough for the front only, why do without a jolie galerie—a thing of pleasure to family and guests and passers-by? And an unimaginative, one-tone front does not appeal to the bayou eye. A man spends no more if he gets part of his paint in a second color, does he? So the wall is red, the shutters, door, and galerie posts are green; nextdoor the combination is yellow and brown, and no one can deny that life is brighter along this way.

There is another reason why the bayou porch is often of a different coloration from the rest of the house (or painted when the remainder is colorless). In the old days the front was carefully plastered over with mud and moss—perhaps whitewashed. That was the way a home should look; a front that appeared like the sides—that was not right. And so the tradition of a specially enhanced galerie was continued. I have seen houses with sides that were handsomely painted, and the front whitewashed. The family, in such instances, had sufficient funds to do the porch like the rest; but who would want a galerie that looked that way?

And I was with the Abadies for a week or two before I realized the full extent of bayou invention. The painter works on only one side of doors and shutters—inside rather than out. During the day, when the galerie is in use and all the world is looking, the doors are thrown open and the inside shows, n'est-ce pas? When it is time to go inside, they are closed. Nobody sees the uncolored outside of the doors and shutters in the dark, does he? Meanwhile, in the house, the family can raise its eyes and see the handsome inside colors!

For some time, too, I passed over an inconspicuous ledge that extends from one side or both sides of many Lafourche kitchens. One of the most persistent survivals of the old times is this tablette, the outside shelf for dishwashing. No one is going to catch Maman Abadie spilling water or anything else on her floor. The tablette is at the level of her arms; she stands facing an opening in the wall, reaches out, and does the wet work in the open air. Papa Abadie, like the other bayou husbands, builds a small roof outside for her protection from sun and rain. There are other advantages. Her head out, she can see what is going on in the world; and, not least, she is in contact with her neighbor, who is working at her tablette across the way. Maman Abadie argues persuasively that she is both inside and outside her house at the same time. Could anything more be asked of a household device? (One of her neighbors had a new kitchen sink, but she still used her tablette for some of the work. The faucet and stopper will never take the place of this listening post.)

Inside, all is economy—a series of little economies. The bayou families—Abadies, Babins, Broussards, and the rest—manage on what seems, to the city man, like an impossibly small budget. The mother wastes nothing, from cream cheese to coffee grounds—pre-rationing and afterward. When the bonne femme has a fair supply of food, she sets part aside; when she has little, she stretches it. The Acadian, like many another rural Southerner, frequently lacks important items of adequate diet and care; yet he seems to me to manage a bit more shrewdly than the American on the same level. As an example: the Acadian knows what the word "wear" means. Many times I have heard a stern order to the little ones: "Save you' clothes." When something is put in place it is "saved," in bayou vocabulary; the child hurries to "save it away."

But there is one thing on which the bayou family has difficulty in making economy—its coffee. Café, it is one of the things that life is made to enjoy—so say earnest men and women as they shake their heads. It is a staple of diet here, a tonic, yes; a fine, warm thing to lift a man when he is low, to quiet him when he is high. The Louisiana lowlander is a coffee man from adolescence to the tomb. With him it is a day-long matter. Some take it eight times, some ten, some twelve. Men carry whisky flasks filled with coffee in their back pockets, and employ them at intervals. Many are in their kitchens every hour or so for a tasse. The visitor, at whatever time he calls, is taken there for his cup. In some Louisiana defense factories men have received permission to bring small pots to be placed at their machines, to help the day pass. They had always had their coffee near them. They could not change.

The newcomer, taking his first sip of Louisiana coffee, catches his breath and looks hard into the container. Black, dripped, strength incarnate, it stains the cup. If he stays in the southern part of the state, he will eventually be complaining when he gets anything else; a lesser mixture is an insult. But the bayou man does not take a full-sized cup, or even half a cup. By actual measurement he gets only a few ounces in a miniature-sized receptacle. True, he consumes more than the Anglo-Saxon, when he can get it; but somewhat less than it seems. In fact, I have heard many a bayou man caution the one who serves: "Just that much. A taste, to wet my mouth." More, and he is angry. He knows his capacity; if several more mouthfuls are there, how can a man resist them? Anyway, it is a waste.

The housewife has her own way for conserving sugar with coffee, and it predated rationing. She puts her sweetening in the pot; no brown crystals are left in her cups. War rules have brought sad plaints from men who say that they do not know how they can get along on "that little-little." Families exchange supplies, puzzle over ways to stretch the beverage, write letters to editors, and ask visitors how they are doing over in the next town, for true? "I feel shaky like an electric fan," one grim Lafourchais confessed to me. "I haven' had my coffee in two hours. How long this war will las', you think?"

With a supervisor, I paid a call at a Lafourche welfare office. The hour was half-past ten in the morning. We were met near the door by the whole staff, just retiring to a side room, followed by a Negro with two trays. "Join us," we were told. It was the regular morning letup for the beverage. We accepted the invitation, but could not refrain from glancing back at the roomful of clients. Would they resent this aromatic interval? The office had emptied. "Where have they gone?" we asked. To get theirs, of course. All had friends and relatives near by; all knew that this was the time for coffee. Look out the window there, at the smoke from the chimneys. The whole town was warming things up for itself and its callers. And the housewives were having "coffee parties," the equivalent of the afternoon tea in other places.

Only when the doctor threatens him with the prospect of death will the true bayou man voluntarily give up his coffee; and he will not always do so then. "The docteur say that to me ten years ago," a seventy-five-year-old patriarch informed me. "I say 'Poo. You drink your coffee, Docteur, non? I drink mine. You not so Goddamn healthy yourself. I bet I outlive you.' He died last year, and look at me." He glared; we all nodded in agreement. He added: "They claim it was the docteur's heart, from too much coffee. But I do not believe that."

§ 9. *Main Street on the Water*

OVER THE 120-MILE STRETCH of the elongated Main Street of Lafourche, men, women, and children are crossing the water during every hour of the day, and by practically every means that mankind has devised for the purpose. It is a place of bridges, with a flavor that is sometimes that of another Venice. After a day along Bayou Lafourche, the caller knows that he has never before seen so many of these structures, of so many types and shapes: crude and costly, public and private, impressive and slightly ridiculous; wide wooden bridges, others that seem to be mere catwalks; elaborate steel ones; floating, lifting, turning bridges. Then there are "bridges" which, in the common meaning of the word, are not bridges at all, but small floating barges drawn by cable from side to side over the small waterway. Skiffs, too, are always at hand, or left-over pirogues—anything that will allow itself to be paddled.

The newcomer is certain that Lafourche has a comically large oversupply of devices for crossing—one every few miles. No people could need that many, I thought when I first went there. After I had been on the scene a week, I was ready to join a delegation to the police jury to demand another installation for our locality. There was nothing to cross on within four miles! When a place is directly in sight, in front of you, I found that you are not happy in making a long horseshoe-shaped journey to get to it and another to return.

A man with an idea and a small supply of lumber frequently gets to work, builds a flat object that floats, and serves his family and friends—and sometimes, in emergencies, his pocketbook as well. Lafourche lives by its bridges, and a neighborhood never realizes this so well as when a brief contact occurs between its nearest one and a well-loaded vessel. On such occasions state and parish officials rush to the scene, start repairs, and order equipment. Newspapers are asked to advise operators of the accident; days or weeks may elapse, while the routine of the surrounding areas is disrupted, and families and merchants complain that they are cut off from the rest of the world. Alex Melancon in the New Orleans *Times-Picayune* has described how a heavily packed barge on one occasion turned two bridges into splintered wrecks. One was across Lafourche at Lockport, the other over the near-by Intracoastal Canal connection. Persons had to travel twenty miles to reach a point two hundred feet away across the water. But here, as in similar cases, the wise bayou spirit showed itself. Some families have never put aside their small boats from the older days, and these came out again and were put to profitable use. In another case, a Lafourchais whom I know ran his own homemade barge near the disabled bridge, and in four weeks earned enough to keep up expenses of the farm for several months. A good, disastrous collision and he might have been free of worry for half the year, he said.

Bayou people have disputed more often over their bridges than over anything else, I would guess. I have met many tired warriors of such disputes—such as Francis T. Knobloch of Thibodaux—and they frown in remembered fury. For years every crossing, floating or stationary, was a toll one. The police jury would locate, then auction it off. On both sides of the question rested the prosperity of thousands. It was the bayou crossroad. At its ends merchants set up their stores, dealers and doctors their offices. Men competed for the privilege of operating the connection. The individual who had most to gain was the owner of a general store; he might have to close if his rival on the other side won the business. His system was "Buy from me and you cross free"; the pass card was an inducement to trade. At one time almost everybody seemed to be in the toll business. A bayou church put up a crossing of its own; those who went to Mass rode for nothing. An old-timer told me, "It helped attendance, sure."

The state has erected its own free bridges at some points. This competition and the work of enraged committees have eliminated most of the tolls. A few, however, still exist. In one case a bank has a connection with such an enterprise, but no effort has been made to determine whether a customer plans a deposit or a withdrawal, as far as I learned! The heart of a bayou village—all of it, frequently, that the outsider can readily identify—is a center composed of the bridge, two or three stores, bars, and soft-drink stands. Here men gather at all hours and debate war, fishing, women, and crops.

It was in such meeting places, from time to time and from place to place, that I learned of another major subject of frenzy among the Lafourchais: the matter of the divorce of the bayou from the Mississippi. Men still shake their fists over this issue.

The bayou floods of the older days seldom raged so fiercely as those of the Mississippi. Some of the iconoclastic veterans remark that a levee break on Lafourche was not necessarily a disaster. It ruined some crops and damaged some property; but a small break, with a wash of rich silt, might make good land out of bad, better out of good. "The crevasse in our section paid the family for twenty years," one man chuckled to me. Others did not agree. When a farmer remarked indiscreetly that he would not mind a "nice, small break," the neighbors watched closely. Armed guards patrolled the levee tops, and they shot in the dark on suspicion.

With the passing years, water troubles seemed to grow worse. The dikes rose higher during the last part of the last century, but an increasing flow seemed to be pushing down; or perhaps the greater development made the losses higher. In one especially bad season of which the old ones often talk, floods struck the main stream and Lafourche with almost equal force. Helen Bowie has told how a rescue vessel was sent out along the Mississippi on that occasion; by some mishap it was pulled out into the overflowed, swampy area between it and Lafourche. Ordinarily, it would have been wrecked, its carcass overturned in the muck. This time the water was so high and the levees so broken that the ship was piloted into the channel of Lafourche and safety. That, as Lafourche says, was a wet year, yes.

From points along and outside Lafourche came strong demands: close the bayou at the Mississippi. The upper section generally wanted the connection left open, for this land was higher and better protected. The lower area, sloping to the Gulf, felt the greatest weight of water. Men fought before the legislature, and sometimes on the bayou banks. Eventually the closing was ordered. Today a heavy mound of earth shuts the Mississippi out of Lafourche. Recent revival of water traffic has brought demands for a reopening, with a dam to regulate the flow. I have attended a furious hearing or two on the issue; but the bayou stays closed.

With the closing, the life of Lafourche has changed, but not so much as some had feared. The doleful said that the bayou would silt up, pass away, and its settlements disappear. Today, from its head to a point a third or more down, Lafourche is stationary—low, dark-watered, lily-covered in places. But it was not killed so easily; it still dominates its country, serving it, giving it its character. From below, the Gulf lends its movement, pushing up its tide and pulling it out; and into Lafourche pour other waters from the east and west. The upper stretches have settled down to a quieter era devoted largely to agriculture, sugar, and truck produce; the lower ones are coming more and more into their own as places of boat traffic, sea food, and oil supplies. The Intracoastal Canal, in its westward extension from the Harvey Canal-Barataria route, reaches through part of the bayou at the south, providing heavier lines of trade than the old days sometimes saw.

Of late an unorthodox thing has been happening—and some of the traditionalists are not sure that it is proper. A bayou without flood danger has no need for levees; today they are in retirement. These mounds, first built up by the stream and then raised higher at the edges by men, have been put to a new use during their declining years. For a time they were untouched; then someone had a thought. This was rich land, as good as any in the South. Make something of it, then. Men started to work with seeds and plantings on the slopes, on the crown, on the edges toward the water. Today tassels of corn wave over many stretches; stalks of cane parade up and down the hills; anything else that will grow to the rear produces with equal or greater richness. Others improved on the first inspiration. If levee soil is fine where it is, it will be as good somewhere else. Owners attacked the small hills and rolled them away in wheelbarrowfuls; the fecund material they spread over every foot within reach over the farm; what is left at the bayou is still available for new planting.

The old Lafourche fostered a method of trade of its own; and all the years and all their changes have not been able to eliminate it—the traveling store. In the French provinces the ancestors of the bayou people knew the cart dweller, who passed through the villages with his items of clothing, shoes, glass objects, anything small and cheap. In Louisiana a counterpart appeared, the caboteur or coast tradesman, providing the same service by boat or houseboat. The Acadians and their neighbors could not get to the big centers; the trade came to them. They had little or no money, and so the tradesman bartered with them for eggs, chickens, corn, hides, and woven cloth.

Eventually, as roads showed some improvements, the packet merchant appeared, carrying his broad bag of goods on his back wherever he could push his way. As he prospered, he bought a cart, a small covered wagon with a high axle, to work along the half-slush of the roads; and in time he acquired a horse. For him, as for the caboteur, the long string of Lafourche settlements made possible a quick coverage, and a heavy return to the mile.

With the modern day came heavy-duty roads. A passage-way now extends along all of Lafourche, concrete on one side, graveled on the other. When it arrived, wise ones predicted a quick death for the trade carts. The families of La-fourche would ride those short distances along the smooth path to town; wouldn't they prefer to deal with the larger stores, that had more to offer? Many families did make trips to town, but not to shop. Let civilization move forward if it wanted, the bayou wife would do like her mother. She would still deal with a marchand who stopped at her door.

I was privileged to spend ten days traveling along La-fourche with several merchants-on-wheels; and I learned of a business with many rules that are special to itself. The mar-chand-charrette (or marchand-truck or marchand-automobile —he goes by several names) has become mechanized and has otherwise fitted himself to the times; essentially, his trade is the same as ever. He has a schedule; the family knows, roughly, when he will appear. As we went along, the house-wives heard his signal—in each case one peculiar to the opera-tor. "Two lil' and then a long one—thas' Alex Corbin, from down; four long ones, Jo-Jo Babineaux." One man, I found, rings a school bell; another blows a cow horn; but these operate in the highly rural areas leading to Lafourche, where the sound must be loud.

From their galeries the families moved toward the road; and here was opportunity for them to mix purpose with pleasure. The neighborhood situation was appraised, and the status of children, funerals, and sicknesses. It was a social event. As the driver pulled to the side of the road, he stuck out a small colored banner—an invitation and a warning: "Serving Customers." Motorists watched closely when they passed. The children crowded around, wanting "candi." The Papas were sometimes there, for such things as monkey blood (mercurochrome), or a rope for their boats. But the Mamans and the drivers were the principals in this trade. The trucks had one side boarded up, the other covered with a canvas flap that was raised at each stop. Inside was the equivalent of the old country store, offering whatever any reasonable man or woman could wish: hats, candles, and razor blades; tea, cake, and mops; lard, belts, and rolling pins. (Was there anything that he didn't carry? I asked one marchand. "I don't carry explosives," he declared, solemnly.) The truck was packed with scores of small trays and holders, above, below, on three sides, each with several articles of one kind, in ready reach. If a rarity was desired, he would bring it on his next trip. He had it at home; he knew just where it was stored.

Dealings were in French in seventy-five per cent of the cases. Even if the housewife knew the other language, she found le française the natural medium for bargaining—and, m'sieu, the more effective one. That soap, it was a cent cheaper the last time. Ah, non. Ah, oui. Two experts in haggling faced each other. Sometimes one won, sometimes the other; or a compromise was struck. The marchand, like his predecessors, was willing and happy to barter; a frank one would admit that he preferred to do so. At the front, attached to the bumper, were large chicken coops, empty in the morning, filled by midafternoon. Inside were boxes with straw, for eggs. Many families never exchange a cent of cash; Madame Babin told me she earned enough from her chicken yard to pay most of the household expenses. And the marchand, in town, sells the farm produce at a neat profit.

The marchand-charrette has at least one other appeal. He is a newspaper of local affairs, a messenger from family to family: You will be sure, 'Zeb, to tell Madame Estève we expect her for the crawfish boil tomorrow? . . . What they think up there, ahn, about the crazy things that candidate is saying? . . . You know poor old Martin is low; we hear he made a second will. . . . And ask Madame Estève when you see her to bring some of her peppers for the crawfish—and some gauze for Co-Co's feets. (The marchand has gauze in front of him, for sale; but he understands his business, and will not push opportunity too hard. Maman knows what she wants.)

War rationing brought various restrictions in the service of such merchants; but the government recognized them as long-established agents of trade in their area. If they did not cover the bayou, their many customers, making individual trips, might use more rubber and gasoline than they do. In some cases butchers, ice companies, and other retail establishments in the bayou towns have sent their wares out by truck, stopping at homes along the bayou. Even ice-cream companies did the same thing before the war came. Rural life with ice deliveries and Good Humors—who could match that?

I had thought, at the beginning, that the life of the marchand-charrette might be a glamorous one. I soon discovered that he is no romantic figure to the bayou girls. It is the bus driver who is the gallant, whose life along all those miles of passage is fraught with gay looks and hand waves. The busman is a man of the world, a man in a uniform; and he speaks French. What more could a jeune fille ask!

In the bayou villages trade moves no faster than with the merchant-on-wheels. Few stores, I found, were younger than fifteen or twenty years. In most cases sons had taken over business from fathers and were training their own boys to take over after them. These establishments are dim, unpainted, signless. Where there are showcases, they are often empty. A man does not need to display his name when everybody knows it, or his wares when everyone knows what he has in the back. Once or twice I asked bayou friends why they dealt with one who gave what I considered inadequate service. I was reproved. M'sieu Claudel was a parrain, or a cousin of a brother-in-law, and a good man. What would he do if they stopped going to his place? No "specials" in the window will answer that question.

Large retail organizations have attempted bayou invasions. I found the corpses of several "up-to-date" stores in the best locations of a number of towns, their brilliant new hues hardly faded as yet. To the side, virgin of coloration or salesmanship, thrived the places of the local M'sieurs Claudel. The chain manager who is sent to a French Louisiana town soon regrets the day. For what, the Abadies asked me, did these people put up a yellow front and showcase? They didn't buy yellow and glass, no.

In one case, an outside organization decided to use strategy and picked a likely home boy as its representative. That, m'sieurs, would not work. The town thought it a very unfair way to deal with M'sieu Claudel. That young one, he ought to have shame. How would he like someone to do that to his père at the bank—put up a new bank nextdoor, all red and big windows, with bargains on Saturday?

Next in importance to the villages along this Main Street are the "settlements." This is the designation—official or informal—of a cluster of farms and houses that takes the name of its main family or citizen—farmer, merchant, or doctor. It is the LeBorne Settlement, or the Settlement à Ledoux. The patriarchal system extends beyond the home. Consciously or unconsciously the neighbors select a man in whom they have trust, for advice and general direction. One settlement leader told me with a grin: "I didn't have a damned thing to do with all this. I just got picked. A lot of times I wish I hadn't." To him, family funds and family secrets are entrusted. Several times bayou farmers told me to write to them "care of him. . . . It might get los', the other way, or go to wrong house. Everybody know him." Packages, farm supplies, tax bills— he receives them for all who live about him. One morning when I called, I found ten others waiting on his galerie, each with a problem. One wanted to see if something could be done about the drainage ditch. Another wished to have a letter written to a cousin in New Orleans; a third needed a tax blank.

The situation, of course, frequently has political implications. The bayou man takes easily to direction in his public affairs. His opinion is that of his chief, his decisions those that the chief makes. On subjects that are very close—the new bridge, the silting up of the canal—his words are strong, and his politician will listen. Beyond that, he has no sharp views; on state and national affairs he will ask how he should vote.

Once he has been instructed, he becomes a fervent, violently loyal partisan of his side. It may or may not be the opposite of what he believed the last time. With families so large and interconnected, a single job can assure the good will of a whole section. I was speaking to one Lafourchais of a widely recognized public thief; he admitted things against him, but concluded, like any city ward-heeler's follower: "He gave my p'pere a nice inspectorship. How I can vote against that man? What you say?"

Those who take office here, generally keep it. It is not unusual for sheriffs, mayors, and district attorneys to continue in their posts for fifteen years or longer. "Political families" flourish with perhaps greater richness than in most places; many believe that the percentage of politicos, professional or amateur, to the population is extraordinary. In some places they seem to be everywhere—in the stores, on the farms, in the boats. A veteran of Lafourche, appraising one of the officeholders of the section, told me: "Thas' a one, all right. I know him for years, but I don' know yet whether he a hard-shell or a sof'-shell." (He was referring, of course, not to the shells of Baptists, but to those of crabs.) Sometimes, it seems, such politicos can change from one group to the other, with all the gradings between. If he has been put back in office with the usual large vote, the bayou official is happy, and that is when his shell is soft. He is vulnerable to the request for favors. But if he suspects trickery, or a rare piece of disloyalty, he can be hard, mes amis, very hard.

However powerful, the bayou politician may not be able to maintain a continuous dignity. His constituents show a large humor in these things. They enjoy their politics. A political meeting along Lafourche is an occasion of roaring laughter. The speaker moves with glee from topic to topic, he imitates, he makes puffed mouth, howls, grunts, goes falsetto. The outsider might call it vaudeville, but this orator makes his points far more vividly than the Anglo-Saxon. He can say in French what he might not be able to present in English—at least with such point; he is adept in playing with words and upon them, in tossing blithe insult at a rival for his resemblance to an eel or the backside of a turtle. There is a surge of giggles, a rush of guffaws, the calling of encouragement from those at the back. A visitor may decide that the candidate has just described some unprecedented thing; that a reputation has been made, or smashed. It is always this way. After some of the searing descriptions, one might suppose that knife or gun duels would ensue. The audience shrugs—and so, generally, do the rivals. They are not Frenchmen for nothing.

It was at a bayou political meeting of some years ago that I first heard about the Irish and English and German Acadians. The program gave a name: E. Crosby, the only Anglo-Saxon among fifteen Gallic ones. Or so I thought, until Mr. Crosby spoke. Then I found that he was Etienne Cr-r-r-os-bay; that M'sieu Crosby was as much like a Bourgeois as a Bourgeois is like a LeBlanc; and that he could not speak anglais. At a bridge, I was introduced to an O'Brien. (Pronounced O'—bree-on.) He was not noticeably less olive-skinned than one of the Babins; though his eyes were light blue instead of the brown of the Babins, his speech was theirs.[1] Using English with difficulty, he told me that he was, assuredly, French. The name? That was just the name of his great-grandfather from

---

[1] Incidentally, some Acadians, being of Northern France, have comparatively light coloring—blue eyes, brown hair. But their ways, as one man put it, are indisputably brunette.

Ireland. Then I met a Lopez. There was no single feature, or anything else, to indicate a Spanish origin; and his speech was French. His father had been able to talk some Spanish, yes; he himself once knew a few words, but they were all gone away. I had a letter, later, for Edward Smith. A man with heavy blond hair came to the door. I meant Edouard Smees? That was him, oui. Come in. How I was? . . . Some had never wondered about their non-French names, and insisted that they were "all French." They became mildly angry at any suggestion that there was anything other than Gallic blood in their veins. It was a kind of reflection.

All this demonstrates another aspect of Acadian prowess. Though they held largely to themselves, through the years the people of Lafourche sometimes mated with others—but on their own terms. In most cases it was a union of Acadian girl with a man of another section, who had moved into the French country to make a living. The outlander married more than his Louise; he joined Acadia in Louisiana. He heard French day and night; the people among whom he plied his trade spoke only that language; he had to learn it for simple self-maintenance, in business, in family conversation, eventually in communication with his own children. His wife taught the young ones, and her instructions included French words, customs, and viewpoints. At the start, of course, she and some of the others would make attempts to learn a few words of the husband's tongue and include them in their exchanges. But when the subject became interesting— Eh bien, who could remember those foreign expressions? The forces were irresistible. In time, he was speaking only French; after some years, he was thinking in the language.

An important element among the Acadians of today are those of French-German mixture. Many Germans arrived early in Louisiana, establishing the "German Coast" along the Mississippi and giving their name to a near-by waterway, "Bayou des Allemands." The Acadians settled near them; some of the Germans moved toward Lafourche, and among them the men and women from Canada made far-reaching cultural conquests. Families which today regard themselves as entirely French have names that can be traced back to the original Germans. Over the generations, the Teutonic names have been altered, shortened, lengthened, transmuted. The stout Jake Schneider was turned into Monsieur Schexnaydre, his first name taken over with the last—and you try to tell one of his descendants that he isn't a true Frenchman! J. Hanno Deiler, who made detailed studies of the subject, found that Herr Schaffer was changed to Monsieur Chauffre; Hans Peter, to Ampète; Hans Jacob, to Jean Jacques.

A French notary found a Zweig before him. Puzzled, he asked what the word signified. "Branch," he was told; and so he set down the proper French form, LaBranche. Herr Zweig, an amiable man, accepted something that everybody could pronounce, and found things easier. And during the Spanish regime, one priest made a modification to the Latin that seems phenomenal. The groom was, by the records, Don Santiago Villenol. As a matter of fact, he was really Jacob Wilhelm Nolte. The bride was not the only one who changed her name at this ceremony.

The Frenchman-by-marriage took other things from his surroundings. It is hard to visit a bayou home for a fortnight, a week end, or an evening and fail to catch something of the Gallic lift of heart. Even a dour attitude has been known to change under the deft prodding of these sprightly people. Vernon J. Parenton, part Acadian, tells how he met an Anglo-

Saxon who was a sunny victim. The way of life, he said, was "easy to catch; and once caught, who in the hell wants to change?"

To many, a great part of the delight of that way is the "ti' game," the little gambling of the Lafourche men. In the back of the stores, in rooms off restaurants, barber shops, and soft-drink stands or bars, they play at night, during afternoon, sometimes in the morning. At home they try their luck on the galerie when the light is right, inside when it is dark. At Saturday night dances, games go on in the back rooms. The stakes are small, the pleasure large; the Lafourchais isn't sure what he would do without such chance-taking. They do not play for nothing— "That is not interesting at all," a white-haired expert told me; but the amounts can be very small. Once, when nobody had any money, I found a group playing for homemade candies in a bowl.

A "gumbo" is a favorite method of gambling in private homes. Word is spread about the neighborhood: "Come to the Trahans' on Saturday." Those who come find poker, re-freshments, and a part of the pool to be taken for expenses. At the high point, everybody gets a plate or two of gumbo.

An equally well-known institution is the "bonco." A man has raised more geese than he needs, or he has extra chickens, or oranges. There is no charge for attendance. Anybody can come and play. Chips will sell for a nickel or a few cents each. The geese or other produce are in the corner. The owner sets a value of, say, $2.50 on a good fowl or a basket of fruit. As soon as somebody accumulates that much in his pile, he can claim one of the prizes. Or there may be a single prize—a hog. Usually the evening ends with half the players taking some-thing home; the owner making a profit on his excess supplies, the losers with at least the recollection of a pleasant evening. A nice bonco, Aristide.

A bonco may be held for a charitable purpose. When a family is in sudden need, neighbors will donate chickens, rice, and other supplies for the games. Also there are political boncos of several kinds. At one which I attended, a candidate was invited, and was expected to buy everybody a drink, in rounds that continued for hours, and to take a hand in the game, and lose with good humor. A political spender solidifies himself on such occasions; one who shows a penurious side can lose an election. Again a candidate will have a bonco of his own. He is host, and everything comes from his large pocket. But such boncos are held on the night before election; all who attend know that they are to spend the evening, playing and drinking until dawn. Then they are herded in trucks to the polls, to vote the right way. It is democracy made comfortable.

One of the joys of this Main Street's country life is that of going to town. Saturday afternoon is the occasion—the high point of the week. The family's destination is only a few miles away, but Donaldsonville, Thibodaux, and Raceland have the glamor of distance and difference. The Abadies had prepared me for the event with such descriptions that I shared their excitement as we got under way one week end.[2]

We crowded into the machine with the others from next-door, making a total of twenty in the voluminous back section—some seated on kitchen chairs, others on the floor. In a near-by wagon four housefuls were packed, all standing, be-

[2] When gasoline rationing came, many turned back to their wagons for these trips. Others husbanded their supply of gas for the short weekly route.

cause that was the only way in which they could fit. By early afternoon the road was filling rapidly. At one point the Abadies recognized friends, yelled greetings, and the two drivers, always obliging, halted for a moment.

"Wait for us outside the show. Don' go in . . ."

"No, we got go to the doctor first. Jean-Jean, here—his gall bladder."

Jean-Jean nodded wanly. Many gave signs of regret and sympathy as we started again. A gall bladder, it is a bad thing to have, Maman Abadie told Maman Delaune. Her brother, the one in the Army, how he suffered. Lean over and she would tell her. . . . Get back, you Ti-Ti; this is not for you.

I learned, meanwhile, that Saturday is the busiest day of the week for some of the bayou town people; foodstands, small restaurants, and other shops stay open until late; some are maintained in business by this week-end trade. For the doctors, lines form such as they never see on other days. People from down the bayou save their illnesses if they can, for their town day. The wife of one of the doctors says that she dreads Saturday like a bad operation.

We had reached the outskirts of Thibodaux. The older girls called to the driver, insistently, to stop. Everybody stretched, put his shoes on, patted himself, and we walked the rest of the way in. The town nudged and whispered: "Look at the gee-gees, with all those children and all that noise!" The girls' efforts had been in vain; we had been spotted, as, I gathered, we would always be. The Abadies sniffed. Half the time, Maman said, it was a former country fellow himself saying that, a tête grande (big head) who didn't want to admit where he was from.

We were in time for the first matinee at the movie house, arranged for the country trade. (The elite town folk seldom attended.) The manager was smiling at the door. "What you got on today, Dieu-Donné? Jean Autray? Bien! Jean Autray, P'pere, you hear?" It must be a cowboy film, preferably with songs. A drawing-room presentation, and there will be loud complaints. Two in succession, and the trade is off for weeks; it will go to the next town. The audience was full-blooded. Les maudits hommes were scorned and given salty advice. M'sieu Autray—quel gentilhomme, that one. "He's a good mans," one eight-year-old informed me and all those about us who would listen. Babies cried, Mamans went to the back with them at intervals, and the proprietor was happy.

As we left, the crowd was quickly filling with new country arrivals for the second showing. It was dark; some were going toward the courthouse square, others were looking in the windows. One of the merchants had a sign across the banquette: "Bargain." The girls insisted on entering; Maman did not wish to go, for she was shy in such big places. But she was persuaded. They tried on hats. Maman whispered that the marchand-charrette had just as fine for half the price, sure. The clerk overheard and assured Madame that that could not be so. Feel that quality. Maman got red. The girls triumphed.

Then we joined another procession for the other major event of the visit, the dance hall. Everybody went, grand-'mère, grand-père and the bébés. I had looked forward to a fais-do-do, the old-time dance, with French music. At the first glance, I knew that I would be disappointed. It was a hall a half-block long; the music was "direck from New Orleans" and non-French; and the dancing, wherever it came from, was in the ballroom-jitterbug variations. Modernism has made large inroads in this direction; the fais-do-do has left the towns of Lafourche. I would have to look elsewhere.

But the amateur traffic officer outside retained something of the old style. He was giving brisk directions: "Retreat your car. . . . Advance to the left. . . ."

§ 10. *Le Bon Dieu*

WE HAD BEEN CAREFUL to bring the old car to church with us this Sunday. Everybody came in whatever it was he had—a machine, a buggy, or a wagon. After the regular service, all gathered at the front steps, and the priest joined us for the annual blessing of the vehicles.

As we bowed our heads, he sprinkled the holy water on running boards, hoods, and tires. The Latin prayer was an appeal for the safety and well-being of those who travel, an old ceremonial dating back many centuries; for us he invoked the protection of St. Christopher, saint of journeys and journeyers. He shook hands when it was over, and the drivers started off, certain that there would be less danger now for most of us. Over the driver's place in most of the machines, from trucks to buggies, a small medal of the saint was pinned.

On another occasion I was invited to the blessing of a store on the main street of a Lafourche town. The owner, a devout church member about to embark on a new venture, accordingly felt confident of success to come. Again, when an auxiliary power station was put into operation, all agreed that a similar benediction was in order. The first radios were given blessings in some towns, until they became too plentiful and obviously non-hazardous.

The church comes close to Lafourche. In many cases it preceded the town or settlement itself. The bayou people have a saying: "Put up the church and the place will build to it." At dozens of centers of population, for many miles of small homes, all are of the one faith. There is no thought of any other. If a man or woman wanted to shift, there might be no other religion available to him for long distances. Tradition governs here in many ways, and in that tradition the faith has a large part.

Masses are held daily, several on Sunday. On the morning of the latter day almost every house will be emptied; and some will attend three Masses. I met a man who paddled eight miles each way by pirogue; he and his family had attended every service for the past five years; they had a record of it.

The language of the services is frequently a conglomerate. The farther from the towns I went, the more generally was French heard in the sermons and the announcements. The old people demand that they be in that language; it is easier for them to follow. In many cases they cannot understand more than a word or two of English, and they feel cheated, they say. But some parents will ask: "More in English, Father. I want the children to learn it good." Sometimes I found compromises. The priest gave the first fifteen minutes of his sermon in rapid French. Then, without a halt, he went on in slower English, simplified so that it would be less difficult for many to comprehend; then he lapsed into brisk French, and ended in English. He made no effort to repeat in one tongue what he had covered in the other; the presentation was a continuous one. No one seemed to think that there was anything peculiar in this method; there was no comment made. Announcements—Masses, devotions, novenas—are given twice in most churches, once in French, once in English. For confessions, almost invariably the language is French. It seems more confidential, several explained to me.

In the homes, too, religion does not hide itself. Holy pictures are in most rooms, particularly the bedrooms, for prayers before retiring and in the morning. Near-by are the green fronds blessed on Palm Sunday. And most houses have at least one small boîte, or shrine, as often as not above the mantel in the main room. In one case—and it was typical—I saw a large crucifix, with two statues of saints to flank it, a set of four religious pictures nailed about them; above, a framed photograph of the parish church; beneath it, two large candles. The floor below was well worn from years of kneeling. The drippings of many candles were at the bases of the holders, but everything was dusted and cleared every day or so; a shrine that needed the attention of the housewife—that was not good.

Before most of the home shrines were receptacles of blessed water. Through the year the holy water is taken from the churches in large quantities. Children bring well-washed milk bottles. When the priest lacks time to accede to the constant petitions for holy water, he sets a special day on which all may call for this purpose; the water is there by the tubfuls.

Every member of the family wears a medal. If the eldest boy is inclined to leave his at home, he will think of the mental travail of his Maman when she makes the discovery, and he will assume it again. In cases of serious illness children are "promised" to saints by their mothers. If St. Anna will intercede to save Emilie, the child will be hers. Later, Emilie will be "dedicated" and until she is fully grown, perhaps afterward, she will carry the saint's colors, in shoulder straps or cords. To leave the house without them . . . that would be wrong, yes.

A family of eight or ten sons will make every effort to enroll them all in the altar boys' society. No O'Learys were happier than the Abadies when they had a team of their own in such service. In their teens, a certain number of the boys talk of becoming priests, more among the girls think of becoming nuns. Ah, it is a fine thing to have a religious in the family, said the Abadies and their neighbors. The neighbors will always remember it, and talk about it. And what does he say in his letter, ahn? When will he be home again for Mass? If a family can send two sons to the priesthood, then it knows that its repute is high.

Religion is nearer even than usual in times of illness. When a patient approaches the end, the priest is summoned quickly. Once when I was calling on a minister in the area back of Lafourche, an elderly woman was brought in a boat from a point forty miles out in the swamp. She had decided that she was going to die, and she had ordered arrangements made. The priest went to the vessel for the rite; then she told her son to start the lugger home again. Several days later we learned that she had died on the way, content.

One of the Abadie cousins fell very ill while I was in their section. From everywhere came neighbors, relatives, and friends to cry and pray. One woman·was an expert in exhortation; the priest could not be present at all times and so she remained in the house. Others joined her; all knelt, for rites that were part-formal, part-improvisations of the prayer-leader, with Hail Mary's, appeals to the saints, and little extemporaneous statements to those above. Some of the women held their babies nursing at the breast, while they remained on their knees. Others stayed for an hour or so, then excused themselves and withdrew quietly without interrupting the service. The intention was clearly one of neighborly assistance and sympathy; the result, I thought, might be, at the least, subversive in its effect on the sick one's morale. But all expected it, the women and the family, and, it seemed, Cousin Abadie himself.

A few days later came word that his struggles were over. Then, as on other occasions, I thought I detected strong similarities between the veillée, or wake, and the old-fashioned Irish variety of New Orleans, Boston, and Baltimore. Friends sat about and talked of death, the sugar crop, and the status of the drainage. One of the more irreverent and distantly related Abadie girls surveyed the rapidly talking crowd and whispered to me to listen to the crowing of "les coqs morts" (the funeral cocks). "They're always there—the same ones," she sighed. In a back room the table was heaped high with provisions of gumbo, rice, and chicken fricassée, with coffee on the stove. Before the hour of the funeral, the great supply had been reduced to fragments. Toward the end, the dead man's sister said that twenty-five chickens had been consumed—"Our back yard is wipe' out; they ate it clean." In her voice was mild regret, and also high pride. It was a tribute to community standing.

Cousin Abadie had once said that he wanted to be placed in the old family grounds to the back; and that meant a funeral by water. Such burials are held every year, though less often than formerly. For most of the participants there seemed to be little that was unusual in a cortege by putt-putt boat. The hearse was the vessel that headed the procession, with the priest and closest members of the family. Other Abadies filled four more boats in the line, and there were five others behind them. We moved slowly, the only sounds the soft lapping, the chug of the vessels, and the lift of paddles as others moved their craft to the side of the narrow bayou when we approached.

The cemetery was near the bayou edge, on a shell-and-earth

ridge, with a small iron fence. It was not, I thought, a gloomy setting, with the glitter of afternoon water reflected on the crosses and the green leaves, and the heavy oaks, dropping moss, as a frame. During the ceremony I looked about at the crumbling tombstones, all in the French style that tells a little more about the person, and sometimes his manner of death, than those of the Anglo-Saxons. "Priez pour elle" (pray for her), asked many, carrying out the friendly and confiding note. This one was a man of great bravery; she was a woman of great graces, a good mother; that one died in a tidal wave of such-and-such year. . . . Pray for them.

Now it was time for the body of Cousin Abadie to be lowered, and as the widow was held up in her grief, each member of the family dropped, not a clod of earth, but a few shells upon it. As we closed the low iron gate behind us, the water was all that could be seen in the gathering gloom, against the sloping line of the ridge and the high trees. The family, said Papa Abadie, should feel better to know that Cousin was near the water and banks that he had known as a boy.

The mourning that followed was a study in degrees and scales; full—all-black; half—black-and-white; lesser mourning "for respeck," by distant relatives and good friends, blue, or blue-and-white. For the husband, wife, or child, it should be worn a year and a half; for brother or sister, a year; uncle or aunt, six months; "close cousin," three months; others, "maybe just two." The immediate family went nowhere for a time; when they visited again, it was only to places at which no music would be played. If by chance someone turned on the radio, the widow excused herself, "always politely," and left. Before that, someone usually realized the error and apologized. "Ah, Madame Abadie, that Marie, she have the head of a duck. I have slap her go-o-od. How you must be sad, chère. . . ."

A widow may remain in mourning to her grave. Sometimes she is no sooner out of black for one member of her family than it is time to put it on for another. At her husband's bedside, in one case of which I heard, a young woman promised that if he recovered, she would never dance again. He lived, and she kept the pledge, never moving to the dance floor even with him. (For one who saw her first fais-do-do when she was five months old in her mother's arms, and had been going ever since, that was a sacrifice.) Widows occasionally consent to marry again, but for the rest of their lives some wear the black of mourning for their first mates. It would be disloyal to take other colors.

After a proper time has passed, few blame the widow or widower who turns to another. When there are children to be cared for, the woman who says "Oui" a second time may be doing only her duty to them, n'est-ce pas? And a husband, he is not a bad thing to have around, Maman Abadie chuckled. But a divorce, non. A separation, perhaps; that is all. A divorced woman would not enter *her* house. As for remarriage after divorce, it was clear that one who risked it was of a daring spirit.

Father Jeansonne meanwhile moved about us. This other Father of Lafourche lives in no moss-hung tower. He is a practical man, who knows what his church wants and how it is to be obtained; he is seldom a fanatic. The influence of "Father" extends to many things; he is considered before most enterprises are undertaken; his opinion is sought by those who are uncertain, or certain, of their proposals. He is of any age from twenty-five to sixty-five; he is probably known as a good fisherman and hunter, especially in the smaller towns, and he goes to the marshes with some of the members of the Holy Name Society. Among his accomplishments should be an ability to laugh at many of the jokes he hears, including an occasional restrained one about himself.

Nor is his church a gloomy taskmaster. It does not frown on a good time in balance. The week end is the bayou man's time of realization, the yeast in the bread of his life. Saturday afternoon begins it, and if he is in bed for a few hours of sleep on Sunday night, and has attended to his church duties in the meantime, he considers that things are well. During that period he will hear music, he will sing, and he will dance; he may drink a little, and he will not feel guilty.

On several occasions I accompanied a number of Abadies on Sunday hunting trips. We always went first to the special service which the church arranged for those like us, the "fishermen's and hunters' Mass," at three or four in the morning. Father Jeansonne got up early and there was a ceremonial before dawn. The lighted altar, seen through the stained-glass windows, was the only illumination along the water for some miles. Outlined in the beam that cut through the dark were the edges of many boats, filled with bait and nets. The service ended, we filed out. Soon the motor was humming and we were turning among streamers of fog on our way to a small lake which the Abadies recommended. If there was room, some curled up and slept. They had been up "late-late" the preceding night; but they would have enjoyed themselves the less today had they started without the service. At home, I knew from previous Sundays, the family was stirring. They, too, had been up until "late-late." That night they would go to another near-by town for another dance; and during the day they would visit down the way. Everybody likes Sunday. "Keep away from the bayou, La-La. You want to fall in before church?"

Regardless of such things as meat supplies and rationing, Friday means that it is practically impossible to get meat from a bayou store. One newcomer, a Protestant, tells of the situation that confronted her on Fish Day, shortly after her arrival. She asked the butcher for lamb. He gazed at her in surprise, then told her: "Madame, you know it's Friday." He was slightly embarrassed, slightly reproachful because of her oversight. She told him that she knew what the day was, and asked the price of lamb.

"Well, I don' know." Silence, cogitation. "You see, it don' pay us to cut meat on Friday. Nobody else would wan' it."

Not entirely satisfied with this logic, she argued further; but she received no lamb that day. Perhaps, she conceded later, it was a matter of economy for him. But she could not overcome her impression that he disapproved thoroughly of the thought, and was determined not to aid in any meat-eating on that day.

For everyone, the most important days of the year are the church days—All Saints', Easter, the days of Lent. Those at the fringes of religion, regardless of how far they have been slipping away, will be certain to attend church on these occasions. During Lent, no dancing is permitted; even the nightly visits from family to family are subdued. People in the back section, normally without means of transportation, band together and borrow a wagon for their trips to church. Good Friday, the Day of the Crucifixion, finds all solemn and subdued. (The man who dug in his field on that day would see blood come from the earth, according to a common belief.)

Nowhere in America is All Saints' Day observed so emphatically. From up Lafourche and down Lafourche, from New Orleans and other places, those who have left home will return for visits to the grave. Members of the family go to the cemetery in advance, cut the grass above the grave, wash and clear the slabs; on the day itself, they place great bouquets before each resting place. Those who watch from above, it is felt, cannot but feel happy at these signs of remembrance. The occasion is one of reunion with the living as well as communion with the dead. Brothers and sisters, cousins and aunts meet to talk over the things that have happened since the last All Saints'.

Particular attention is given to the "shadow boxes" that are everywhere about the cemeteries. These are small white containers with figures of saints, crucifixes, or other holy objects. Peak-roofed, glass-fronted, the boxes also contain "permanent flowers" of tinted metal, shaped and colored by nuns or others, or of beads and other materials. The boxes are dusty during most of the year; on All Saints' Day they shine.

On last All Saints' Eve, I remembered an old custom that is compounded of distance and faith, and directed my course late in the afternoon along the road toward the Bayou des Oies, Bayou of the Geese. The church bells were tolling, and the sound of feet echoed from around the bend. In the dusk came a file of men and women, each carrying a flickering candle, which had been lighted at the church. There they had knelt and heard the prayers for the dead. Now they followed the priest through the gate to their graveyard. As he reached the first grave, he dipped his hand into the holy water and gave his blessing. Next he offered benediction at another grave, a few feet away, and soon he had completed a circle about the cemetery.

Now the place began to shine in the night. Almost every grave had a candle, or a long row outlining it, most of them brought by those in the procession. As I watched, men and women were lighting more and more of them. On one resting place, I counted forty points of flame. From the gateway it was a glowing scene: the jumping lights, the faces outlined in the circles of illumination, bayou gleaming to the side, and the passing of an occasional boat a few feet away, its passengers leaning out to watch. A hum of conversation rose; children ran out for more candles, and there was visiting from grave to grave. Friends came to admire, and the call was returned. About some of the resting places were dozens of people, talking quietly, or with animation. Here and there a lone man or woman knelt before a row of candles, and sometimes a child or two did the same thing. Such a family, the others told me, had suffered a "new death"; and those about them were silent and respectful. A member of a group with many candles took one or two of them to a near-by, forgotten place. "They would be here if they could," he said.

For hours the place was crowded. Then slowly the visitors slipped away. Most of them stayed until their last candle flickered out, then made the sign of the cross, and left. Others remained, lighting new candles, maintaining their long vigils. By one o'clock there were only four of them, single figures huddled at widely separated graves, each outlined in the surrounding darkness. By then I felt that to stay further would have been an intrusion on the privacy of sorrow, and I went away.

Since then I have asked the meaning of this custom. No one is certain about it. The likeliest explanation is that it grew up in earlier years when such places were held in tight isolation. The priests could not reach them for the All Saints' services. Yet this was an important day to the people; and so the candles were lighted, and men knelt as before an altar. Today the church is nearer; but the people have not forgotten the older way.

The church went early to the old Lafourche, and over much of the water's length their records are interconnected. The towns of the upper bayou form a string of "dedicated villes," each placed under a saint of its own. Thibodaux is dedicated to St. Valérie; Plattenville, to St. Faustine; Labadieville, to St. Philomène. Thus it is, the devout are certain, that they have escaped hurricanes and yellow fever epidemics when others about them have been stricken.

At the old point of contact with the Mississippi stands Donaldsonville, a quiet place of less than four thousand population, which was, strangely, once the capital of Louisiana. Its location has been a rather important one for trade to the watery west of the state. Originally it was called Ascension, when a Capuchin, settling down in 1772 among the Acadians and others of the area, wrote in his church register: "This parish is dedicated to the Ascension of Our Lord. I have this day witnessed its founding." In the early 1800's William Donaldson, an American of Scotch-English descent, appeared there with large plans. He bought land and announced to the French-Spanish settlers that he was ready to make this a great center. They smiled. He succeeded by a display of ingenuity that might delight a modern manipulator.

Donaldson "worked with" merchants, banks, and officials. He gave free space and favors, bestowed presents; his principle was "tit for tat." He played upon country hostility to

New Orleans, and within twenty-five years his town had become the capital and bore his name. His plans worked, but only for a few years. The capital was taken away, and Donaldsonville lapsed into a more staid period. His town reflects some of the circumstances of its history. Other bayou towns have winding streets, like those of France. He set his out in Anglo-Saxon squares and angles; but the population remained largely Gallic.

Another kind of place is Thibodaux, largest modern city of Lafourche. Its pattern is the older one, with curving passages, some of them so narrow that two cars can move abreast only with difficulty. It is quiet, French, and conservative. Other Louisianians sometimes smile and describe how it hurt itself because it was certain that the upstart railroads would never supplant the steam vessel. When South Louisiana received a long-awaited railroad after the Civil War, it was scheduled to pass through Thibodaux. But the city had its own thoughts on the subject: railways dirtied up clean houses, and woke people out of their sleep; also the residents feared such direct connection with New Orleans, then a place of yellow-fever visitations. Mass meetings sent the line three miles away, and the railroads have never come to Thibodaux.

This city was long the religious center of the bayou, and a full-fledged legend has grown up about "the Apostle of Lafourche," Canon Charles M. Menard. A man of roaring energies, he served the area from his ordination at twenty-five until his death at seventy-nine, riding a white horse, using skiffs, steamboats, wagons, and sometimes his feet to get to his long-separated destinations. The missionary gave short shrift to effusive talk of such things as heroics. One of his former parishioners remembers him as, fixing his eye on the men of his classes, he beat his hands upon the table: "Obedience, that is the thing. It is better to obey than to sacrifice!" "We generally obeyed," the old man recalls. His sister tells of that burning day when Father Menard decided that too many women of Lafourche were inclined to serve a bit of meat on Friday because they had failed to save up for other supplies. Arm extended, index finger quivering, he pointed a lesson: "The good housewife will start on Monday to save eggs for Friday. Let me hear no more of such trifling." Today, fifty years later, she still starts the week by thinking of her egg supply.

Father Menard went to Rome in 1867, with a determined purpose. He wanted a noted religious relic, something that would inspire the young women of Lafourche, "for the future of the church will depend largely upon them." He had little success at first; the Pope had put a halt to distribution of such objects because there were so many demands for them. But Father Menard was not one to take even an ecclesiastical No. He questioned, petitioned, investigated. Eventually he called on a Cardinal, he argued, and won. The Cardinal was the possessor of two prized relics: the head of St. Prosper, and part of the arm of St. Valérie, V. M., Virgin Martyr, tortured and beheaded in the Flavian Amphitheatre. Father Menard knew well what he wanted; he took the latter.

Then he placed Thibodaux under St. Valérie's protection. There ensued a great procession, with the relic encased in a wax, red-velvet-garbed statue of the saint. For years it was thus carried in an annual ceremonial, marching behind it the girls of the parish, garbed as "Little Valéries," or "Little Martyrs" in white, the color of virginity, with ribbons and head wreaths of red, that of martyrdom. The event had a climax in the old cemetery of Thibodaux, under the tall oaks; and thousands of the men and women of Lafourche who accompanied the procession would remain afterward with their families for picnics among the trees.

This old cemetery touches the life of its section at many points. Its grounds provide place for outdoor events and assemblages. In it are held open-air Masses and programs such as one in which three thousand men, each carrying a candle, stood among the oaks at night to renew their baptismal vows before the Archbishop. (When the prelate arrived, he was greeted with firecracker tossing, as an evidence of high festivity.) I remember the cemetery in particular because I was shown about it and its resting places of many priests and nuns by the mellow Monsignor Barbier, retired successor to Canon Menard. He took me to a fresh tomb and asked: "How do you like it? It's brand new. It's mine." He had planned and supervised its construction, approving the last detail of the lettering which told of his life and death, omitting only the concluding date. For a time the inscription was uncovered; but many people raised questions, and it had to be hidden. "But everything is ready," he shrugged and smiled.[1]

Such is upper Lafourche. The bayou is low here, within high banks; for miles, one may paddle along it between remaining levees, or parts of levees, and see only the tops of the houses to the side. To the south, the banks are lower and the waters rise. The Gulf slips upward, and the life approaches that of the seacoast.

---

[1] The Monsignor had received two witty oil paintings from France. They dealt with the experiences of a gourmet. The first showed him zestfully opening his lips to receive an oyster; in the second he was lifting a piece of lettuce, but discovering at the last moment a good-natured worm an inch from his mouth. Monsignor Barbier agreed that the pictures were delightful. "But too many people kept looking at them when they called." So he put them in the garage, which became the best-ornamented one on Lafourche.

The last town on the bayou is Golden Meadow, in many ways the antithesis of the settled upper places. Its history is a postscript to tragedy, going back to Chênière Caminada of the Gulf.

In 1893 many of the broken people of the Chênière went up Lafourche to a small settlement, Leeville. A second Chênière developed, to be left alone by men and nature for fifteen years. Then another September, and a hurricane blast wiped out most of the village. A short way up Lafourche was the new town of Golden Meadow, then a handful of residences. One of its present-day natives told me of that hurricane, and of the way he looked up to see "whole houses being wash' up the water by the wind." The ill-fated families followed, and they have stayed since then in their new homes. The idyllic title of Golden Meadow was given by an American organization that established itself here to reclaim the land. It dried large areas and dug a ditch which the natives dubbed Yankee Canal. The Yanks left, and their town became largely a sea-food center—a far-down border town, the end of the road in more respects than one. It won a reputation over South Louisiana as a place of raw fish and raw deeds. A resident carried a knife or a gun because he needed it; feuds thrived, and men slashed each other at the wharves.

Later developments did not quiet the area. It became a major center for rumrunning along the coast during Prohibition. As in Lafitte's day, as during the Civil War cotton blockade, men slipped through the meshes of bayous and inlets. They carried thousands of cases of whisky, rum, and champagne from Cuba, British Honduras, and other points; and the modern legends of lower Lafourche include heroic concealments of caches that could be reached only by thread-like passages and "secret" canals. Golden Meadow still talks of this and that exploit: the dropping of alcohol in sacks at the bayou edges; split-ups of shipments in the marsh, hijackings, killings of natives or government men, and in one or two instances, daylight kidnapings and disappearances of men suspected of tip-offs. Several retired leaders of the trade told me that many a Federal man was "worth about $100 in them days." "Just a bill, and most of them would look the other way," one said. This man had formerly been a trapper; he now wears silk shirts, and we were served imported beer as we sat on his high porch. He seemed to miss the old days.

Golden Meadow learned about easy money then; the town ran wide open. Other events helped. In 1931, at the site of the lost Leeville, from which the families had fled, oil was discovered. Production spurted; millions in investments were poured into the field, and water-going wells rose over the flat landscape. The beds of many of these bayous, lakes, and other bodies of water have been found to contain vast stores of wealth, needing new methods of capture. Barges are floated into place, filled with water, and sunk into the soft bottoms, to become machines for drilling. Other vessels carry oil to beached ships which serve as storage tanks; catwalks stretch for thousands of feet from one well to the next, and "roughneck" crews go to the job in boats. As we passed the field last year, two slim egrets circled the derricks.

Many Golden Meadow men were accorded places with the oil companies, but much of the skilled work was allotted to imported crews. This brought new conflict. The oil workers were Texans, Oklahomans, and others, not gentle men nor men necessarily in sympathy with French ways. A number of the local girls liked the free-talking, free-spending oil men; Golden Meadow youths, proud of their status as wild bucks, were ready to meet their rivals anywhere, and did. Golden

Meadow was an oil-rush town, with shootings over the jangle of music. In time some of the natives grew bitter toward "les Texiens," and every stranger was called "Texien." (One newly arrived Acadian youth lamented to me that though he was from Donaldsonville, he heard the grating word used of him.)

Golden Meadow has settled down in recent years, but it is still a combination of Louisiana French village and Texas oil town. The Lafourche pattern has not been lost; it is a three-mile chain of houses on one side of the bayou, one street long for the most part. Its businesses and its smells seem to be three: fish, oil, and cows. Ice houses, shrimp factories, and supply houses line the water, and men and their families tie up their houseboats and live in them between seasons. The family washing flaps on the narrow bank near the road. Many things are informal. Walking after dark, I stopped at the sight of a passenger bus parked alongside a house which it dwarfed. Inquiry disclosed that the driver lived here; and why shouldn't he put his company's bus in his own side yard, ahn?

Oil has moved into the town itself. Many buildings, including the Catholic church, have derricks and slush pits in their yards. For it was discovered one day that the Leeville oil pool lies under the settlement. Leases were made in small town-lots, and sometimes a house has been shifted back or to the side. Gangway for the derricks. Some marsh men have a new source of wealth, receiving thousands of dollars an acre in leases and royalties. They install telephones, import bricks for homes, and do not hear when friends call them big heads. Grand Isle has cows on its beaches; Golden Meadow offers them its sidewalks. During the day the herds go into the marshes; with nightfall, the mosquitoes drive them inland. Having learned that the highway is not a safe place, they move quietly into the footpaths, in the glare of bars of flimsy construction and imposing neon lights. The soft notes of the French girls mingle with the sharper tones of the Texiens around the juke boxes; to reach any one of the numerous establishments, one has to skirt cows and cow dogs. And above the blare of music comes the sound of long moos over the evening air.

Between the two extremes of Donaldsonville and Golden Meadow is the middle Lafourche, the part that I remember longest, from rides in the putt-putt boats. In the late afternoon I found the bayou and its people at their happiest. As we headed downstream, we could see along parts of both banks. For a time some of the levees were in the way, but these declined, and eventually the view was clear. On the galerie of most houses was a crowd: old men in the corner at their cards; girls and boys in the center, getting ready to go to the dance; Maman and the little ones and the women guests around the slowly moving swing. Shrill sounds echoed as one housewife called to another across a fence. Men tied up their boats just ahead of us from time to time, and held aloft packages of fish, amid the excitement of children who ran to greet them.

As we passed settlements, men were lounging outside, arguing, chuckling, waving hands for emphasis. Here was a cemetery, gleaming in the dusk; there a shrimp factory, identified promptly by the nose. On the near bank, a bench, and on it sat a girl in green, a youth in tan, which might have been a soldier's uniform or merely his working attire. They called out a greeting; we called back. A mother strolled out of a house, asked where Térence was, and shrieked when she discovered that he had jumped in the water with three others and was now headed toward our boat.

We turned off the motor, the boys returned to shore, and Térence cried in anguish and embarrassment as Maman hauled him up and out, still naked, and started him running across the road. The bridge tender gave us a "Bonsoir" and said to watch out for the new barge, tied up around the bend. As we made the curve, the last trace of light came through the leaves of a willow, trailing slight draperies in the water. In a few minutes, all was blue about us; the final red cloud was disappearing. On the galeries men and women were moving, and a hum and a buzz arose about them. We heard a sharp crack, a dull retort. By craning, we could see what had happened. A swing had fallen, and its fat male occupant had crashed with it. Twenty or more people laughed, and the victim slapped his rump and roared with them, and all twenty talked; and he talked louder than any, and what he said must have been the funniest of all.

Lafourche, having a good time in the evening; Lafourche, being itself. . . . People come back to the place year after year and look again and feel better. That's what it's like to be a Lafourchais.

Part III: *"Garden of Eden"*

TILDEN LANDRY

§ 11. *The Opulent Teche*

BEGINNING HIGH toward central Louisiana, in a terrain of bluffs and slightly rolling ground, a stream rambles downward through the geographical heart of the state. It curls and recurls, occasionally twisting back upon itself in indecision, until after nearly 150 miles it widens and deepens into what many have called a noble river. It is Bayou Teche, most richly storied of the interior waters, and the most opulent. Its land is thick and wide, as wide in some places as that of the Mississippi Valley; often as fertile. But for many centuries the area has had no direct connection with the great middle passageway of America, and it has lived aside and to itself.

As much as any other part of the state, to my way of thinking, the Teche is the Past in Louisiana. It has seen and heard excitements, near-civil wars at times, tempestuous sayings and doings of elegant men and poor men, priests and duchesses.

Now it has settled down to a period of serene rest. A visitor from another section, calling late in the last century, remarked that the place had about it an air of "afternoon." He struck an appropriate note. The Teche country gives the impression that it has labored and fought and conquered, with great reward, during a crowded morning; now, in the deepening light of the day, it remains among its trees, and remembers, and reminisces of other times.

Lafourche has been largely the place of the habitant; on the Teche the measure of things has been broad and expansive. A tradition of affluence developed during the first days of settlement. A system of great holdings was established. Acadians came here as to the other waterways. Some stayed, and their children are still here. But many of them did not stop. They moved into the adjoining prairie stretches and streams, leaving the Teche banks for others. The Americans arrived early in small numbers, then in greater crowds, and here they have entrenched themselves as on no other large bayou of South Louisiana. Yet this is the section with which is identified the greatest single legend of the Louisiana French land—that of the Acadian Evangeline. And that will be a story in itself. . . .

Today over the Teche spreads an alternation of elements—one part that of the older Creoles; another, that of the Acadians; but predominant over many miles, that of the Anglo-Saxons. The various groups settled near each other and competed for dominance. The result is often a curious juxtaposition—a strongly Southern-American town next to a cluster of small Acadian homes, and then a grande maison bearing a shining name of Creole civilization.

Here arose, and here still stand, white-pillared monuments to another life than that of most other parts of the lowlands—

The Teche is the most handsomely endowed of the bayous.

E. M. Morgan

The "Shadows" is the preserved grace of another era.

But the Darby home is a place of tragic memories.

Weeks Ha

Stern-wheeler up the Teche.

L. P. Resweber

Along this tree avenue was held Louisiana's most opulent wedding—"spider webs for decoration."

Study in light, oak and Spanish moss.

E. M. Morgan

Evangeline waits on pedestal beside the Teche for her lost lover.

Amid the splendors of the Teche, the Acadian House remains.

the life of the great estates. Here thrived a style, French and American, that was not that of the rural places, nor yet of the cities. Away from the Mississippi's concentrations, yet in spirit closely related to it, the men and women of the Teche made a rich existence for themselves—the high manner in rustic environment. Some have compared this era, in surface appearance at least, to that of the Russian provinces of Czarist days—days of heavy magnificence in the distant reaches.

The years brought their modifications, many sudden and harsh, others slow and perceptible only to one who comes back after long absence. Some of the towering establishments have been torn away; some are deserted, slipping toward the earth and their own doom—a balcony gone, a shutter hanging crookedly. But others continue in mellowed preservation through the years, outlasting the way of life of which they were symbols. The Teche clings whenever it can to the things of these earlier days. The basis of its living has changed and it sometimes carries on new trades, especially in its lower reaches—tapping mineral and water resources little suspected in past centuries. It does not, however, thrust forth such evidences of future promise. The country is prouder of the tokens of its former glory than of that prosperity which may come to it in the present and future.

Nature provided for life on the Teche a setting that is not only lush in fertility but also possessed of handsome physical endowments. Unlike many of the other bayous on which men live, the Teche has no artificial earthworks against high water. It is an old stream—older, for instance, than Lafourche—and its land slopes slowly and easily to the water's edge, with broad green meadowland stretching in both directions. One man, it may be remembered, thought that Lafourche looked like an artificial ditch; others have found the natural surroundings of the Teche so symmetrical that in their opinion they could have been achieved only with the assistance of man. Some at first sight have decided that the land resembled nothing so much as a vast park, cleared, and studded with hedges and other growths. The native of the Teche will assure you that she is a Louisiana grande dame of superb attributes, who does not require false aids that others might employ. Lafourche laughs a warm housewife's laugh; the Teche smiles quietly and moves in serenity.

The trees along the stream's course are seen first and remembered longest. The live oak makes here its greatest stand in Louisiana: patriarchs in stately rows, long files for several miles; double avenues, with branches arching high above the heads of passers-by, leaves mingling with leaves; clumps at the banks, hanging over the water. At the bayou bank rise palmettoes and canes, their sharp spikes unaffected by the breezes that lift the moss edges. Against them drift the ever-present water hyacinths on their way to the Gulf. Along the easy slope of the soil to both sides spread white fences to mark the property lines, and barns and other outbuildings also adjust themselves here and there to the line of the ground. Thick hedges of roses, orange trees, magnolias, vines, and small wild flowers give proof of the fecund base. But the oaks are the mark of the Teche. Some are fantastically twisted giants, thirty feet or more in girth, of a heavy fiber that seems impenetrable. The arms often stretch out practically at right angles from the trunk, 150 feet or so, and from each hangs the moss that is sometimes a yard or so longer, trailing to the grass or to the water. Among the trees and the flowered growths sing the cardinals and the mockingbirds.

When highways came to the Teche, they did not press

close to the water, as in other places. Instead, there is a distance of several hundred yards to the crest of the soil and the roadway, and those who pass along it see the bayou through the frame of her green-and-moss borders. Between the road and the bank, and among the oaks, are the homes of the Teche. The oldest among them face the stream that made them possible; others look to the road. In either case, the gardens and the orchards decline to the water's edge, permitting the family to "live to the bayou," away from the outer world. The design is a pleasing one.

It was in such a setting that I began a series of revisits to the country. The place was "Shadows on the Teche," one of the stateliest mansions of the Deep South, and to my mind the best conserved on the bayou. For this, one man is largely responsible, its present owner, Weeks Hall, of New Iberia, descendant of the original builder. I first met Weeks some years ago when, with others, we saw the arrival of King Zulu by coal barge for Mardi Gras in New Orleans. This time I arrived in New Iberia at half-past ten at night, and proposed that we meet the next day. "What's the matter with now, too?" asked Weeks. And so we passed through one of the great gates, and sat down in the garden chairs, with tumblers of Scotch and Weeks' dog, and we talked of the Teche and its meaning, and especially of "Shadows" and its people through the years.

The family, of Scotch descent, went early to the bayou. The first owner received his large grant of land from the Spanish government in 1792, about the time that John Marsh went to his new Avery Island holding. He prospered, acquired plantations that doubled, then doubled again, in the vicinity of the Teche, and not far from the Marsh property. In time the holdings included five properties—Weeks Island, Cypremort, Richohoc, Acadie, and, last and greatest, "Shadows." On Weeks Island, as on Avery Island, salt was eventually found in large supplies. The son of the family was David Weeks, a man described as seven feet tall, with plans and projects to match his size. In 1830 he set up his edifice on the Teche, the one which I was now visiting. It was not so large nor so ornate as some plantation structures with their emphasis on bulk and profusion of ornament. The builders were content with perfection in its place—eight columns beginning at ground level and continuing for the two stories, behind them a red brick structure of delicate line and pattern.

The builder, David Weeks, spent some rewarding days here with his wife, who planned the broad plantings and the walks among the oaks. Then a few years later he visited New England and died there. His widow remained on the estate with their son, and it grew greater with the years, until the Civil War. A Federal general occupied the home at this time, and it was then that Mrs. Weeks died. Some said that it was the shock and sorrow of these days that took her. In any event, she was buried in a small family cemetery that still remains. Her son, William, took over, and later, his daughter and her husband, Major G. L. Hall, became the owners. Worse things than war came for "Shadows." The other holdings dropped away as the estate approached bankruptcy; eventually only this plantation was left, and much of it is no more. The last of the old slave buildings disappeared; the town itself crept up on the property and reduced it to three acres. Only the great house remained, with its back to the bayou. Then, for a time, the family left it. A single caretaker watched it all fade and sag among its weeds and grasses, until some thought that "Shadows" would soon be with the many other reminders of the past that had crumbled to wreckage.

Then young Weeks Hall came back from Europe, where he had been studying art, and took over the home in the early 1920's. He summoned trained men, and they repaired and restored it. Surprisingly little major change was required; walls held firm, old cypress was intact, even the blinds were in good state, after nearly a century. The oaks and camellias that the first Mrs. Weeks had planted were still in place. Since that time Weeks has lived there, with a servant or two, giving most of his days to the preservation of the place.

He and his helpers erected high walls of bamboo and trees about the edges, and it was hard to remember, as we spoke that evening, that only a short square or so away the town was passing by. The moonlight struck the great, unornamented columns, outlining them to the classic cornice, then beyond, along the tall and sloping roof with its three dormer windows.

Beyond the deep porches the interior remained in the style of a French château; its marble loggia, its wall drawings of the house as it appeared to artists in the last century. It all looked little different in these sketches from the scene that presented itself to us that night as we sat in the garden. And yet it was now another place, because the things and the kind of people that had made it what it had been in those days were no longer here.

As we watched, the moon transfigured the house and the half-seen, age-stained garden statuary about us, altering a line, sending a curve into new dusk. Through a garden house, at the back, bits of the silver Teche shone at intervals; and occasionally a boat passed, all tawdry light in the dimmer blue. We talked of these other Weekses, of the ripe compensations which their lives brought them, and of their heartbreaks and bafflements at the treachery of time. A fountain tinkled a few feet from us, and a light wind stirred the surface of the long, rectangular pool. From outside came, suddenly, the backfire of an automobile and the loud, laughing exchange of several men and women—good Cajun voices. I wondered what another caller, here another few decades into the future, would be able to say and think of this scene and its neighbors, Americans and Cajuns.

On other occasions after that, I stood before other gleaming galleries, half lost in their tropical greens; and almost always it was with one or two or three persons who lived in houses built for fifteen or twenty or more. We enjoyed pleasant meals at long tables beneath sixteen-foot ceilings. "Right where you are, he rose and lifted his glass, and then he fell. . . ." "This was where they were when the bullet came through. . . ." At such places I heard, again and again: "It was . . ." "We remember . . ." Everywhere was a feeling of life in a reflected light, of aloneness in a place so obviously meant for the sound of many feet.

The Indians told the first stories of the past of this bayou. Scanning its many curving passages, they created a legend that a great silver snake had once twisted over the country. Red men, terrified, retreated; until one day they decided to destroy him. From a distance a thousand warriors sent arrows into his body and then used clubs to crush out his life. In his writhings, he cut deep grooves in the soil, in which the waters accumulated. The stream then took the name of Tenche, Indian for snake, later to be softened by the French, and pronounced Tesh.[1]

Geologists, following more prosaic theories, have another explanation. The Teche is a stream with almost as many turns as the modern Mississippi, and there is a reason. Many centuries ago, it appears, this was a course of the master waterway itself, before it took the Lafourche and other routes in its final portions. Through a series of connecting passages to the north of the Teche that have largely silted up, the surging river drove its course. It followed this line for many centuries, and here is the explanation of the very wide natural levees. Then the river shifted to the east. Another stream, the Red River, inherited part of this course of the parent body, and then it also deserted. To the trained eye, an unusual picture offers itself: the spreading Mississippi levees, within them a smaller area of scarlet-brown soil brought by the Red from Oklahoma and Texas, and in the center, the present, smaller Teche. To the east is a string of lakes of great size, a series of bayous and swamps of the Atchafalaya river system; to the west, the drier prairie lands. Toward the Teche, men have gravitated through several centuries.

The region suffered for years because it received a bad name. About it ranged the Attakapa (pronounced Tackapaw or Tuckapaw) Indians, subject of gruesome rumors. The name in the red man's tongue means man-eater. About 1720, according to the Frenchman C. C. Robin, a vessel missed the Mississippi mouth and was carried to the west along the Gulf. Five officers went ashore and lost their way. Four died; the

---

[1] Some hold that the stream's name comes not from the Indian but from "Deutsch," after some of the Germans who settled about the time of the Americans on the lower Teche. This element was soon absorbed. Dr. William A. Read has pointed out that in South German dialects Deutsch is pronounced Teitsch.

last, Belle-Isle, wandered about until he found himself among some of the Attakapa. They were smoking food at the time, and were puzzled about what to do with the newcomer. They took the clothes from his shrunken frame, prodded him, and finally offered him something to eat. Reaching out, he found that it was human flesh. When he rejected it, they gave him fish, and this he accepted.

The tribe decided to keep him, and made him a "slave to a widow." He had an additional function, that of carrying the bodies of enemies scheduled for the feast. He lived with the Attakapa for two years, helping them in battles, and though he became somewhat accustomed to the sight of daily consumption of human flesh, he was never induced to eat it himself, says Robin. Eventually he was rescued. An imaginative artist has shown a touching scene in which the widow bade him good-by.

The usual French-Indian relations were reversed in this area. White men did not seek out these Indians for trading; the Attakapa went to them, and were rejected. There was that matter of cannibalism; the French also believed the Attakapa to be shiftless and too nomadic in habit. The Attakapa promised to reform, but dealings were few. The year 1760 saw what was probably the first permanent settlement near the upper Teche, fixing a tone for later colonization. Gabriel Fuselier de la Claire bought the site of a village from an Attakapa chief. Within a few years he had a neighbor, the Marquis de Vaugine.

The Marquis' plantation was a large one: forty arpents wide on one side of the Teche and twenty on the other. Many habitants could have found a living in this space. The "maison principale" was a raised cottage of three large rooms, with rear sheds for the drying of indigo, and a protected court. An inventory of a decade later listed crystal, silver, porcelain, carved furniture, and thirty-three slaves among the Marquis' possessions. Another surprise among the listed objects, as Henry P. Dart noted, was "Big Louis," a slave. The Marquis and his neighbors were in the habit of sending this emissary all the way to New Orleans alone, on a trip that might take a month or more, to collect their debts, large ones in some instances.

With the early years of the Spanish regime a military post was established at a convenient point on the upper bayou—a minute settlement with a commandant, a priest, a shop, and a petty force of soldiers. It was the Poste des Attakapas, taking over the name of the "cannibal Indians." Many men of many elements came to the Teche, among them military officers, government appointees, others of rank and wealth, including Creoles of New Orleans. From the first, these last-named formed a separate group of their own. About the same time that the Canary Islanders were taken to the Terre-aux-Boeufs section, other Spanish settlers were brought to the Teche and started on acreages of flax and hemp. Like others of their race introduced in this fashion, they had difficulties. The crops failed, they shifted about, and many gravitated toward something else that appealed to them—cattle raising. Today various Spanish names can be found, especially about New Iberia—Viators, Prados, Lopez, Romeros—and there is a trace of the national heritage: sharp noses, particularly brilliant eyes. But unlike those of the fur-bearing area, these Spaniards have intermingled with others, French and American; there is no separate "colony."

Meanwhile the first Acadians had reached the Teche. The year 1765 brought a party celebrated among the former Canadians, headed by Joseph Broussard or "Beau Soleil," his nickname growing out of his ever-beaming countenance. Other French came, early and late. Santo Domingan racial upheavals, which sent thousands of plantation owners and their mulatto and Negro slaves to Louisiana, brought more settlers to this area. With the French Revolution, many holders of titles and their sympathizers saw the then-Spanish colony as a welcome retreat. A large group of the latter element found their way up the Teche to the Poste des Attakapas, and here they left a particular impress.

The last years of the 1700's and the early ones of the next century saw the blooming of a hothouse plant without counterpart, perhaps, on the American continent: "Petit Paris" of the Teche.[2] The barren Spanish post was expanded, given new colors. The émigrés elected to continue much as in France; they would fit this New World to them, not them to it. They created a background which would serve them: "A pretty little village . . . called also Little Paris and full of barons, marquises, counts, and countesses," in the words of one traveler. These expatriates held great balls, with minuet accompaniment taught to willing local musicians; gave entertainments alfresco, and attended a theater at which French vaudeville and Italian opera were offered.

Françoise Bossier, whose diary was first presented to readers by George W. Cable,[3] has given a sharp picture of this rococo place and day. As a young girl she went there, in 1795, with her father and sister. The trip by flatboat began in May. Working their way through bayous that were often covered by fallen trees, over lakes in which they nearly drowned, they finally reached their destination by July. They found pomp in

---

[2] This eventually became St. Martinville.

[3] *Strange True Stories of Louisiana*. Charles Scribner's Sons; New York, 1889, 1917.

a bandbox: men in court attire, women in wigs and "covered with costly jewels," who visited each other in formal calls at the theater, between acts of "The Barber of Seville." The sisters were guests at a reception in a home with a drawing room, wide galerie and garden "crossed and recrossed with alleys of orange and jasmine." Servants in livery bore salvers of fruit, while the hostess, a countess, played at her harpsichord. There followed dinners, fetes, a picnic on the shore of a lake, a soiree on a bayou bank. On the occasion of the soiree, the interested newcomers heard music as from a distance, and beheld a floating vessel, covered with flowers and greens, on which the musicians sat. On shore, the trees were lighted, and to the music of the anchored vessels, couples danced on a pavilion about which were placed blooming magnolia trees joined by garlands of flowers. The belle on this and other occasions was "Ton-Ton" de Blanc, married at thirteen to a doctor forty years her senior, who died within two years and left her a well-to-do widow. Presiding over her inheritance in splendor, she was arbiter of style and manners for her contemporaries, inventing headdresses, breaking rules of attire, and keeping the less glamorous supplied with tidbits of gossip.

The climax of the Bossiers' visit was a grand ball. The women planned costumes to bedazzle each other, keeping materials and design secret until that evening. The little settlement talked of nothing but the event; the ball, Françoise learned, would be held no matter what happened. In Petit Paris no one had ever heard of a storm bad enough to hold off a dance. Again, much greenery and flowers, with countless colored lamps and a platform for formal greetings and acknowledgments. The chairman was a young gallant, enamored of "Ton-Ton." His costume was memorable: hair pow-

dered, with pigeon wings held by golden pins, queue ornamented with ribbon of rose, vest of rose with black trimming,
almost to the knees; coat of "frosted rose silk, with broad
facings of black velvet"; rose knee-breeches fastened in black
velvet, diamond buckles, stockings "shot alternately with
black and rose"; and diamonds on throat and wrist, shoe
buckles, and shirt front. As a good country Acadian would
have said, "Thas' a man!" It was all distingué, and from the
distance of today faintly pathetic.

Many of the elegant ones were certain that they would be
back in France before long. But the glad day seldom if ever
came. No sympathetic government summoned them home,
with praise for loyalty. Their light conversational plannings
wore thinner and thinner. Some had to dispense with their
dances and their picnics, then with their rings and their furniture, and settle down to another kind of life. Often a pair of
Creole eyes proved more attractive than would any offer
from the Continent, and various émigrés married into Louisiana families, and managed estates that did not decrease with
the years. Some went to farms and toiled like other new settlers; while some sat alone through the long Louisiana evenings and wondered what could have happened to their last
messages, and asked themselves if that final source of friendship and funds had also forgotten, or died. . . .

With mixed elements of Latin temperament in close proximity, troubles might have been anticipated. Word came that
Louisiana was being shifted back to France. Some of the nobility in exile were shocked. Napoleon in control of Louisiana! What would happen to them! But others were French
to the core, and they rejoiced. In Petit Paris older rivalries
and resentments broke out, and the French colonial prefect,

waiting to take over from Spain, sent a peppery account to Napoleon. One side, he said, was "unable to conceal its joy at our return"; but there were others who played a Spanish game. In Petit Paris, M. St. Julien, a planter, used the word "Citizen" in a letter. A conspiracy, said the Spanish officials; but before they could arrest him, something happened at St. Julien's home—the basis of a cause célèbre. As Monsieur and Madame St. Julien enjoyed the evening on their porch, Madame was fatally shot, and her husband was found injured. He charged the crime to the other faction. It said that St. Julien had killed his wife and feigned his own condition. The Spanish authorities arrested him. The French prefect, breathless, told his government: "Men are shot here (the Attakapa area); civil war reigns."

Then, to the consternation of both sides, the upstart Yankee republic took over all Louisiana. What worse thing could have happened? men asked each other. American officials were soon puzzling over ways to handle this excitable population; and l'affaire St. Julien was not the least prickly of their problems. St. Julien was an innocent victim of Spanish spite, said one side; St. Julien was a guilty wretch, said the other. One group sent a memorial to Monsieur le Président in Washington. Spain's representative offered a flaring accusation that his country's honor had been impeached in the matter. The dispute widened at Petit Paris; the clergy were involved in the pulling and hauling. Two rival priests appeared, and raging factions backed up each one in his claims to the church.

One Sunday, each pastor made a descent on the church building, attended by "partizans who were numerous and very much inflamed," in the Governor's words. The civil commandant rushed to the church, shut the doors, and would not let either side enter. The Governor commented that all

Americans, new and old ones, had freedom of religious choice, but that the house of God in this case had become "a temple of discord" and that Christians had "deviated from the mild precepts of their Heavenly Master to become the Sons of Riot."

Gradually the church war was settled, but when a grand jury met for the first time under the American system, at St. Martinville, tempers cracked again—this time at the expense of the Americans. An outsider appeared and made the mistake of offering a document in the strange English words. He read it in French, but French that was gibberish to natives. Robin, the writer, was one of the jurors who heard the man run on; he understood only that regulations were being presented against such scattered crimes as sodomy, rape, gouging of eyes, biting off of ears or other organs. The highly sensitive Frenchmen rose to declare that they were not "cannibals" and would resign in protest against barbarous regulations implying that they were Indians. This they did. There was no law in the area for months, and Washington must have wondered more and more about the wisdom of its acquisition of Louisiana.

Soon the French of the Teche had another subject of concern—the fast-moving Yankee invasion. The Americans had been there at some points for years, but now they came in greater numbers. The upper parts of the bayou were becoming crowded; the lower half stretched invitingly, and the newcomers saw there some of their best opportunities in the new state. A series of American bridgeheads was established. Yankees, sugar, and in time, steamboats—it was a triumvirate that was to change many of the aspects of the Teche. Until then most of those who lived about the Teche had raised cattle, rice, and indigo, with some cotton. F. D. Richardson has described in his recollections how the Americans went "rushing to the sugar gold fields." Within a six-year period at the close of the 1820's, the agriculture of the land was overturned. Soon practically every plantation on the stream was in sugar. Each American had his own plan for making a fortune by outstripping the less-bustling Creoles. The latter had assets and advantages of their own, and they held firm.

Between the two elements, the feeling was sometimes strong. For years they met only at business, and as seldom as possible at that. An elderly woman of the upper Teche told me of her mother, a member of one of the first of the Creole families, who had the daring to marry an American. "It was a terrible day when the word spread; often I heard her talk of it," she shook her head. "Her father had finally consented, but the relatives! They called in delegations. Several of her friends would not speak to her. For years she knew that behind their fans the old ladies were whispering. She realized that she had to be proper in everything; they were all ready to say—'And what do you expect of one who married an American?'"

Others told of their mothers who said, "Ces sacrés américains!" and they added: "They didn't mean 'sacred,' when they used that word." One woman, I heard, had a room to which she would retire, tight-lipped, if any of the aliens happened to enter the house. "This is a French room, do you understand!" she would storm at her more easygoing sons and daughters. "None comes in here but French." (Sometimes the children talked of bringing a Yankee barbarian in to her, to see what would happen. "We never found the courage," a grandson said.) Meanwhile the French children called the little Anglo-Saxons "Ti' coquins yankees" (little Yankee ras cals), and the Americans retorted with that flaming term, "gee-gees."

All elements, French and American, found themselves handicapped for years by the watery distances between them and the center of the colony. Before the steamboat came, a man thought twice when he undertook a trip to New Orleans. Large barges provided transportation, and nothing else. The passenger brought his own food, servants, bedding. Through long days the heavily laden vessels moved by oar or sail or both. At night they tied up, and the passengers slept, or tried to sleep, on shore; or they played cards and drank with their friends. When bad stretches were reached, they had to get out and pull with the crew, from the bank.

The steamship brought improvement, but not so much as the modern man might believe. Topography was still against the people of the Teche; there was no straight-line passage to the Mississippi. Over the mixed marsh-swamp-waterways that lay between, men worked to develop a series of routes, trying new bayous and short-cut canals—one advantageous in low water, another impassable except at high stages. In floodtime it was possible, perhaps, to chance a run over a little water connection that, lo and behold, cut off thirty miles. For days the country would echo with the tale. C'est impossible. A man could not do it. "But I saw that Frenchman wash right over it with the boat; and then he turned and said he had never thought he would make it! . . ."

The whites of the Teche imitated the Indians' mode of getting places, by using portages between streams which the red men had first established to cut off distances here and there. Eventually they developed their own portages. It was cheaper and easier to move a supply of materials a few miles by land to the next waterway than to float it all those extra miles. The problem always was to find land dry enough to permit such operations, and so the water remained the main path. Two main routes developed: Lafourche was often used, but this was closed off during the drier months because of the natural deposits at its point of contact with the Mississippi; Plaquemine, the large bayou above, was more dependable, but in time it developed so strong a flow of its own that it flooded plantations below, and it was curtailed.

In either case, the passenger had first to go down the Teche, then up again for a distance that might be longer than the first lap, to find an entry to the Mississippi, and then down the Mississippi again. It was a series of arc-like turns that were costly and time-consuming. The whole trip would have been cut to a fraction by a direct connection, but none was possible.

The Teche thrived despite its handicaps. The New Orleans agents appraised its cane, when it finally arrived, as unsurpassed in the state. From the Teche, too, came great quantities of hides, beef, and other produce; and, in time, shipments of heavy timber cut from the near-by swamps and banks. Long rafts of wood were floated along "runs" in the swamp, to bayou paths that led to the mills. At one time the state was supplying building materials to perhaps a third of the country, and a Louisiana Senator boasted that it could provide enough for all the world's navies.

With these years before the Civil War the Teche came into its own as a stream of prosperity and shining splendor. For mile after mile stretched a procession of estates, every foot of ground seemingly in cultivation, or the site of a great home and great garden. On the west side, freer from any danger of overflow, were the mansions, the rows of whitewashed slave cottages, the tall stacks of sugar mills, the stables, dairies, and herds of cattle; and an occasional spread of lighter emerald, half-inundated acreage, that of rice. Frequently a house of a small Acadian was almost lost from sight under the wide arms of the oaks. To the other side of the bayou extended the rest of the holdings, the same lines of cane as far as the ground was firm; and between them were wide floating bridges, with openings in the center for passing vessels.

The manors of the Teche had gone up or were going up now, to dominate their scene. The earlier Louisiana plantation homes of the French-Spanish period were usually raised cottage-type structures, with porches and slight columns, all of them simple though large and comfortable. The American period and the prosperity that came with it brought the Greek Revival with its templelike façades and other elegancies. From the swamps were taken the cypress for the buildings, but only after it was first ringed and allowed to stand for seasoning during two years or more. From the bayou came heavy supplies of sand, and kilns were set up on the grounds to bake the bricks. From New Orleans arrived wrought-iron work of delicate pattern, and carved woods, and friezes, and chandeliers, and furniture; and with it all, men to help in designing and laying out a house and its surroundings. The exuberance of the land and the system of plantation operation gave a heavy supply—even though it was sometimes only temporary —of funds. The owners hesitated little over costs, and sometimes, it seems, gave little thought to the future. But the results justified the exertions, men decided, as they watched the last installations from their garden benches on the banks of the Teche. It was something to show, by God; something to leave behind to the children—and also something to enjoy. Richard Taylor, the Louisiana Confederate officer, looking back on those pre-war days, said: "In all my wanderings, and they have been many and wide, I cannot recall so fair, so bountiful, and so happy a land."

The years ahead held the end of the traditional plantation era; but few could know it. There was no pensiveness, no sadness at that time, in the opulent mansions of the Teche.

§ 12. *Two Gentlemen of the Bayou*

I STOOD last summer at two points along the Teche, one in the center of the "American," or lower area, the other in the upper, or "French," part, and heard of the lives of two men, and saw their heritages. Neither was a native Louisianian; one came from Ireland; the other about the same time from France. Each found well-being on the bayou; each made a strong impression on many who lived about him. The first has left an imposing edifice to remind later generations of his presence; the other has bequeathed only a site, a scenic vista— and a fine tale. I leave it to others to decide which man wrought the better, or which may be remembered the longer.

Alexander Porter was a Celt whom the French liked. He might never have left the old country except for a tragedy that came to him as a youth in the late 1700's. His father, a Presbyterian minister and a chemist, was executed on suspicion of connection with the Irish revolutionaries. With an uncle, brothers, sisters, and cousins, Alec came to this country. And because friends who preceded them had recommended the place, they settled in Nashville. Alec at the time was sixteen. He had had the beginnings of a good education, and now he went to work, fitting himself to become a lawyer.

He showed an ability to make friends, and practiced for a time in Tennessee. But there were few openings there for an obscure man. Alec knew Andy Jackson, and the General thought well of him and gave him occasional advice. Riding one day, he met Jackson, and spoke to him of his desire to move to another place. The General, yet to go to New Orleans for his Battle, warmly suggested Louisiana. There was a place of opportunity, rich and unfilled. Alec thought well of the idea but delayed action. The General saw him again:

"What! Alick, not gone yet? This won't do. When you determine, act quickly; someone may get in before you. And remember, Alick, you are going to a new country . . . a different people from those you have grown among, and you must study their natures, and accommodate yourself to them. . . . Look for a good place, and when you stop, stop to stay. And let all you say and all you do look to your advantage in the future." [1]

The career of Alexander Porter might well have been based on that advice. He studied the nature of the people, and he accommodated himself to his chosen area as well as any man who went to it. First he had to find his exact place. He went to New Orleans about 1810 and heard of the fine lands of the Louisiana to the west. They sounded much like those that the General had in mind. He went up the Mississippi to Donaldsonville at the entrance of Lafourche, hired a man to take him by skiff to the nearest courthouse, then another to get him through a canal to the intervening lake area, thence to a landing in the old Attakapa territory. A final stage of transportation brought him up the Teche to Petit Paris, soon to take the name of St. Martinville. He stayed about the more or less

[1] W. H. Sparks, *The Memories of Fifty Years,* and Wendell Holmes Stephenson, *Alexander Porter—Whig Planter of Old Louisiana.*

settled French towns for a time, and then he learned of the open bayou just to the south, fast filling with Americans. Before long he moved there and set up practice at Franklin, a place so named for old Ben by a fellow Pennsylvanian, turned Techian.

The fledgling had an experience not calculated to develop his regard for the French. During one of his first trips, he spent most of a day rowing a small skiff on the bayou. Worn out, he came to the mansion of a leading Creole; on the galerie were neatly attired people of all ages. He entered through the gate and walked forward until a sallow-skinned man came out and waved a hand at him: "Arrêtez!" The word was strange, but the manner was unmistakable. The unwilling host ran on in French; the newcomer spoke in English; neither understood the other. The owner called Pierre, his Negro, who acted as interpreter. Learning that Porter wished water, the Frenchman gave a haughty direction: "Tell him to get it from the bayou." Porter, not an Irishman for nothing, relayed a new inquiry: "Then can I get a little buttermilk?"

The master waved his arms, and Pierre warned Porter that he had called the dogs. A dozen animals chased the newcomer to the gate. Porter resumed his rowing, came to a friendly household, and over food and drink, asked the name of the other man. He remembered it. (His experience had been a somewhat unusual one; however suspicious, neither Creole nor Acadian was normally ill-mannered.)

With other Frenchmen his relations were good from the start. Most of the French like to laugh; so do the Irish. The French appreciate charm of person; the young Irishman had much of that. He worked, too, over the shifting, confused jurisprudence of the new state, part French, part Spanish, part pure Louisiana; he became eventually the leading attorney of his section. He moved among the French as freely as among the Americans. He was as choice a raconteur as any Creole, and a favorite dinner guest and gallant. If French mothers were not able to win him for one of their daughters, at least he was an ornament to their guest list and galerie.

At twenty-five, though technically still a British subject, he was chosen as representative to a state convention. Wendell Holmes Stephenson has described how he became a go-between, trusted by both sides, in settling furious differences among the French and Americans. The young man of the Teche drew attention in other parts of the state, too. With his future widening, he took out citizenship papers. During his first year as an American, he was chosen to represent his district in the state legislature. And all the time his heavy practice was growing at home. He was probably not surprised, one day at his office, to look up and find before him the man who had in those early days turned his dogs upon him.

Neither gave any indication that he recalled the earlier meeting. The Frenchman wished Porter's services in an unusual affair for the Teche. His wife had brought divorce proceedings; her part of the property was large, and if she won, he would be bankrupt. Porter asked why he had come to him. The answer was gratifying: all the caller's friends assured him that Porter was "the best lawyer," and he needed the best. Porter listened, then announced that he would take the case for $1000. The Frenchman was stunned. He could not think of paying so large a fee. Then he must employ someone else, Porter informed him. But there was no one so good; the next best man had, alas, been retained by his wife. That reminded Porter; he had just received a note from the latter counsel, he said, who presumably wanted him to work with him on the case. The caller quickly agreed to pay Porter what he asked.

Porter won the case, and his client visited him again. Fee in pocket, the Irishman told the Creole that he had fixed the first $500 of this payment for his services on the case at hand; the other was for a previous incident. The Frenchman nodded; he had been thinking that all the time, he shrugged.

At thirty-five, the bayou Irishman was made a Justice of the Louisiana Supreme Court, and after a dozen years he went on to the United States Senate. He was a Whig, the party of privilege in that day. As such, he became one of the firm opponents of the man who had started him on his way to Louisiana—Andrew Jackson, the commoner. Before long, Porter was known as one of the wealthiest men of the state.

It was during these years of his early success that he began the erection of his masterwork, Oaklawn. No one, French or American, could claim a vaster palace than this. Five years in the building, it arose in sumptuous height and spread, with not one splendid portico, but two. They were identical at back and front—tall Doric columns, with another gallery for the second floor, across all the building front, and a third one before the windows of an "attic" which was a full floor in itself. There were massive doorways with carved archlights, and spiral stairways, and imposing marble mantels. A hallway ran the full length of the building; the top floor was given over to a ballroom. The Judge selected and approved each item, and inspected the materials as they arrived up the Teche from New Orleans, sometimes after a trip from Europe. To the side was a separate, smaller house, almost a duplicate of the main one, and connected with it by a stairway between the two upper balconies. A French landscape gardener arranged parks and flowered walks, with statuary and growths enclosed in ironwork, much of it in the style of the Versailles gardens. The mansion was reached through a double row of oaks extending for a mile and a half—a line which English visitors declared had some of the most magnificent trees they had ever seen.

Life was semi-feudal at Oaklawn, with acres of cane, and herds of imported stock with which the Judge sought improvement of the Teche breeds. Older slaves were at work manufacturing cotton and woolen goods. One caller, E. C. Allen, found that "even here ice is regularly brought by the steamboats from New Orleans, a distance of nearly 300 miles by the route taken. Thus the Yankees, by their accustomed shrewdness, are indirectly driving a brisk trade in exchanging the congelations of the wintry North for the crystallizations of the sunny South."

Here Judge Porter became a brilliant entertainer of the American great, with Henry Clay and other statesmen, with literary and other men of ability and promise spending weeks as his guests. W. H. Sparks thought that his hospitality was "not surpassed by any gentleman in all the land." The section, in honor of Porter and his neighbors, became known as Irish Bend. Another visitor, Charles Daubeny of England, has left an account of the difficulties of travel in the 1830's, which made even an Oaklawn a far outpost. The Judge and his friend were two days on a Mississippi steamer going between New Orleans and Bayou Plaquemine; there they found the water too low to permit entry into the bayou for the journey south toward the Teche. They would have to wait at least a day. A smaller steamer, bound for Texas, made the crossing, and they might have transferred to it, but the vessel looked "rickety" to the Judge and, furthermore, it would take them no nearer than twenty miles to Oaklawn. Two more days passed, and the Captain still would not take a chance; so the Judge hired two free Negroes to row them the last fifty miles, along bayous, rivers, and lakes. They spent an evening or two on shore along the way. Even then they were not carried all the way. Eventually they found themselves three miles from Oaklawn, separated from the estate by a swampy wood or slough, not quite wet enough for rowing; and the renowned jurist and his English friend waded through the slush to the elegant porticos. (Presumably, in this state, they used the back door!)

Judge Porter became slowly less well in health, and spent his declining days in the shade of his columns upon the Teche. On his deathbed, in 1844, he remembered many names. He had made his enemies; prominent among them was Attorney Thomas H. Lewis. He referred to his opponents and said that he was forgiving them. Silent a moment, he boomed: "Yes, Lord, even Tom Lewis."

The master left; his masterwork, Oaklawn, remained. Yet it continued for only a few years in the hands of the Porters. The Judge's wife and children had died before him, and he left the estate to a brother.

The Civil War came on, and two of the tales that I heard several times along the lower bayou concern it and a second Mrs. Porter, the Judge's brother's wife. She was one of those in this area—settled in part by Northern men—who were not in sympathy with the Southern side. One day she took a position in the carved doorway and watched a furious clash between the two armies—the Battle of Irish Bend. She had a grandstand place in this elevated porch, and peered, fascinated, between the pillars, as between great curtains. Not once did she seem to consider such a thing as danger, but remained at her lookout post to the end.

According to the second account, the Confederates were retreating past the house at a time when Mrs. Porter was watching. A Union officer galloped through the entranceway and on up the driveway. Emerging from the long line of oaks, he found Mrs. Porter at the edge of the steps, smiling, bowing. He spoke quickly. The rebels had passed here; which way had they taken? Mrs. Porter, eager, pointed. The officer nodded briskly, turned, and led his men in the other direction. These Southern females were transparent, sir!

Mrs. Porter went to Europe, and the mansion passed from one owner to another. After some years it fell into a state of shabbiness. About the gardens, weeds were untended; insects nested in the intricate carvings, and paint cracked. A large Acadian family occupied the place for a time; then Negroes, descendants of the original slaves, tended it and collected a fee from visitors, sometimes wondering what they saw in this sad old carcass. Oaklawn dozed on.

Many years earlier, a young man of Indiana had passed the stately property on regular trips he made as captain of a bayou lumber boat. He looked and looked at the magnificent galleries, until others guyed him and asked if he were in love with the place. He just couldn't keep from wondering what life could be like in such a place of glory; and he made up his mind then that if ever he could, he would get himself a house "something like that Oaklawn up there." That young man was Captain Clyde Barbour. As the years passed, Captain Barbour became a citizen of Texas, and by the time the late 1920's came around, he was a millionaire, and a man of strong impulse. He remembered the beautiful mansion on the bayou and he began to make inquiries about it and about the Teche. Eventually he made up his mind that Oaklawn itself was what he wanted. He was not discouraged when he beheld it again, so dishonored. He engaged assistants, removed time-worn woodwork, installed new foundations at several points, and retrieved some of the original decorations. Then, one day, when the work of restoration was almost completed, the building burned down, to smoke-scarred stonework.

The Captain stood in silence, shook his head, and then he said that perhaps it had been for the best. He wasn't certain that they had done everything just the right way anyway; now they could profit by their mistakes. "Let 'er go, boys, and we'll make it better than ever, and fireproof, too!" New architectural aid was enlisted, and persons with drawings and photographs of the old place, with any information about it, were asked to come forward. Cedar, cypress, tapestries moved up the Teche again. The Captain added some extra touches of his own: white marble staircases, ironwork that had not been there before, inlaid marble floors instead of wooden ones, and a few other things that the Judge had overlooked—polo grounds, a golf course, and a landing field. Eventually, friends said, the venture cost $300,000 or so.

To a gala opening the Captain summoned officials of Louisiana and Texas, neighbors, fellow millionaires, and small Acadian farmers from bayou and prairie. (The New Orleans *Item* reported that the banking-industrial wing represented a conservative valuation of $300,000,000.) Forty private guests stayed at the home, where fourteen bathrooms had been installed; they and hundreds of others ate at an "open-air table" the length of a city block, set out under the oaks. Among Judge Porter's 310 oaks were lampposts, newly erected; six ·miles of poles and cables had been constructed to provide electric and telephone service from near-by Franklin. This would be no outpost when the Captain finished.

For entertainment, an airplane did stunts; two Louisiana professionals competed against two Texans in an exhibition golf tournament on "the South's largest private course"; speedboats were available for runs up the Teche, to admire the estate from the proper points; and a jug-and-reed band from a Teche town offered musical selections. The Acadian farmers moved about and looked at the "Henry Clay room," a replica of that in which Clay slept, an adjoining chamber containing a bathtub hewn out of a block of solid marble; a great marble dining salon, with an overpowering table, hand-made from a solid slab of Italian marble, mounted on wrought-iron pedestals; a Napoleon desk; original tapestries of Aubusson and Gobelin; a Corot and many another rare item. Available accounts give no comment by the small Frenchmen on this new neighbor.

The Captain had what he wanted, Oaklawn with modern conveniences. It was his for five years, until his death. He knew now just how the Judge had felt up there behind those porticos.

And now, I have found, Oaklawn has become something of a museum. One pays fifty cents to enter the grounds, and another fifty to inspect the house. I gave my dollar, and as I walked about, I thought of the Judge and the Captain—and especially of the Judge; and of their living quarters that are filled with precious things, but cold and empty of the spirit of the old owner.

Later in the week I traveled up the Teche to a place on the outskirts of the old Petit Paris, and looked at another great procession of trees. These lead to no mansion; where there was once a house, there is now only grass—and a small history of a planter, two wives, and two daughters.

Monsieur Charles Durand was "an original," in the words of his granddaughter, Mrs. Stella Madère, who rocked in her rocker and told me about it that day. He had his own notions, and not all the Madame Grundys of the bayou could dissuade him from the smallest of them. He came from France, shortly before 1820, already wealthy; and his first actions on arrival were broad ones. He established one of the most extensive plantations for many miles about. He bought scores of slaves. He wanted many trees about him, and he decided to have a long avenue, three miles in extent. Once they began to grow, the alternate pines and oaks became show-things of the upper Teche.

Along with the trees, the Durand family waxed. An addition came almost every year, until the children numbered twelve. He, his wife, and the smaller Durands led a spacious life and a mirthful one, for Monsieur Durand believed that wealth was to be enjoyed. Some were certain that, as he sat before his massive desk, he tried to devise ways of spending his riches that no others had ever conceived. He came close to success, his neighbors thought.

He acquired a set of carriages with ornaments of gold, including the harness. The countryside stopped to watch them, glittering in the sun, as Monsieur Durand and all the Durands bowed right and left. He gave orders that the family was to be waked in the morning with sprays of perfume. More and more pleased by this fancy, he installed large supplies and bathed in waters well strewn with crystals which gave off those fine aromas. He suggested that the other Durands follow his example. They did, and they liked it, and insisted that their guests do the same thing. Papa had such gay ideas!

Then the first Madame Durand died, and Papa was as extravagant in sorrow as in everything else. Never would he see the face of another woman without thinking of his poor lost wife; never would he marry again. He swore it for the world to hear and be guided thereby. Daily he went to the cemetery across the Teche and knelt before the tomb. He made his trip in good weather and in bad; when it rained, he wore a covering against the elements. To perpetuate the memory of his grief, he ordered an artist to create an iron statue of him, on his knees, hands crossed, clad in his raincoat; the statue, too, was protected. At the base was an inscription telling of his oath never to be false to the dear one.

Within less than a year, Charles Durand met a girl whom he liked and was married again. The town tittered. Boys of the area, doing what their elders did not dare do, crept into the cemetery and tossed stones at the statue until the head dropped. Someone scrawled over the graven words at the base: "Do Not Tell Such Lies!"

But Monsieur Durand was not one to concern himself with over-meticulous consistencies. His second marriage was as undisturbed, as undilutedly jolly, as his first. Again a child came with every year or so, and again the total reached twelve. His granddaughter said that he had informed everybody: "The number must be the same as before. I cannot be unfair to either lady." There was a man with a delicate sense of the rightness of things.

A few years before the outbreak of the Civil War, two of his daughters simultaneously accepted the marriage proposals of members of native Louisiana families. Bayou Teche looked for something unusual from Monsieur Durand for the occasion. Few expected anything like the thing that they experienced.

The planter sat long at that desk, and concentrated, before he conceived his project. He chose spiders for the basis of the ornamentation. One source says that he imported a cargo of enormous creatures from Cathay. His granddaughter insists that he sent merely to the woods near Catahoula, Louisiana. In any event, they were large spiders, capable of large deeds.

Shortly before the marriage day, the spiders were set loose, while the slaves watched, big-eyed, among the trees in the long avenue. For days the spiders worked, lacing the spaces between the trees with yards of delicate webs. All wondered; would it rain between then and the wedding day, and his efforts melt away? Monsieur Durand was not one to fret over trifles. It would not rain.

It did not rain. On that morning, the planter called his slaves, gave them bellows and supplies of silver and gold dust. Over the long canopy of cobwebs, says the tradition, they spread this gossamer covering. ("It must have been superb," said Mrs. Madère, softly. "So many times have they told of it. . . .") Others worked beneath the canopy, laying a series of carpets to cover most of the three-mile passage under the trees. At one end of the avenue they placed an open-air altar; between the trees, at the sides, were tables covered with food, to be served by as many of the slaves, domestic and field, as could be fitted with aprons and drilled for the occasion. Bands played from strategic points. The wedding was open to all— French and Americans—up and down the Teche.

Thousands attended and watched. Toasts, dancing, songs, and the giving of gifts continued until dusk. Then up the bayou came a steamboat, to take the two couples on their honeymoon to New Orleans. The crowd accompanied them to the landing, shot off fireworks, and bade the young people good-by; and the four stood at the rail and waved until they were out of sight.

Charles Durand had made his last grand gesture. The war came, and he fought in it with sons and grandsons. His slaves were freed, his sugar mill was seized, his home was damaged; and the golden carriages also went. He did not survive the war by many years. In his last months he talked of money that he had hidden somewhere, perhaps under the oaks and pines, perhaps somewhere else. The children asked him many times: "Where is it? Where?" He never told. Later, one of them dug for months—and found nothing.

The house and the sugar mill fell away with the years. A barn and a few slave houses are all that can be found today of the former grandeur of the Durands, among the trees. These, too, have been reduced to about half their original number. The spiders? I tried for a time, but I failed to find more about them, whether they were truly imports from Cathay, or merely from Catahoula; and just how well they performed their assignment.

In any event, Monsieur Durand was "an original." He had less material wealth than Judge Porter; fewer knew his name outside Louisiana. But, of the two, I wonder if, after all, life wasn't a lot more fun for Grand-père Durand, yes?

§ 13. *Time and the Teche*

EVANGELINE, a sweet lady who never really was—at least in the way that the world knows her—is the strongest force alive for miles along the upper Teche of today. She is a secular saint of South Louisiana, and especially of her home-in-death, St. Martinville. There may be irony, or satisfaction for some in that fact; for it tends to show that occasionally the meek can inherit their earth.

Petit Paris and its titled ones have disappeared; their place has been taken by the figure of a girl of the Acadians. Were it not for her and what America thinks of her, St. Martinville might be a forgotten spot on the map. She came into being by accident, out of a union of the printing press and the unspoken yearning of Anglo-Saxon America for a legend of the New World. Yet when I talked with many of the men and women of the Teche, I was told that her trail goes back farther than Henry Wadsworth Longfellow.

For many years the Mouton and Voorhies families of St. Martinville had passed along a family story that began in Nova Scotia at the time of the "grand dérangement." The grand'mere of Judge Felix Voorhies befriended and reared an orphan girl, Emmeline Labiche, in the Canadian home of the Acadians. A few days over sixteen, Emmeline was about to marry a young man of their village, Louis Arceneaux. The banns had been published. Then, the day before the marriage, the blow crashed upon them. Louis, resisting, was injured and carried away; Emmeline screamed and fell to the ground. She and her benefactor were taken to another ship, and their party landed in Maryland. There they had a somewhat less difficult time than was the lot of many of the others, for they fell among families who were sympathetic and helpful.[1] But Louis was not there, and often the saddened Emmeline talked of him, and wondered whether he had lived; if so, where he was

[1] One of the families who aided these Acadians were the Brents. The exiles had good memories. Eventually some of the Brents moved to Louisiana; the Acadians helped elect and re-elect one of them to Congress from their district.

now. After several years, the party heard, like others, of Louisiana and, after much debate and over the protest of their Maryland friends, they made the perilous trip, by land and water, to the Attakapa country. Here, contentment awaited most of the party; for Emmeline, there was something else.

She stepped off the boat with the rest, but she paid little attention to the scene or to the exclamations of the others. Her face as usual was sad. Suddenly she halted. There, under a heavy oak, was the man for whom she had wept during these drab years. She ran to him; he rose, recognition and then pain in his face. She reached out; he turned half-away, and spoke in muffled voice: He had pledged himself to someone else. He had waited . . . but after all that time . . . He walked away.

From that day, as Judge Voorhies has recounted it, the life of Emmeline was lived in dim light. Her manner became strange, alternating between melancholy and tremulous excitement. She wandered along the Teche, picking moss from the live oaks, flowers from the edge; and then she wept and talked of the old land and of her marriage the next week to Louis. Again she would shriek that Louis had been killed by the soldiers, and ask what would become of her. Her physical health gave way, and one day, clinging to her aged friend's hand, she died. Almost until her own death in 1830, at 103, they say that her guardian visited the girl's grave.

Some fifteen years later, in another part of America, Nathaniel Hawthorne had breakfast with the poet Longfellow. Another friend, a Salem minister, mentioned that he had been urging Hawthorne in vain to make an Acadian study, telling of a girl who was separated from her lover at the time of the exodus, and spent the rest of her life in search of him.

Longfellow was intrigued; if Hawthorne were not interested, could he try a poem on the theme? Hawthorne agreed to attempt nothing until Longfellow had worked at the subject. The poet was soon engaged upon his "idyl in hexameter." At first it was to be called "Gabrielle," then, perhaps, "Celestine" or "Evangeline." It emerged with the last name. Longfellow had never seen Louisiana. He read histories, geographies, studied pictures, talked and corresponded with those who knew the country. A number of Louisianians, including a descendant of Emmeline's guardian, have told of communications with him at the time; a St. Martinville youth, student of the poet at Harvard, declared during his lifetime that he had passed on to Longfellow, in addition to scenic data, the Voorhies family tradition as he had often heard it at home.

The Longfellow story, of course, deviates from the Voorhies account. His Louis (Gabriel) was not forgetful of his Emmeline (Evangeline). Evangeline came to Louisiana, as did Emmeline, but then she wandered about the country, seeking until she found him, dying, in a faraway hospital. But South Louisianians cite many similarities and point out that the first parts of the two versions show little difference. They are certain that the Evangeline of the idyl is the Emmeline of the Teche.

The poet himself was amazed at the warmth of general response. "The public takes more kindly to hexameters than I could have imagined," he said; and there was something of understatement in that remark. His pathetic Acadian became part of American folk tradition, a companion to Barbara Frietchie, Pocahontas, and Hiawatha. Copies of the poem spread over the country, in edition after edition, including one in Attakapa cloth. Afternoon clubs and lecture organizations presented it, and when the bonnes femmes of the morning coffee parties took it up, it had come home. Men and women made trips to St. Martinville and its environs; to many, all the area became known as "the Evangeline country."

Meanwhile the fates had been dealing harshly with the older St. Martinville. A town may hold up under one calamity, perhaps two, but not a series of them. It maintained itself until shortly before the Civil War, then slipped quickly. It was high up on the Teche, and steamboat operators gradually found that they could obtain and dispose of cargoes closer to the Gulf without uncertainty over low water. Still, St. Martinville was the port of a rich prairie and agricultural country and it clung tightly to its advantages. In 1855 came a yellow-fever epidemic of unprecedented proportions, wiping out much of the population. Shortly afterward a fire burned down her business district, and then a hurricane killed acres of crops, destroyed buildings and cattle. The war itself struck hard; the town shifted from one army to the other, and was damaged with each transfer. Finally the railroad made its incursions, and the steamboat owners found fewer and fewer reasons to go so high up the stream. The bayou silted up, and little was done about it.

For years, however, St. Martinville's social éclat diminished but little. I have talked with old ladies, some still there, others in other towns, of those charmed days when St. Martinville still drew the elite for their vacations; when the French Opera Company singers made annual journeys up the bayou from New Orleans for a "second season on the Teche." Music festivals and theatrical entertainments continued much as in the days of the nobility. Some of the players found St. Martinville so hospitable that they married there, and a few of their children remained. It had a flavor of its own— a colony of singers, organists, composers, of "select schools for young ladies," elocutionary and amateur dramatic organizations among the natives. Judge Felix Voorhies, the attorney and writer, was a playmaker, acting in his own entertainments, drawing in most of his own family as well as the sheriff, merchants, and others of the town.

Marcelle Schertz, who has made a thorough study of the Judge's works, has cited the case of a favorite player, George Sillan, émigré of France; and Monsieur Sillan represents the St. Martinville tradition at its most favorable. Cultured, witty, fond of reading, he delivered milk in a two-wheel cart with a pony, singing operatic arias in the dawn. For years he saved his money for a return trip to the continent; and at last he had enough. Then, walking down the street with his passport in his pocket, he collapsed and died. There were others like Monsieur Sillan, before him and afterward, who adjusted themselves to the demands of their scene; who hoped to see home again, and never did. And quietly the population of St. Martinville was falling away. Some of the great names disappeared; property values declined, and less affluent families moved in from the rural areas. Yet I met some of the descendants of the celebrated ones, who have never left; and in the old church I was shown their carefully preserved coats-of-arms near the altar.

In the interim, Evangeline was in the ascendance. If anything replaced the steamboat for St. Martinville, it was she. America came and it asked: Where did Evangeline arrive? Where did she walk? And St. Martinville told, and still tells, all about Evangeline, and Emmeline too. The two jeunes filles are connected and related many times a day until they have become as one. The visitor may be able to distinguish them at the start; the task soon becomes impossible. Emmeline is

Evangeline; Evangeline, Emmeline. That is all you need to know.

Across the Teche bridge lives Monsieur André Olivier, Evangeline's minister, with or without portfolio to the world. A friendly source once described André as a "live, piquant bachelor." He is that, and more. When I met him, he was wearing a blue shirt open at the throat, safari-fashion helmet, black-ribbon pince-nez; and he was lecturing on the heroine to a group of callers. Official cicerone of the town, he also runs a small grocery and general store that bears the banner, "Evangeline Enshrined Here." He sells gumdrops, beans, bedsteads, Attakapa Indian baskets, and most other things; to the rear is a museum of Acadia, at which he gives Evangeline free. Part Acadian, part Creole, he is a descendant of Hugues Charles Honoré Olivier de Vezin, who helped the Spanish Governor of Louisiana when he led the French in taking posts from the British during the American Revolution. Before he was out of knee pants, André was taking people to the bayou for little talks on Evangeline. The family, he said, had been "badly bent" by the Civil War; another conflict, the First World War, made it possible for him to Enshrine Evangeline. Using surplus military commodities, he opened his establishment; until recently, some of his first supplies were still available.

With André I visited the "Evangeline Oak," under which Emmeline (Evangeline) is said to have found Louis Arceneaux (prototype of Gabriel), in her moment of joy and anguish. The old church had part of its original chapel of 1765; just outside, in a setting of Spanish daggers, stood a small grave, surmounted by a life-sized statue. Here, said André, were the remains of Emmeline; the inscription also bears the name of Evangeline.

Near the park entrance stood a group of Negroes, talking excitedly, with much movement of hands. Their words were French; they knew no other tongue. The French-speaking black man is common through much of South Louisiana, particularly in the areas of the former plantations. He is proud of his language and of his background; and here, as in other places about the bayou land, I thought I detected an easier relation between white man and Negro than in other parts of the South.

There was a last stop, at the Longfellow-Evangeline Memorial Park, with its Acadian House museum; and here, perhaps, was an ultimate irony. Who had lived here? None other, say the natives, than Louis, the lover who did not wait. It is a handsome structure, two-and-a-half-storied, with heavy columns below and more delicate ones above. Louis prospered, I would judge.

For dinner we went back to André's store, then through an alley that led to a garden. The background was a cottage in the Acadian style, but about it André had packed a series of wonders. I thought for a moment of that other enclosed green place, Weeks Hall's "Shadows on the Teche"; here was one in the same spirit. About an area the size of a moderately proportioned rear yard, André too had placed a circle of bamboo and trees, pecans in this case, to shut out the modern scene. It was an exercise in economy, ingenuity, and simple joie de vivre; André's Acadian blood told. In front was a fountain; its border, the rim of a plantation wagon wheel; the bottom casement, a pre-Civil War syrup vat; the pedestal, several old pipes and rocks. Concealed somewhere was the differential of a Model T Ford. In a New Orleans restaurant, André once saw a rubber ball tossed into the air by a jet of water, falling back, to be caught and sent up again. He studied how it was done; his homemade fountain behaves in approximately the same manner. Near-by stood a "spotlight" for his night scene, his "outdoor floor lamp," a tall pipe surmounted by a phonograph horn of Edison cylinder-machine variety, with blue reflector to produce his moon rays.

"Supper is coming down," said André. His statement was a literal one. I looked up, and prepared to duck. From the top branch of the tree descended a circular object held by several chains. It dropped into position over an upright piece of metal; André dislodged the chains and drew them back up into the tree, and there was the table, fully set. Over the excellent cold meal I learned that Evangeline had been translated into ten languages; that one of the Acadian spinning wheels in his shop had "spent six months in Paris" (André was patently envious of it), and that, rich Gallic accent and all, André is a Son of the American Revolution by virtue of that distinguished ancestor.

On the way out, I met one of the Misses Olivier, a gentle, dark-eyed woman, who helps at the store. André's other sister teaches catechism. The three have always lived in St. Martinville; they will never leave. I was also introduced to a new kitten, who was being retained to replace a pet that had died. "I regret that cat," André said.

If fortune has seen fit to slow its tempo, modern St. Martinville at least will make its walk a graceful one. Age has settled becomingly upon this place of 3500. New houses are few; many seem considerably older than they really are. Whether large or small, there is unity in these buildings; most are not Acadian homes, but town adaptations and elaborations. Nearly all are white and galleried. At several points there are smaller versions of the columned mansions, their long porches almost level with the sidewalk; long doors and windows opening a few feet from the passers-by, behind narrow pillars.

To the other side of the bayou from the main street sits the cemetery; and several St. Martinville residents repeated, with a certain local pride, the saying that there are many more under those slabs than on the streets. I sensed a gratification, too, that practically everybody who finds his place within the graveyard was born in St. Martinville and was preceded here in birth and death by others of several generations. For more than seventy-five years the population of the town remained stationary. Few new people came; not many old ones left, except across the water to that quieter place. Here, in crumbling marble, I came upon names that Françoise Bossier and others mentioned in accounts of the faded Little Paris, and some dating back to the first Poste des Attakapas, among the "man-eating" Indians.

On the street corners, nailed to the posts, were black-bordered papers that I recognized as funeral notices. A boy handed me one, slipped another under a door. This was a Louisiana town custom, now passing away, which St. Martinville has never lost. A man or woman who wants to keep up with the "veillées" (wakes) need not bother about the newspaper obituary columns; he watches the posts. As soon as the boy appears, a crowd gathers, to discuss the details, the adequacy of the service, and who thought that poor Soo-Too was so old. The notices are heavily formalized. One that I have before me now shows an attractive, dark-clad widow, leaning against a tomb surmounted by an urn; a mournful willow shelters widow and resting place. Leafing a day or so ago through some records of New Orleans in the 1870's, I found one such notice of a funeral in the old French section. The design—widow, urn, and willow—was identical.

There is death also about the Darby home, a short distance away. Françoise Bossier, in her diary of 1795, mentioned a "Saint Marc d'Arby," engaged to "little Constance de Blanc," among the gay ones of the society. The family was not originally French, but English. To François St. Marc Darby the Spanish government gave a large land grant, and he married a French girl of high birth. Their son in turn took a French bride, Félicité de St. Armand, a belle of her day. The residence that was built for them predated the Greek Revival tradition. Erected between 1815 and 1825, it was in a simpler Louisiana colonial style, its base flush with the ground, with stuccoed brick pillars, impressive doors and entrances.

For the beautiful Félicité and her husband, the days were golden. The family had a home in New Orleans, another in Paris, and the children were sent to France for their schooling and the finishing processes. In the Louisiana capital, the Darbys had their opera box, their carriages, their entertainments. They and their guests repaired to the country place for weeks of pleasant times, hunting, fishing in the near-by lakes, dancing in St. Martinville. When the Civil War arrived and the early days gave few hints of the grim ones to follow, the Darbys are said to have brought up "troops" of soldiers for amusement in the home and environs. Then, by contrast, ensued the somber years: the failure of the plantation enterprise, death for the older members, and decline for the others.

Eventually three Darbys were all that remained—two brothers and a sister. Used to luxury in their early lives, they grew to hate the fates that had soured their world; they hated, too, their old crumbling home and, not least, themselves. The last servants disappeared. No more town visits, no opera box; they had only one place, and one thing left in the world, and this was it. Natalie Scott has described these tragedy-shaded years. François and Octave Darby ignored each other, though they had to see each other throughout their days. When a cow that one owned broke into the small green patches of the other, the latter sang a song about it—to inform the brother with whom he would have no communication. The other would reciprocate. Octave turned of necessity to selling milk, but wore a frock coat during his deliveries. François attended to chores at the house. The sister quarreled with one, and informed him that she would leave her possessions, such as they were, entirely to the other. For a time these two formed a bitter pact against the third remaining Darby. At her death, the friendly brother took her sealed will posthaste to his attorney. In it was an unmarked sheet of paper.

Then Octave, too, died, and François lived on, the master of the Darby heritage. He stayed to himself for years, alone in the wreckage of his family's glories, the subject of whispers through the countryside. Those who ventured too near ran the risk of injury, by him or his dogs. Some said that the bearded old man ran out of the house at them with a hatchet. Superbly designed furniture moldered, under layers of newspapers, pushed into corners away from holes in the roof. Beneath tall oil paintings of his ancestors, the hermit cooked his meals in the fireplaces and ate them off the cracked marble mantels. The high four-posted beds were thick with dust; he preferred straw in the corner of the room. Then François, too, was taken to his grave, and most of the furnishings, last traces of Darby possessions, were removed.

Several years ago I visited the ruin in bright sunlight; even then it had clammy disaster about it. Past the remains of a once-graceful entrance gate, I fought my way through weeds to the neglected body of the home. Stairways rotted, half exposed to the open glare. Bricks had fallen away; rats and other unseen animals stirred in the accumulating debris. Each heavy wind had left its mark, each winter had added another dark stain. A cur dog stood guard at one corner, as jealous of the sanctity of his temporary refuge as if it were again a mansion. I was not reluctant to go; the sight left much the same impression as that of a once-beautiful woman, cruelly scarred by the years, on her deathbed. Then, on my most recent trip, I saw the Darby place again, and found that it had received a reprieve from final destruction. It has been repaired here and there, and made livable for tenants. A tin roof gleams where the shingles gave way; the windows have panes. But the marks of the years have not been erased. The bricks remain badly eaten away, the old wood is unpainted; at the back, where a great tree crashed in a storm, the galerie is gone, and one extension juts into the open air. Another tree remains on its side, its root system exposed to the wind; and pigs and chickens move about the yard among the clotheslines.

Some time afterward, an elderly man of the Teche opened his collection of records to me, and by accident my eye fell upon the words "St. Marc Darby." It was a "Reminiscence of the 60's and 70's" by Louis Paul Bryant. His mother was Hermance de Laureal, native of the French island of Guadaloupe; her parents died when she was young, and she was sent to Paris by her brothers, to be educated until she was eighteen, in the Convent of St. Clothilde. Her brother, Dr. David de Laureal, graduate of Le College de Louis le Grand in Paris, had come to Louisiana, first to New Orleans and then to St. Martinville, a place "known for its exceptional culture and gayety." Young Hermance joined him in the Teche country, met the Darbys, and she and the beautiful Félicité became intimate. The Darbys were also friendly toward a young Virginian, a Bryant, whom they met when the family spent some time at White Sulphur Springs. The cordial, enthusiastic Darbys told Mr. Bryant of their place, and he came to visit the Teche, and eventually he was persuaded to move here.

From the time of his arrival, the son tells us, the father was "identified in one way or another with the Darby family." In their drawing room he met pretty Hermance de Laureal, and quickly fell in love. "At that time," says the son, "my father had a very meager knowledge of French and my mother a very meager knowledge of English, and this courtship must doubtless have been beset with lingual difficulties." Before long they were married, and then young Bryant was further adjusted to the Louisiana scene. His patrons, the Darbys, won him to the Catholic Church; St. Marc Darby became his godfather, Madame Dubuclet his godmother. Five bright years ensued, years of visiting and dancing and all-day picnics for the Darbys and the Bryants and their circle, and always the center of the festivities was that shining house of the Darbys, behind the inviting gateway. When war broke, the men left; her husband away, Hermance de Laureal Bryant took her son and lived with the Darbys. Some accounts have told of Federal depredations in the house, of men using their swords and axes on the rich furniture. Louis Paul Bryant, who remained through these troubled days, gives a different view. He remembers no damages; the Union men treated the household with "kindness and consideration."

A soldier once appropriated a saddle that belonged to him, a boy under ten. His captain learned of it and had the child's property returned. There follow, in this account, descriptions of horse racing, of showboats that came up the Teche, and other memories; but there is no more regarding the Darbys. It is a more pleasant way to leave them—in their period of happiness—warm, generous, and unaware of the darknesses ahead.

Down the Teche lay my course, along a road from which the water could be seen at intervals. With each few miles, the American influence grew stronger. Soon came New Iberia, where these trips had started, home of Weeks Hall, his "Shadows," and other things; and this was probably a good time, with St. Martinville fresh in mind, to consider something of that thriving city of 14,000. Part of the life of the later Teche is a tale of these two bayou cities. New Iberia came rather late as an incorporated center—not until 1839. It was in this area that early Spanish colonists were placed, and to it they gave the title "Nueva Iberia." In time, English-speaking settlers moved in among the Spanish and French; today the former influence is only minor and scattered.[2]

New Iberia for many years was a stepchild to the grandeur of St. Martinville, the capital and tribute-taker of the area. But New Iberia's location told. Closer to the Gulf, it was a logical point of transfer for traffic from east to west, and its deeper water made possible year-round travel. Eventually it broke away from the domination of the older city and became the center of its own parish. Today it continues to grow, as a gathering center for trappers, moss pickers, and fishermen, as headquarters for oil men, and as shipping point for heavy volumes of salt from the near-by mines. Yet since it is a city of the Teche, it does not flaunt its industry. That stays quietly on the side.

[2] Mr. Edward T. Weeks, Sr., has recalled one Spanish custom that continued through the years: the long funeral processions for leading citizens, headed by brass bands playing solemn music. On the way home the same musicians would blare out all the livelier tunes they knew.

Farther south lay small towns—sometimes French, sometimes French-American, or largely American: Franklin, Baldwin, Centerville, Patterson, Jeancrette. The older houses gradually thinned out, though some had interest: Arlington, built by a mulatto plantation-and-slave owner, Euphrazie Carlin; Albania, erected by a French Royalist, now owned and operated by the city of New Orleans; and Shadyside, Dixie, and others. Here, too, was an unexpected connection or two with the bayous of other areas. A sugar man of the lower Teche, an American, went fishing in the near-by Gulf waters early in the last century. A bad wind came and he thought drowning was near; and then into view hove none other than Jean Lafitte. True to his reputation, the corsair was a gallant gentleman; he picked him up, fed him, gave him a warm drink, and sent him home with a supply of pirate whisky. Also, I was informed by members of several old families, Jean and his crew "worked" the Teche as they did Lafourche and the Barataria waters. Here they had two suave planter-intermediaries, who provided any amount of slaves that the plantations needed. And since others improved their means of transportation, the buccaneers did the same thing, digging a canal of their own to reach their customers. Curiously, one of the names of the Lafitte agents is the same as another mentioned by young Françoise Bossier in the story of her visit to Petit Paris. He received the family with kindness and assisted them on their way. Françoise was in the midst of more things than she suspected.

Below, Morgan City spread itself, and here one Yankee entrepreneur above all others set his name upon the area in post-Civil War days. Charles Morgan had more faith than many natives in the ability of the quaky terrain about the adjoining marshes to hold pressure from above. Over the eighty miles of half-land from New Orleans to this point, he fostered a direct railroad connection. Many smiled at the weird thought. (Some had held their breaths when the first "skyscraper," of three stories, went up in New Orleans; and had watched to see if it sank suddenly into the soft ground.) The railway supports maintained themselves, and easy overland passage to the west was eventually possible from this point. For the time steamers waited at Morgan City —powerful ones for the Gulf trip to Texas and Mexico, and small ones for the route up the Teche; and much of South Louisiana remembers old Morgan for his part in opening up vast territories. He also had reason to remember Louisiana; his profits were fabulous.

The Teche pours here into wide Berwick Bay, an extension of the Atchafalaya from above. The water is deep, so deep that officials had many troubles when they put up a bridge. To erect one span, it was necessary to build it on barges and sink the barges until a stable bottom was reached; one of the piers has been described as "the deepest foundation in the world." In the Morgan City of today I heard French accents, Spanish, Italian, and others, but they are often those of the visitors, the fishermen, trappers, oystermen who bring their produce here for shipment to all parts of the world. It is a place of wharves, of long lines of boats, and of packing houses; each living by its strategic water connections. But, as befits its newness and also the memory of its former patron, it seems more an American town than anything else. The gentler, older Teche and its spirit are not far off, but they seem many centuries and many miles in the distance. This is the end of the line.

E. M. Morgan

"Hi, Etienne—Mass, she is over right now!"

F. M. Morgan

You can always pack another one in, if you try.

*Grand'mère washes dishes at her outdoor tablette. (She says
she can thus be inside her house and outside, too.)*

This mail also gets through; but it sometimes waits.

Mère

Grand-père

Parrain

Oncle

FACES ALON

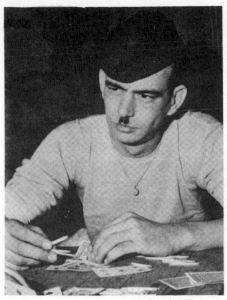

Charles Genella

Fils

Farm Security Administration

Bébé

Fonville Winans

Garçon et Jeune Fille

E. M. Morgan

*Every old family has its chinaberry tree, "topped" annu-
ally for fuel. Note the thick body and small branches.*

Mechanized prairie agriculture—feeding machines for rice.

But the old also holds an ancient, man-and-horse syrup mill.

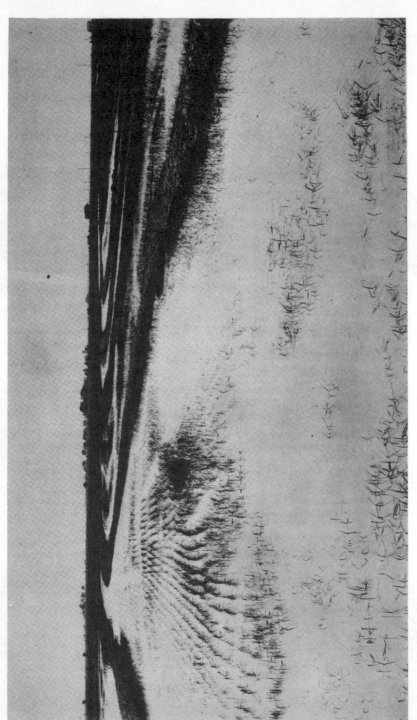

Man-made flood—a rice field, with new shoots above the water.

Part IV: *Where the Buggies Roll*

TILDEN LANDRY

§ 14. *Back Lands of Grass*

FOR MANY YEARS, a large percentage of all the buggies manufactured in the United States has gone to the prairies of Louisiana. A Middle Western firm, largest in its field, once estimated that it sent to this area a larger part of its output than it shipped to the rest of the country. War has been mechanized, and so has peace; but the Louisianian of the prairies clings to his horsepower.

To the west of the Teche, covering 3500 or more square miles, are the grasslands that provide the greatest concentration of Acadians in America. The appearance of the place may seem related to that of the marshes to the south. Once it was little different from the trembling terrain. Slowly it drained off, and the flow of its streams was slackened; it is now a territory of smaller bayous, with wide pasturage between them, and of frequent coulées—side streams that are sometimes dry. A man may have a coulée, or minor bayou, in his own back yard, a private waterway of his own.

As elsewhere, it is these waters that bring trees to the countryside. Along each stream are belts of timber like darker currents through the grass, with knobs and extensions reaching out into the prairie. The original settlers clung close to such wooded places, for fuel and protection. But eventually the patchworks of farms and homes spread into the open acres. All of it remained in tight self-containment; some yet call it the place "behind the backlands." Over it, from early days to the present, the horse rather than the pirogue has been the means of travel.

Today almost every family has its buggy, sometimes two of them. In the night, thousands of the small vehicles jog along the innumerable back roads, and the only sounds to be heard are the clop-clop of hoofs and the clack-clack of conversations. On the main highways a long and steady file of these older vehicles moves slowly among the heavy-powered delivery trucks and occasional passenger cars. With gasoline and tire conservation of the Second World War, the prairie man could not be blamed if he grinned as he spurred on Loo-Loo or Jacques. "Didn' we 'ave smartness all the time, you and me, M'sieu Cheval?"

The automobile, as a matter of fact, never threatened to replace the horse over most of the prairies. The main establishment of the town and village has been the buggy shop; the latest available models and the old reliables that the trade always wants are on constant exhibition. In normal times the arrival of new displays has meant the equivalent of the city automobile shows of affectionate memory, with connoisseurs testing footboards, balancing on seats, and checking to see how many pumpkins or children can be fitted under them.

While a line of the buggies awaits repair at the combination buggy-and-blacksmith shop, men debate their respective merits. That one is all fanciness and paint; and the company used to be a good one, yes, says one of the elders. Another observes that his would have been good for ten more years if that accident hadn't happened the night Ludovic had the Jérémiads.[1]

Doctors put up hitching racks before their offices; so do dance-hall proprietors; so do midwives and parish welfare officers. I inspected the first drugstore that one town had ever known—shiny with fountain and black chromium front; it too had a long rack for the trade. At several Sunday church services our automobile was the only one among a hundred or more buggies stretching up and down the road. When Mass ended, an incredible number of people fitted into each conveyance. A seat meant for two accommodated five; behind them, others squeezed themselves, and below them, still others; and everybody with an available arm or lap took an additional small one. Papa or Maman looked around to see that all were wedged in so that none would fall out (a thing that was now manifestly an impossibility), then clicked, and they started off. How to get out in such cases would seem a harder problem than how to get in; but once one of the elders handed down several armfuls of the children, openings were created in the solid mass and the descent was accomplished.

Families pass on their buggies from one generation to the next. Euzèbe, who courted his bride twenty years ago in his new one, sits and watches Ti' Zeb start off in the same vehicle on a similar mission. It creaks louder; but it has been well polished and it will do until the boy has his first six or seven chil-

---

[1] This expressive term, denoting strong lamentation, refers to stomach cramps.

dren, or longer. After years of use, the top will wear and rip, and reluctantly the family will take it off. But the buggy will not yet be given up. A topless one is better than none, and they will ride on indefinitely in it. When it rains, they will all put paper over their heads, or pull in out of the rain and wait. They have patience.

The buggy makes its stand here because it is favored by the topography, the economics, and the people. Built high off the ground, away from the mud, it has always been the simplest means of movement over the green ground. When the automobile arrived, it could not match the buggy for the rear roads and paths, which were most of the thoroughfares. This buggy knew the hard life. Also, it was cheap; $100 or so would buy the sturdiest kind, and grass was ever a pleasant substitute for gasoline, rationed or pre-rationed. Finally, the prairie man had the potent argument—"Je fais comme mon père." Nobody here wanted a thing simply because it was new.

A short distance from the Teche the scene changes sharply. The estates and the remaining plantation houses are gone. Sugar holds its own for a time, but then it becomes the small crop of small men, cultivated in plots along with corn and sweet potatoes, greens and occasional other vegetables. Refineries disappear. When a farmer wants his cane processed, he takes it to the back-yard mill of a friend, who uses the open-kettle method of the old days. To the west and north, even stalks disappear, and for a time the cotton bolls rise over the ground. But no miles of white—the Mississippi Delta scene of the planters—can be found. These are brief lots, surrounded by other crops. Eventually this alters, and the wide fields of America's great rice-producing section are at hand.

The soil has thinned, and its base is a clay pan that holds at the surface the water that is needed by the peculiar crop. Louisiana has all too much liquid in some of its Southern reaches; but here it has to pump additional water over the greenlands for the benefit of its rice.

And for many miles, from east to west, cattle graze. From almost the first days of white men's memories, the prairies have been a place of livestock, moving slowly, in heavy herds, across the horizon. With them roam Acadian cowboys, speaking French to their stock, singing placid or witty songs. On the streets of the prairie towns I have seen the boys move with what they obviously felt was the swagger of those Texiens just to the west, wearing jeweled belts and hats of many-gallon capacity, which seem larger than ever on the slighter, shorter French youths. Many older Louisianians feared the Texas influence; much of the younger generation talks of the place as a land of free and gallant adventure, which most Texans will readily admit that it is. So the Gallic ranchers practice with their lariats while their girl listeners sigh at the glamor of it. The prairie version of "Gjingle-Gjangle-Gjingle" has a rare and special ecstasy about it, full of Yips and Yies, and as western as, say, "Alouette."

The Louisiana prairies begin at the east from a line of mild bluffs not far from the Teche, which the geologists declare are the edge of the alluvial plain through which the known courses of the Mississippi can be traced. The beginnings of the prairies have a series of slight and pleasant rolls; and in these, too, the scientists have found traces of the great river. Many years ago, they are inclined to believe, the wide stream and some of its tributaries moved through the grasslands. Today most of the channels have dried up; and these lost levees and valleys account for the gradual lifts and falls of the soil.

Early visitors were reminded of wide billows of a vast sea; viewed from a point on one of these mounds, the uniform surfaces of grass change like waves as the wind slips over them.

The Acadians also were impressed with this resemblance. When they came upon a dark patch of wood, surrounded by the lighter grass, they called it an "île." Where the wood jutted sharply into the prairie like an edge of land in the water, it was a "pointe." A section partly protected by extensions of the trees was an "anse" or bay. The Acadian, of course, had a background of life at the water's edge, and this he demonstrated in other ways. When he wanted to cross the prairie, he used the word "naviguer" (navigate). He said that he would "embarquer" in his buggy or "mettre la voile" (set sail) on the green; and he "moored" his mount. André Lafargue heard an Acadian mother exclaim proudly when she beheld her daughter in bridal attire: "N'est-ce pas qu'elle une göelette bien gréee?" (Isn't she a fine little boat, all rigged out?)

Venturesome Frenchmen pushed their way into the prairie margins during the formative years of the Louisiana colony. A trading contract for the Opelousas area was recorded as early as 1738 before the Superior Council; soon afterward cattle brands were being registered with the authorities. North of the Poste des Attakapas on the Teche was another for the prairies, the Poste des Opelousas, named also after the neighboring Indians. About these two points centered the official life of the grasslands through many generations. Non-Acadian Frenchmen came first, but most of them did not go far from the Teche. Spanish officers, following them, also remained largely in the vicinity of the established places, as eventually, too, did the American arrivals. The Acadians were to have the grassy areas largely to themselves.

To one of the lower stretches, the Acadians gave a descriptive title, "Côtes Gelées" (Frozen Hillsides). One explanation is that the settlers, coming in winter near a place of slight mounds above the prairie, camped in the vicinity. Rising the next morning, they beheld all of the scene outlined in a white frost; the Acadian girls called out the name, and it was never forgotten. A more prosaic version declares that the shivering arrivals looked in vain for wood and used the words in mockery.

The presence of the livestock made the life of these settlers different from that of others to the east. The original cattle and horses apparently came from the Spanish possessions of the Southwest, and many were offered to the French by the Indians. All proved hardy and well fitted to the scene. William Darby early in the last century described the horse of the Attakapas and Opelousas as "small, compactly built, and inconceivably durable." This durability continued through the years; wild ponies were always available for the catching and taming. The cow of the prairie was, Darby thought, "high, clean-limbed, and elegant in its appearance." Elegant or not, it multiplied almost as rapidly as did the Acadians.

Cattle-raising was not a difficult occupation; the owners turned their stock loose on the grasses, let it move practically at will, and gave it little or no care. Once every year or two they made a roundup; the calves were branded when they followed the others, and there was nothing more about which the owner need concern himself until the next time. When he wanted meat on his table, he picked out a likely animal; when he saw a chance to reach the market, he and his son spent a day or so in the open. Soon there arose the "vacherie,"

French equivalent of the cattle ranch, and many could claim several thousand head of cattle. Those to the south, where the dry prairies declined toward the sea marshes, had even less about which to worry. When winter arrived, their stock shifted to the wet areas, where they learned to hold their footing on the crustlike covering into which others would sink. This led some to claim with pride that such animals had webbed feet. Strangers who watched them were inclined to agree.

About the prairies were hundreds of wet spots. Some were low boglike flats in which water accumulated; others were clear natural ponds, which the Indians said were created when the animals stamped down small depressions and widened them. The clay pan prevented the water from seeping easily into the ground, and these water holes were always available for the livestock. Many Acadians learned from nature, plied their shovels, and had their own back-yard ponds or "digs." Others, finding large wet places, used them for the planting of rice; a name developed for this prairie crop—"Providence rice." It grew easily, and seemed to depend mainly on the will of le bon Dieu. If rains fell and made possible a good crop, its owner was happy. If the precipitation was light and the rice failed, he shrugged.

The wet sections were the main hazards to travel over the prairie. The animals left trails that the settlers followed; in time the men made their own; but generally, until long after the Civil War in many places, the simplest and often the only way of passage was to set out across the trackless green and hold toward a previously fixed direction. For individual transport, a man got on his horse and went forward as well as he could; everybody, in fact, learned to ride, from mother to young daughter. For freight, oxen drew heavy carts by slow stages; and I have talked with old settlers who recall how these conveyances looked and sounded. Wheels were solid wooden disks; axles were unoiled, and the grind and squeak echoed a mile or so off. Prairie people were wakened in the night by the approach of such vehicles over the open land; and it might be an hour or more before the last shrill note was lost in the opposite direction.

During the early days of the American regime the common carrier was the calèche, predecessor of the modern buggy, a topless, all-wooden vehicle, held together with pegs, its body hung on rawhide strips. Thomas Nicholls, whose father received a government post in the Attakapas, said of them in a memoir: "These strange, lumbering carriages would appear before sunset, filled with young ladies and old ladies on their way to the coming ball. On the floor of the carriage would be one or two shot bags filled with dollars, intended by the old ladies to furnish the means of indulging in their favorite game of vingt-et-un." Young Nicholls was delighted with the place: the French neighbors were hospitable, though they knew not a word of English, and the newcomer was pleased in particular with the Saturday night dances. The girls were "beautiful and fascinating, with a total absence of all parade and etiquette." Among less happy reminiscences was an evening on which his carriage broke down in the middle of a bog while he and his brother were trying to follow directions across the prairie to attend a ball. They spent a fretful night among the mosquitoes. It was not for nothing that men warned strangers to keep out of the grasslands after dark.

Others have described the balls of this prairie land. There were few public establishments, but regularly a few people met and decided to "make a dance" at a private home. A man and woman pushed the furniture from one room to another, put something to cook on the stove, and all was ready. One family could not bear all the expense, certainement; and so everybody would contribute a little as admission. First, though, the neighbors must be informed of the arrangements. A young man jumped on a pony to be a messenger of the ball. He attached a cloth to a stick and galloped past every house for some miles, waving the banner as he went; it would not do to make enemies by skipping friends who were out of the way, no. As he went, he called out the tidings; and sometimes, for emphasis, he fired a gun in the air. When he had made his run, he fixed the stick at the gate of the proper house. All knew what that meant, whether or not they had seen the rider.

On the appropriate night, men and women came in carriages, in wagons, or in anything else that would support them. If there was a near-by bayou, some arrived by boat; and often many walked in their bare feet, their shoes hanging over their shoulders, with the laces tied at the neck. At the entrance everybody brushed off or washed his feet, put on his shoes, and went in. The mamans watched the girls at their dancing and also looked after the younger children. They saw that the dancers followed a rigid code. Toujours la modestie, mademoiselle; you can be with the boy during the dancing, but between the numbers, stay to yourself—boys to one side, girls to the other. You come with your family, and you leave with it. The young man had one opportunity to whisper with his girl. In the middle of the evening, somebody called out from the next room: "Gumbo paré!" There was a small charge, for the house, and nobody could stop a boy from talking to his sweetheart over the thick chicken and rice mixture.

The musicians were fiddlers, accordionists, and assistants

who struck at the "ti' fers," or "ting-a-lings," little irons or triangles. The musicians were bowed to, complimented, and flattered by the audience, for on them depended the party's success. Many times during the evening the players would threaten that this was their last number; they could not produce another grunt or wail. Somebody would coax, and the dance would continue. Finally, the musicians would reach a decision. One or two rose and went to the front. Out came pistols, and bullets went into the air. "Le bal est fini!" And fini it was, no matter how many protests broke out.

The horse, meanwhile, had found a specialized use, as a helper in the pursuit of love. There developed a "courting tacky," a particular kind of prairie pony. Young Jean, acquiring one, taught him to turn, prance, and dance. After intensive rehearsal, Jean ventured forth and put the tacky through his paces. Jean waved his hat and felt impressive; horse and man seemed one, bowing, rearing up, making circles. Marie Elizabeth stood in her window and smiled and smiled, while her sisters giggled. It was a formalized art, enjoyed by man, girl, and beast. She could not go out and thank him, or talk with him—that would be a boldness, yes; but everybody knew that such a performance meant something. A man who went through it and did not plan marriage, that was a scoundrel. He would hear from her brothers.

Visitors found here the same Acadian house that grew up in other places, and a surrounding farm scene that differed hardly at all in detail from mile to mile. About the immediate grounds was a fence of pieux—split cypress fitted into holes in the posts, without nails. The pieux were staple articles of trade; a man who was near a wood cut down a large supply for sale to those who were more isolated in the open grasses.

Cypress sellers, like others, took eggs, poultry, and meat in exchange for their wood. But few of these merchants went far out into the prairies. The distances were too great. So persistent farmers found ways through the years to get the lumber that others had. They tried many plantings. The live oak seldom did well; the clay pan retarded the roots. They experimented further; a smaller tree, the unpretentious chinaberry, managed to hold its own, and it became one of the true marks of the prairie home. The light growth, with its feather-like leaves, was a reassuring sight to those who traveled the broad expanses. Some of the prairie men have shown me, with a pride approaching that of the Grand Islander, the lines that their grandfathers planted.

Nothing about the farm worked harder for its keep than did the chinaberry tree. It gave shade; its seeds became beads and ornaments; its flowers were a substitute for camphor balls; it provided heating and building supplies. But the wise man did not destroy a tree that he had taken such care to plant simply because he wanted wood. He topped it, and for a time it was a grotesque sight, its branches gone, a procession of trunks thrust into the air. After a while it grew again, and the owner had his tree and his lumber too. It was not until after I had seen a number of these cropped trees that I realized what was so uniformly odd about them. The bodies are thick, with the girth of many years, but the limbs are young and scrawny.

The prairie was a well-enclosed, busy, small world to itself. From year to year the only cash that left the house was for coffee, and often the housewife traded her eggs for that. The bonne femme played a large role in the prairie economy, and it was not confined to the house. She worked in the field with her husband. She separated the seeds from the cotton and wove her cloth. The loom was massive, the size of a four-poster bed—and it seldom had a rest during the day; she saw to that with her daughters. In his patches the farmer grew a row or two of yellow or "Nankeen" cotton; this gave the housewife a color for her designs, or she used bark, indigo, and peach leaves for her shades. There was nothing light or delicate in the product; a thing to be used was a thing to last, whether it be trousers, blanket, or curtain. The cottonade of the Attakapas "wore like iron."

(Though it has largely disappeared, I recently came upon one authentic survival of the older day—a "battoir" or bat for clothes washing, on the edge of a pond. The housewife used it to beat the clothing until she conquered or they did; and the cloth had to be heavily made if only to survive this treatment. The elderly owner looked affectionately at the implement: "I kept my family clean for forty years with this; it is my good friend.")

It was a tranquil country, the smoke curling from the chimneys among the grasses, the cattle at the edges of the pools. The vista shifted with the hour. A heavy cloud left an irregular splotch on the light-hued plain as it moved across the sky. In the strong sun, part of the land seemed a brilliant yellow, against an area of gray blue, or one of a dark brown, and the proportion changed with the hour. On a dark day the prairie could be cheerless; a group of oaks on the shore of an île of darker green was a symbol of melancholy. But in the clear light of the wide green spaces there was usually little that was sad.

Smaller divisions of the countryside appeared, separated by the spurs and belts of trees. Each was known as a "prairie" or an "anse" (bay), with a name of its own, taken from the

Indians or from the nearest stream or from some aspect of its topography. Thus there were Faquetaique Prairie, so designated from the original red-skinned residents; Prairie Mamou, from a natural growth; L'Anse aux Pailles (Straws); and others. Some titles are minor mysteries; as an example— Prairies des Femmes. Sometimes, it seems, the settlers had spells of humor; one water trail became Bayou Queue de Tortue, Bayou of the Turtle's Tail.

The southern prairie developed a center, Vermilionville, near the main stream of its area. Among its first settlers, about 1755, were two brothers, Jean and Marin Mouton. Jean wore a hat, Marin wore a yellow homespun cap. Two branches of the family rose, one the "Chapeau" or Hat Moutons, the other the "Capuchon" or Cap Moutons. For generations, when one met a Mouton he asked, "Are you a Chapeau, or a Capuchon, Mouton?" Jean set out the town, and ranks as a kind of father of the territory. The family grew with the land; when one of the later widows died, she counted ninety-seven grandchildren. Vermilionville eventually became Lafayette, capital of a large part of the prairies, a place high in the affection of the people for miles around. The Mouton descendants prospered and went far in Louisiana public life. One became Governor, while others took rank as leading soldiers and lawyers.

To the south also grew Abbeville, and the manner of its creation is indication of the influence of the church. Abbé A. D. Megret, a Capuchin, decided about 1844 to establish a place of worship at a small, older point, Pont-Perry, or Perry's Bridge. The best that people there offered him was a section that would overflow. He thanked them, and went away; a short distance off he found a spot that he liked. He built a chapel and announced a land development, laying out a tract and inviting all good citizens to move there. The rent would be an annual payment to the church. The place thrived. Pont-Perry slowly pined away; today it is a half-forgotten speck. There is no record that Father Megret ever expressed anything but pious regret.

On higher land at the north, the older Post of Opelousas held its place as a trading center and a place of transfer on the westward trail. It eventually had cosmopolitan ways of its own, attracted a Creole population, and developed as its port Washington on the Bayou Courtableau—jokingly described by others as "Washington D'Ici, District of Courtableau." The Courtableau was an important connection point for steamboats with the rest of the colony; for Opelousas it became a Frankenstein. It threatened to outstrip its parent, and demanded that it be made the parish seat. But eventually it dwindled; its bayou was closed off, and Washington now sits stranded, a pleasant little place of decayed landings. Some term it "Washington Deceased." And Opelousas has remained.

For years a pastoral quiet hung over the broad acres. Men watched the skies and their soil, and worried little about the outside. But in 1859 there broke over the region a series of internecine clashes that led large bands of men to defy the force of the state. It was a Louisiana version of cattle stealing and its counteraction, the work of comités de vigilance—a part of the state's history that has received comparatively little attention. The place remained in many respects a frontier, and eventually it attracted a scattering of men from other places, ready to work with some of the natives to turn advantage to profit. At roundup time, some of the cattle raisers discovered that they had many head less than they had expected.

They were inclined at first to blame the winter weather, or disease. Then they noticed other things; they heard prowlers at night, and saw strange men galloping away in the distance. A family might leave the dance at night to find its mounts gone; a young son sobbed as he told of dark-visaged men who took off most of the herd before he could get help.

But the prairies were so large, the law so far off . . . The settlers did little. Sometimes, too, they suspected sons of their friends, and how should a man act in such a case? The marauders increased, accordingly, in numbers and in scope of operations. Men were stopped in the day hours, relieved of their stock, and told that they were fortunate to be let off so lightly. Town stores and crossroad settlements were attacked, looted, and burned, and men were murdered on both sides. Officials finally intervened, and brought cases to trial. Suspicion had been growing that higher-ups, of intelligence and material resources, were connected with the bands. At the bar for the accused appeared several of the most prosperous men of the area, and coincidences indicated other ties of a political nature.

Juries were weighted, witnesses "fixed." Alexandre Barde, who gave a contemporary account, offers an instance. One night an Acadian found a bandit in the act of removing one of his most valued pieces of livestock. They eyed each other; the owner told the other that he "had him at last." Not yet, said the second man. "You have better sense than that; you know this is my cow. You sold her to me, and I paid you before witnesses. I can prove it by ten of them." When the matter went to court, the accused man brought forward fifteen; he had underestimated his ability to obtain backers.

In St. Martinville, a great fire broke out in the night and spread in several directions; eleven men died in an explosion in one building. The country people, coming into town to inspect the scene, found pieces of clothing, laces, and broken liquor casks on the roads. The flames, it became clear, had been set by looters for their purpose. Feelings reached a high point. Through the territory men met and argued, then announced that they had formed comités de vigilance, one for each prairie area. "Crime has its army in our midst," declared a proclamation. . . . "He that sows the wind shall reap the whirlwind." Each group organized as a "court" to try violators. Men were taken from their homes on "warrants" of arrest, or pursued for miles into neighboring areas. The "sentence" might be the same as was imposed by the courts; again, it was more severe. Many were given short periods in which to leave, or they were placed on boats or stagecoaches for Texas or New Orleans. Others were stretched on the ground and lashed. The vigilante groups were anxious to "try" men who had been freed by fixed juries or by other means; and the complainants carried out the verdicts against the men who had supposedly robbed them. Accused men sometimes fled, or died in battles with those who sought them out; and now and then bitter moments came, when cousin faced cousin, or uncle stared at nephew on the night of judgment.

Private armies were formed by the committees, with three to four thousand men under march and drill. "Anti-vigilance" groups rose and also collected arms. Open war was imminent. The issue stirred men about the state; the Governor rebuked the vigilantes and demanded that they disband. He and others asked how it could all end. Who could say that the committees were correct in all their actions? [2] The vigilantes denied

[2] Some claimed inequities in the committees' work, and asked why higher-ups went unmolested. One man was lashed and banished, according to Barde, merely for "denouncing the comité de Vermilion." Yet three others

that there were abuses, and went ahead despite the Governor. The use of troops was threatened, and meanwhile the two sides lined up.

The "anti's" gathered ammunition at a farm along the Bayou Queue de Tortue. About 1800 of the opposition assembled there, ostensibly for a barbecue; the other side declared that the "anti's" planned to march on Vermilionville, rob and burn it. All the comités sent representatives to a central band of about 700 soldiers; these descended on the farm, with a cannon. Through loopholes in the wall, gun muzzles waited for them. A parley, under a flag of truce, failed. The vigilantes fired their cannon, and the "anti's" broke away in panic, men, women, and children running from the house to the bayou and woods. Two hundred were captured; most of them pledged themselves not to offend again. About eighty, said to be ringleaders, were stripped and placed on the ground, one next to the other. The vigilantes, taking whips, then vented their fury upon them.

Despite the gunfire and angry emotions, only one man had died, and he took his own life to avoid capture. The "anti's" had left behind a thousand pieces of unused equipment. The brass cannon, heroine of the day, had the name of "Betsy"; the event lives on as the Battle of Turtle Tail Bayou. The comités dissolved, and the prairies had peace after a year of turmoil. The respite was brief; soon the natives of the bayous and prairies were fighting other brothers, men of the

were ordered only to leave after they were said to have indulged in "robbery, sometimes murder, often burning and perjury . . . piracies, night expeditions, and cattle stealing"; as a final offense, they had celebrated an improper acquittal by going to the funeral of an adverse witness and singing obscene lyrics to the music of psalms. The "Franklin Banner" declared that "none but poor men" had been punished, and asked if the movement, good in origin, had not been "run into a speculation" by which some obtained control of property at sacrifice prices.

North in the Civil War. But never since, in war or in peace, have the prairies seen the organized rage of those days.

The later years have brought their changes, in agriculture, in cattle raising, in further settlement. The prairies are no longer quite so open. Farms press in, and the countryside does not raise so great a volume of cattle for market, though many still have small domestic herds, and efforts are being made to return the industry to its former state. Over the northern part, about Opelousas, cotton has become the main crop; cane has further decreased, and men have had to devise substitutes. Dudley LeBlanc introduced me to the aged Madame Gary near Abbeville, and she said, sadly, that things were harder now than in the old days. "Everything was so fertile then. . . . So many cattle; cotton with its bolls high in the air, and birds everywhere. When people talked then about needing commercial fertilizer, we laughed. We don't laugh now." The prairies, it seems, are a part of the South which for too long mined its soil and forgot its future. But most of the families hold to what they have received from the past, and hope for better in the days ahead; and the buggies still jog "behind the backlands."

§ 15. *The Bride Had Paper Flowers*

PERHAPS IT WAS because I was there during the spring; but I heard more about l'amour et le mariage in the prairie area than in any other part of South Louisiana. I was privileged to watch several weddings with their many accompanying fetes; and they were demonstrations in mass pressure, mass curiosity, and inherited custom.

Everybody is expected to get married, and the sooner the better. Older accounts tell of weddings at twelve or thirteen, and of grand'mères in their late twenties. Time has sent the scale upward; today the ages on the priests' records are more often sixteen and seventeen or higher. One of the favorite nursing songs of the mothers, addressed to "Minette" (Kitten), tells her:

> Go to sleep, my little one
> Until the years to fifteen run.
> When the fifteen years have fled,
> Then my Kitten will be wed.

Many have heard the young husband, not out of his teens, address his fresh-faced wife as "ma vieille" (my old woman). The attractive Clothilde Gautreaux, with whose family I visited, explained the situation: A girl expects several proposals before she is twenty-one; if she reaches twenty-three without a wedding, she has reason for alarm. She is edging into the ranks of the poor old maids; her friends will be arranging little parties at which she will meet acceptable prospects. "At twenty-six—c'est too bad!"

Double weddings are common. (Old M. Durand of St. Martinville was no innovator in that respect, with his spider-and-gold-dust affair.) Triple weddings are not unknown, as a result sometimes of the adroit persuasion of friends who feel that such a thing is joli. Clothilde Gautreaux was to be married that summer, and so was one of her friends. Clothilde's younger sister, Annette, was being pushed toward agreement to a third simultaneous ceremony. Mildly annoyed at the moment, Annette told me: "You don' have a mind of your own aroun' here. Everybody make' it up for you. They think a bad marriage is better than none." Her aunt, who listened near-by, had a retort: And how did somebody know a marriage was bad, chère, until she tried it? A little later, I overheard some of the arguments placed before Annette. "Come on, 'Net. You know you like Gros Bosco. What do you want to wait for? Sure he like' you. I know. I aksed him myself, already. Why you getting red, 'Net? Everybody know' you and him are going to make mariage sometime, ahn?"

But Annette was a stubborn Acadian, and she was still resisting Bosco and the community when I left. She was still going to and from the Saturday dances with her family; and that meant much. Once she let Gros Bosco escort her, all would know that there was an engagement. Custom, to be sure, is not quite so rigid as formerly; but even today a girl who lets herself be taken to a dance by a boy runs the risk of the old women's chatter.

In any event, only a two-couple wedding could be held, with Clo and her young man—who was soon to go into the army—and her friend Amélie and Amélie's farmer-fiancé. I thought that I had watched joy in chaos when I saw and heard families meet and talk on Lafourche; it was a quiet sight and a whisper compared with the gathering of these four households to plan the events. As in most such cases, it developed that relatives on all the sides were previously connected, somewhere, and would become more closely intertied by the latest nuptials. Zu Gautreaux asked Papa if he knew that Nonc Boots was already cousin to Bosco; and Tante Sappho, she was cousin secondaire, for true, to Ti' Dado. What did that make him, he wanted to know?

Days before the ceremony, the families were deep in preparation and in flour. For the bride's family, the ceremony meant, above most things, cakes. Next to bride and groom, that was the most essential item. For days the girls and their mothers and friends labored over the stoves, preparing dozens of them—small, large, massive. One room in the house of each bride became the cake room; one of the girls was assigned a vital function, that of maintaining a watch against ants. Her weapons were woolen rags soaked in kerosene and tied at the feet of the tables. The prairie people know of no better insecticide. Meanwhile Clo and her Maman were worrying over the supply of the cakes. There could not be too many; their concern was that one of the connoisseurs of weddings would look around and sniff. . . . "Hm. . . . Not so many gateaux with the Gautreaux, ahn?" That would be a wrong start for a marriage.

The day arrived, Saturday, always the favored one because everybody can attend early and stay into the night for many happenings. I arrived at the Gautreaux house as instructed, shortly after seven in the morning, and helped Papa and the boys move most of the furniture from the two front rooms to make places for the people and the dancing later in the day; Maman, meanwhile, was checking over her carefully husbanded supply of wine and coffee and food on the stove. This was not to be a house wedding; the nuptial Mass at the church was set for ten o'clock, and soon the bridesmaids were gathering, to make final changes to their costumes of red, green, and yellow. (In some cases of which I had heard, the husband-to-be purchased the wedding gown; once he bought the whole trousseau. It might, I thought, be a happy augury of generosity to come; but the Gautreaux looked down on the practice. That was only something that gee-gees in the swamp did, Maman assured me.)

Finally, I had a good look at the bride. Clo was brilliantly attired in her white satin, with white gloves and veil; and in her arms she carried a large bouquet of flowers, made of paper. It is the invariable custom; a bride who marched in with real blossoms . . . people would look at each other; that would be a big head, sure. There are no florists in such places; garden flowers are often not available. At least they were unavailable in the old days; and so the practice has continued. Each maid, too, had her paper bouquet, to match her dress, in red, yellow, and green roses.

It was, of course, to be a buggy wedding. The number was overpowering: I lost count, but there were probably more than a hundred. I found my place with the rest and bowed right and left with the others to the men and women who stood at their gates and called to us. The other bridal party preceded us by a few minutes, from its house, and was waiting. The bride and rest of our group had difficulty for a moment in getting into the church. The little building had been filled long ago, and friends now covered the front steps. We forced ourselves inside and crowded into some of the already tightly packed pews. The two grooms awaited the two brides, and they were a study in formalism: black suit, heavy black gloves, a flower of paper in the buttonhole. (A renter of wedding suits does a brisk trade. Sitting next to me, a man told me that he had outfitted five in the Gautreaux family with this same suit. "The Gautreaux always come in the same size," he nodded.)

The ceremony, in French, was highly effective, and the two Mamans did the expected thing by crying, and several tantes and both nainaines of the brides joined them. The service, however, was slightly curtailed. Father Gardelle had just received word that somebody was dying, and he had to hurry things a bit. As we left, the wheel rolled off a buggy, and one tante who was in it had a nerve attack. Clo's groom remarked anxiously that it was a good sign, yes? and added, Or a bad one, ahn? Everybody in earshot assured him it was a good omen.

We went around a bit, just for the ride, and finally we were back at the Gautreaux home—both brides, both grooms, and the others. Tables were covered with food, drinks, and of course the cakes. Everybody had to eat and then eat again, and make toasts and jokes. A pleasant surprise was an old-time band of young men from a neighboring town, célébrités de musique. I heard them from eleven in the morning until half-past seven at night, with hardly a letup, and I had opportunity to learn directly of the subject.

The ancient Acadian notes and the ancient Acadian words still lived here—French, but their own kind of French. Irene Whitfield put it well when she called it "music in dialect." It was jerky, of irregular beat, slurring from one note to the next. Neither the singer nor the players were purists; when they decided to add a sound, they added a sound, and no one noticed the difference. The accordion was king, the violin his prime minister, and the man-of-all-work was the holder of the "ti' fers" or triangles. To add to the rhythm, the musicians used their feet, and so did some of the old people while the young ones danced. The accordionist, one Ti' Dan, was also the singer, and a man of unquestionable personality. Used to the spotlight, he took charge, inserted the brides' and grooms' names in his songs, made jokes to and about them, and called for more wine. It did not matter that he lacked a voice of much pretension; he did many things with what he had. Anybody could hit notes and look sad, but he went falsetto, grunted, squeaked, and smiled, gyrated in his seat, cocked head to side, winked, and raised eyebrows. Throughout the day, when they were not dancing the girls watched Ti' Dan, open-mouthed and impressed.

We heard songs of longing, of jubilation, of boasting; new songs, old songs, ballads in antique style, others that showed the American influence; and always the subject was l'amour, with a masculine view. I cannot say why, but few Acadian songs are those of women; this is a man's world in music as in other things. Everybody wanted to hear "Jolie Blonde," that favorite about the fellow whose blonde turned away from him. He sings of her cruelty; his plaint is tragic until he reaches the last line or two. Then he quietly informs her that he has found another and lets her know that he is managing quite well. A lament that ends on a note of revenge, it is definitely not in the romantic groove. I remember also that the players offered "Bye-Bye, Fedora," in the traditional vein; and one finds a true story there, as Miss Whitfield has noted. Years ago, Léonce Trahan of Rayne, an accordionist, loved Fedora Uzée. Fedora preferred Arthur Lagrappe; and in the proper story-fashion, Léonce agreed to play for their wedding. He had a song which he had written for the occasion; he offered it to her and to the world; and as she heard it, the bride quietly dropped her veil, so that all would not see her crying. . . .

The day and the music went on. Two or three times the players took a rest. In each case, someone turned on the Gautreaux phonograph, and we had more of the same music. When the first phonograph arrived on the prairies, many shook their heads. It was another blow at the good français; soon only those American words and music would be heard from morning to night. The Acadians did sit for hours before their machines, but it was Acadian song that came forth. One firm made a few records and sold every one of them, several companies for years have issued volumes of them, in the patois. Inns and restaurants along the road have their juke boxes stocked with Acadian records; and on this day the Gautreaux guests played a collection of a dozen, over and over, with unflagging enthusiasm.

The other couple eventually left for a party at their home, and after dark, the Gautreaux fete reached a climax. Nonc Tel' rose, and the noisy ones were nudged, for quiet. It was the event which all expected—the "addresse aux mariés." A traditional talk, it was a simple lecture on the new life that was before the young ones. Because of its lack of ornament, and the warm humanity of its lines, it was a highly affecting thing. Everybody told his neighbor to watch how ol' Nonc's eyes were crying, too; and how Clo had put her lil' hand into the hand of her new husband. For days afterward, people would be saying how well Nonc did it. Now the crowd prepared to leave, with kisses and handshaking. There was one more event on the day's program, the wedding dance—the bal de noce. It was to be somewhere else, at a near-by dance hall. After some unsuccessful attempts to locate a real fais-do-do in other sections, I had been assured that I would find one here.

I wanted a good look at the dance places, and so I preceded the bridal party. There were at least four other halls within a radius of a few miles, and all were in full operation. Each looked the same—a long, unpainted, unornamented wooden rectangle. Connected to it was a one-room store or grocery, and usually an additional chamber on the other side, for the card players of weekdays and week ends. Immediately inside the main door was a large bar; behind it stretched the wide dance floor. On three sides ranged a series of windows, along them and below them a double row of wooden benches. The first arrivals sat on the top bench, to be in the cool; latecomers packed themselves beside them or reluctantly took the lower place. Whole families were in attendance, mères, pères, m'mères, p'pères, tantes, noncs, bébés. Maman got to work at once in most cases to feed the smallest one at her breast; it was better that he be satisfied now and go to sleep.

I had heard often of the old days when a "parc aux petits" thrived, as a separate side room in which the Mamans deposited their children while they danced. This is passing away; only one hall, the oldest and smallest, had it on this occasion. There, a dozen and a half of the youngest progeny were sleeping or crying or fighting on a large bed, in the charge of one of the older women. She explained to me that she paid her pew rent at church with her fees; and she pointed out the children's mères as they moved about the floor. It was difficult to tell most of them from the other young girls. There is a well-known saying among Acadians about children who look like neither mother nor father. "They must sure have gotten them mixed up at some fais-do-do." The old woman sniffed at the legend; she had never confused bébés in her life. Then she excused herself to serve as arbiter in a bitter dispute among three of the larger enfants.

At the other places, the family looked after its own. Maman passed the youngest to a sister or a friend when she wanted to dance; if she were a popular matron, someone held him for her all evening. Those in whose custody the child was left watched warily to make sure that none of the dancers came in contact with him. Once I came upon the ultimate in baby protection. A grand'mère brought an egg crate with her. Over it she had carefully fashioned a screen cover; Bébé went inside, safe from mosquitoes and crowd, and Grand'mère could watch everything about her with ease.

At the dance hall in which the Gautreaux party would appear, someone handed me "the announcement," a printed dodger with three-inch letters telling of the event. The arrangement that had been made was based on common sense and public demand. Clo and her husband knew that people for miles about wanted to see them; they themselves had been to many such wedding dances. The operator sought extra crowds.

Competition for the event had developed as soon as rumors spread that the banns were to be published. Rival dance-hall managers "requested" the event; each promised something, usually a cash minimum, plus percentages of the receipts or a free-will offering taken from the crowd. A good bargainer, I was informed by one of them, could get $10 for a couple; in rare cases, with large and popular families, the figure could be run to $15, but hardly higher. I had heard part of the dickering over Clo's wedding, and it was a deal between hard traders. It ended at $12 and the privilege of the collection from the audience. (The other couple had been "taken" by another hall; the Gautreaux family confided that these received only $8. A four-dollar difference in family acclaim was something to be proud of.) The operator said he was sure that he would lose at the $12 figure. When I looked at the crowd, I put his remarks down as talk for the record.

The bar was lined up two deep. The men could stay there all evening, if they wished, and watch the dancing over a rail. To go on the floor meant payment of admission. All women, children, and old men could go in free; for the younger men there were differences in rates. Young sprouts, in fact bachelors of all ages, paid more than married men, twenty-five cents instead of fifteen. The gatekeeper, it appeared, had to know his neighbors; his ruling was seldom questioned. Strangers like me were assumed to be single, at a quarter a head, unless they could prove otherwise.

Between dances the girls stayed to themselves, the men to the other side, much as in the old days, all under the surveillance of the older women. A girl who moved among the men would be "showing herself," and would regret it. The women saw that things generally were as they wished; if they disapproved, they could move in a body to a rival place, and ruin the proprietor. Now the hall was filling, and some were restless. What was the delay, M'sieu Naquin? Was it true that other fellow got the bride and groom away from you? Hastily M'sieu Naquin denied it, and sent a second messenger to Clo's house. Such rumors are heavy when rivalry for a bal de noce has been particularly strong; and sometimes they turn out to be true.

In the middle of the dance number the crowd at the entrance stirred, and word spread quickly. The wedding party had arrived. I hurried with the others to the front door and peered as M'sieu Naquin conferred with them. The bride developed shyness; and that was not hard to understand, with all those eyes watching and mouths moving. Clo protested that she would rather go home; she had a bad headache, yes. The groom thought that it would be a good idea; see how she was nervous, everybody. His own hands trembled as he glanced at the throng. But the manager and the relatives were firm. At last it was agreed that the couple need stay only a short time. Clo took her husband's arm, the maids those of the groomsmen, and M'sieu Naquin, with his arms and a stick, pushed a way through for them.

The music stopped and all rushed forward to see and comment. The bridal party was in full attire, veil and paper-flower bouquets, black gloves and the rest. This was part of the requirement; it must be just as it was at the ceremony. Clo took her veil in one hand and her flowers in the other as she elbowed in. Several women reached out to feel the material of her costume; and many made audible comment on the appearance of the other members of the bridal party. The group reached the floor; M'sieu Naquin raised his arms and his stick for silence, and signaled to the musicians. It was the grand march for the bridal party. Everybody else was ordered back, while the couples circled the room. "Slow! Slow!" M'sieu Naquin directed them, but they continued at a pace far in advance of the music. These were no gracious masquerade monarchs, sweeping scepters in proud splendor over all about them. They gazed earnestly ahead, moving their lips only when someone yelled "Allo, Clo!" or "Hi there, Goo!"

Back at their starting point, a half chorus ahead of the accompanists, they asked what to do next. M'sieu Naquin, hovering protectively, motioned to the players. The first dance for the bridal party; the couples formed partners and moved about to a livelier tune. They were at greater ease now, and Clo giggled at something her husband said. By the time the next dance was over, Clo's cheeks had regained their normal color, and the groom was no longer wetting and re-wetting his lips. They went on dancing with the crowd, and stayed through most of the evening. Before long, the others lost their avid interest; Maman Gautreaux took the paper flowers and held them carefully. They would be put away as a souvenir of the occasion. She still had hers in her trunk.

Where was P'Père, Adele? Outside, smoking with his friends, as usual; he was in an argument with that farceur Dezain. M'Mère shook her head; wouldn't he never understand that Dezain made jokes with everybody? "Look there on the floor," one of the Gautreaux children told me. Pierre, who was eight, was dancing with Cléonie, nine, just like they were grown up, and all the crowd was smiling. "Ain' that fine, Papa?" asked Maman. "Look to Cléonie, Papa! Papa! Eh bien!" Maman sighed. That man, he was always more interest' in his cards than his chir'ren, she would tell anybody that. . . .

Midnight came and then one o'clock, and the bridal party was ready to leave. M'sieu Naquin raised his hand. As everybody knew, the nice little couple were about to start the new life; and the way to start off a new life was with a little gift. His son would pass around, and everybody ought to give. Nickels and dimes came forth from friends and from strangers; the amount was almost as large as the operator's own payment. Clo and her husband slipped out a side door. They had planned to go at once to his family's, to a room set aside for them. But friends with a larger place had provided a more private one for the first few days of the mariage. Then they would set up their things at the other house. There would be no honeymoon. The husband could afford nothing like that. Besides, his père never had it, had he?

In the rural corners, I learned of another kind of marriage, without music. It is a mariage de contrat, a kind of semiformal recognition of a common-law relationship. The two partners call upon an attorney and sign or mark an agreement, with affidavit, notarial seal, and other embellishments. Worded with "wherefores" and "let it be knowns," it declares simply that the couple have decided to live as man and wife. The custom is declining; the church works hard, of course, against it. I saw two such "contracts," and a former attaché informed me that a couple once filed such a document with him in court. The practice developed, an elderly prairie woman explained, when "the impediment was there. . . . She found a man who loved her but had a wife, or something like that; and they usually moved together to another place." Years later, in some cases, when "the impediment" was removed, the couple went to a priest for a ceremony.

"Jumping over the broomstick" is another way in which a man and woman have inaugurated an informal connection. The two stand together; "witnesses" hold the stick a foot or so above the floor, and the pair hop over together. In one case, dating back some years, an English-speaking neighbor was invited to such a ceremony; one man, directing it, went through a kind of service in which he asked the partners whether they were willing to stay with each other. There followed cakes, drinks, and kissing of the bride.

More recently, a French welfare worker happened to arrive in an outlying area at the time of a rite combining "contract" and "broomstick." The neighbors had gathered. The bride had a white dress and long veil, tucked in her belt for convenience, and her paper flowers; and she also wore tennis shoes. The groom was attired more simply, in tan shirt, tan trousers, and tieless collar. After the broomstick was jumped, an "official" wrote out a brief statement in French, to which the others attached their marks. Then the bride, groom, and older men took penknives and fixed their marks on the door of the nuptial chamber.

The Second World War further discouraged these practices and simultaneously brought an increase in "late marriages," as the local term has it. To establish a claim for dependents' pay, it was necessary to establish recognized dependents.

§ 16. Prairie Good Time

THE WORLD has heard much of the New Orleans Mardi Gras, with its tall floats of papier-mâché, kings riding high above the populace, and costume balls with tableaux. For generations the prairies have had their rural version, less formalized, less costly, and in one instance, as I know, at least as much fun.

"Courir Mardi Gras" (running Mardi Gras) is the name of the observance. This Fat Tuesday is almost a race, and a daylong one. A thing primarily for men and horses, it consists of impromptu hell-raising that has no place for the girls; no queens on balconies, no costume ball with court of honor, although there is a happy fais-do-do in the evening.

I had talked over the subject with some of the old-timers and others who knew only the Mardi Gras of their later day. All said that the custom, unfortunately, was slipping away. Once it had started early and gone on for days; now it was reduced to a single day. Some of the localities that had continued it were giving it up, one by one. Be that as it may, a country friend remembered me a week in advance, and I arrived in his section for the occasion of man's final fling before the forty days of Lent.

Down the road that morning came the runners on their mounts, ten to fifteen of them, masked and in clown's attire, in stripes and dots and other raffish garments of reds and yellows. One fat man had donned two potato sacks, which did not quite encompass his poundage; another wore what was clearly a borrowed, well-pinned set of curtains. Several sported about in women's clothes, with toy parasols and dolls; and these had donned wigs, bustles, stuffed brassières, and other added attractions. All were "acting the macaque" (monkey). They stopped at a store, waltzed together, sang, and asked for contributions from the grocer for their coming ball. On the road, when they met a lone man or woman, he or she was the object of fulsome attention. One of the clowns requested the honor of the dance. The lady might decline, but she was danced with whether she liked it or not. If the man rejected the offer of a waltz with one of those in female attire, he was paddled, or lost his pants for a few moments.

With the roving band went a fiddler, blowers of cowhorns, and wielders of other noise-making devices. As they moved about, their calls drew families from their houses to the road. One man was in charge of the runners, and he went forward in each case to inquire if the household were willing to receive them. The answer was almost always "Oui," and the Mardi Gras men dismounted and surrounded the family and the farm. They danced about the yard, sang, frightened some children, delighted others, and guyed the adolescents. "Eh there, Ti' Jean, when you goin' ask that lil' brown-hair girl to marry you?" At the house of the girl, one of the maskers would inform her that Ti' Jean had announced himself as bored of waiting for her, and was looking for a blonde.

Soon, as everybody expected, the party approached the important matter of "the request." A traditional song, a series of doggerels that has been used for generations, was offered. In it the Mardi Gras was asked whence he came. Why, he came from Angleterre (England), and in midwinter. He went on to tell of his prowess as a drinker, of his various feats; and the singers declared themselves "good gentlemen" and made a formal petition for a "little fat hen"—always a fat one by tradition. If the farmer agreed, the men scrambled after the fowl, and it went into a large bag that one of the younger members carried. A drink was in order at each stop; when the host had none to offer, he was invited to take a mouthful or two from the bottles of the runners. The visit ended with musical merci's to the mesdames et messieurs, and a request to be with the revelers that night to dance and "manger le gros gumbo." [1]

Several times, I noted, the stop was at the home of a member of the party; and here he was at his gayest, disguising voice and manner with special care. Invariably, Maman and the rest knew him from the first moment or two; to please his vanity, they pretended that he was, in truth, a stranger from England or some other weird place. Finally, in most cases, one of the bébés murmured, "Allo, Papa," and the spell was broken. Everybody had the laugh on Papa, who said that he knew they knew all the time.

The spoils had been gathered by late afternoon, and the wives of the runners went to work upon them. Iron washpots were brought forth, fires were built under them, and gumbo was started. Hours of preparation, salting, tasting, exclamations when feathers were found in the thick soup; and then the women went home to dress before serving the meal. All the runners boasted of their powers of gumbo consumption; I saw one tired and soggy Mardi Gras consume seven heavy dishfuls and move on to the rest of the evening without visible

[1] Mrs. Kollitz of Crowley has preserved a record of a Mardi Gras song which she heard years ago. It agrees in most verses with the one that I heard—though the latter was shorter—and with the ones used in the neighborhood of Nilas Young of the northern prairie. Others at Southwestern Louisiana Institute have contributed recollections of the older Mardi Gras, and Lauren C. Post, who has given much study to the prairie country, described the Mardi Gras in the *Louisiana State Alumni News* of January, 1936.

mishap. Later I found that he stayed in bed for a week afterward.

One prairie man who was a great runner of Mardi Gras decided a few years ago to take a trip to New Orleans for the much-touted day. He came back in disappointment. He thought it a dull affair—"no spice."

Only one other South Louisiana institution can match the Mardi Gras in its semiregulated horseplay, and that is the French-style charivari. The custom has been common along many bayou areas, but it seems to have survived in particular style along the prairies. It is the matter of inequality, or lack of balance, that makes for charivari. A widower of fifty-eight takes a bride of eighteen. Ho-ho, he has a noise coming to him, that one. What you think, ahn? Les' make charivari. . . . A widow with seven children mates with a stripling, or any man not previously married. Ha, this will be *a* night, Maman! Yet when widow and widower marry, there is no cause for such a serenade in roughhouse. That is a "new marriage"; the two start with the same status.

Things are at their best when those to be charivaried do not like it, and show their feelings. If someone has a good friend in the household, one who enjoys a joke, he may arrange to slip in on the wedding day and "fix" the nuptial bed. It may be adjusted so that it will collapse whenever the couple place themselves upon it. Or heavy cowbells are attached to the springs; and the crowd will be below the window in the evening, listening, perhaps tossing in suggestions. "Ah, there, Alphonse!" Many a wedding bed has not been slept in because of those in attendance outside.

I had been talking about the custom with several prairie friends. There had been none in their neighborhood for several years, though some had heard of a recent one several miles away. If I had only been here a few months earlier . . . they were very regretful. . . . Then one evening, a knock woke me, and a breathless man was at the door. I wanted charivari, I had told him? I wanted charivari, I answered. Well, for Chrissakes, come on; they were ready to start one just outside the nearest town. I hurried into my clothes; on the way he gave the details. This old fellow, a merchant, with ten children by his first wife, who had died eight months ago, had married a young girl just out of convent school, and had returned with her a short while ago from New Orleans. They were just having supper, and the serenading band could get there before bedtime. The new husband was something of a skinflint by general reputation, and the thought of a charivari had developed spontaneously during the day. We stopped when we saw—rather, heard—a crowd. More than a hundred men were gathered along the road.

They carried buckets and heavy spoons or bars of metal with which to beat them; cowbells, dishpans, horns, saxophones, anything else that gave promise of making noise loud and long. One man waved an alarm clock, which rang without letup. Another had borrowed an oil company parade drum with cymbals. As we took our places with the others, a fellow came up and asked whom the charivari was for. (No explanation of the purpose of such a gathering is needed; a man spots a charivari at once.) When he heard, he admitted that he knew nothing of the bridegroom, but he wanted to take part. He had a brother on the fire engine, and if we would wait a minute, he would borrow the siren. He was an important addition.

The charivari had twelve leading members. "It's like a law," explained one of the older men. All of this elite group must be over twenty-one, and it is customary that they be at least acquainted with the couple. They started the march, the drum beater and the siren man close behind them. It was a clamorous procession from the start; but when the house came in sight, the whooping, howling, singing, and caterwauling intensified. A light that had been on, suddenly flicked off. Oh, oh; so they were going to be mean about it, were they? The crowd was not displeased at the prospect of a clash of wills.

For an uninterrupted hour and a half, the unwanted visitors screamed, whistled, and made sounds of all varieties. The siren whined, the alarm bell rang, the drum boomed, the spoons clanged. From the neighboring farms others came out; few would sleep until the couple gave in. Still the house remained dark. The crowd did not enter the gate or go up the steps. The rules warned against trespassing, my friend told me. How long would we stay? I asked. Oh, another few hours, maybe. And if they still had not come out—we had lost? He smiled at my naïveté. "Hell, non. We have right to make noise thirty nights in success," he pointed a finger. "After that, it is too much."

One of the neighbors, smiling, called over to ask when it would stop. His wife had sent him; he confided that he was enjoying it. The crowd made its determination clear to him, and he volunteered his services. He went up the stairs, knocked several times, explained who he was; the door opened a crack. A muttered conversation, silence, another consultation, and then he returned. They admitted defeat! The crowd yipped and beat harder. Out came the husband, in his suspenders. Everybody realized that he was in a rage; but he dared not show it. He stood alone, waiting for the noise to diminish. But the crowd was not satisfied. He knew the regulations; there would be no end of it until bride as well as groom appeared in symbol of joint submission. Reluctantly the husband went back, and the girl appeared with him.

"Kiss 'er!"

The bride demurred, then agreed. The husband turned to ask the question that is a standard part of the ritual. "What do you want, gentlemen?" It was up to the twelve leaders to answer. They knew, as usual, the financial status of the couple, and they were always reasonable. They would not ask a poor man for too much, but a rich one . . . Wine, they told the merchant. Well, he didn't have so much in the house, he thought. That was all right; we would use that while he sent to the store for more. And he might as well call for whatever cake, sausage, and cheese he had—and a little beer; some of us mightn't like wine. The miser almost blanched, but he had no choice.

"Entrez!" called the leaders to the crowd, and everybody trooped into the house. For the next hour there followed jokes and speeches, while the couple tried to look happier than they felt. The lady had the pleasure of a series of toasts by those who had been charivari-ing her. These were followed by others according to an old formula:

"A Dieu les mariés!" (To God the married ones.)

"A Dieu les noces!" (To God the nuptials.)

Eventually everybody had his fill, shook hands, and left. The couple were now "free." The understanding is that once a charivari crowd has been thus recognized, the event cannot be repeated. The pair sighed in relief and went inside. In a few minutes, according to spies who had done a bit of preparation, the bed fell under them.

I learned of other cases. An amiable acceptance of a charivari, in spirit as in letter, is vitally important. One bride, who had accepted (or taken) a man eighteen years her junior, swung open the door and went quickly through the pre-scribed routine. But she was surly and made the mistake of saying, "Come in, rats!" The next night everything began over again. She apologized and addressed the tormenters as "gentlemen."

When a couple have separated and now come back to-gether, they can be ready for a small charivari to celebrate the new wedding night. Such an event may not provide the best atmosphere for a reunion, but neither husband nor wife has much to say about the matter. And a man and woman need not be married to get the charivari. The countryside may decide that they have been dallying too long, and that a serenade is in order to shame them or hurry them. Sometimes there are whispers that a lady under such circumstances has plotted quietly with the crowd's leaders to push on a slow suitor. That, of course, may merely be the talk of the old maids who have never blushed to the serenaders' raucous shouts. In one instance of which I heard, the uproar had the opposite effect. A man was calling on a widow. He was not really infatuated, "but trying to get himself in love," his brother said. The scheme shamed him, but in a way other than was intended. He went away and married another widow.

Sometimes a kind of fake charivari may be staged by the sly groom himself. The usual events are classed as "charivari "d'ennemi," of an unfriendly or not-too-friendly variety. An-other, less common one is the false type, or "charivari ami-cal." Sensing the inevitable, the new husband will call to-gether a group of his friends and select the twelve leaders. They will come out of the dark on the proper night, engage in polite and courtly serenading; he will open the door in amazement, find out what they wish, and invite them in. Others, who may have been thinking of a charivari of their own, are estopped. There can be no second charivari.

The boucherie, or cooperative country butchery, is the prairie correlation of good fellowship and good meat. It arose out of a supply of cattle, a hot climate, and the prairie man's trust in his fellows. The meat may be scarcer than heretofore, but the other elements are unchanged. Cows and calves, unfortunately, do not come in one- or two-meal sizes. Even a family of twenty can eat only so much in so many days. And there would be that fine animal, So-Soo, going to the bad. It was many years ago that one of the first Hébert sat down with one of the Thibodaux, consulted the nearest Broussard, and had an institution in the making.

Spring makes the family think of fresh meat, and soon Papa is conferring over the fence with his neighbor. When would be the best night for all of them to get together? They ought to start soon; Papa says that the kids are talking boucherie at him every time he walks into the kitchen. The heads of the families in the arrangement usually number from fifteen to twenty-five. They meet and make plans in advance. Each one has a share; one who can write will make out small slips of paper with various future dates upon them, and each will draw a paper out of a hat. Jo-Jo comes first, they find. That means he will bring his on next Friday. Caza comes after him; then you get ready, Cousin Bay. As a farmer outlined it: "They ain' no kick, and no fuss, and no mixup. They can't be, this way."

A good animal of sufficient weight to supply everybody is produced by each man on the allotted date. The job of preparing the animal is not for the amateur; one expert is chosen to serve for all the killings. He need provide no meat of his own; in return for his contribution of supplies and skills, he receives a full share each time. An order for obtaining sections of the animal is now set up—loin, then rump, flank, etc. The man at the top of the list gets this part this time, the others the next, in turn. On the following boucherie day, each man advances a step around the carcass to the adjoining section. None can complain; everybody knows what part of the animal is next. Again, "no kick, no fuss, no mixup." And through the season, every family has a sufficient supply of meat when it needs it, and none goes to waste.

The day of boucherie has a holiday atmosphere. It starts early; the butcher is up and routing out his helpers at one in the morning. I have been present at a number of them; once the operator took pity on a city man and woke me after the harder preliminaries were over. In the other instances, I arose with the others and, like them, cursed the moment. But Madame had hot water for the men and animals, coffee on the stove for the former, and eventually we were awake. Knives flashed, rags and mops worked, and nineteen or twenty neat piles of meat, weighed, sometimes wrapped in paper, were there for all callers. Some liked to come in their buggies, pick up their meat, and get home to start their chores at the usual time; others preferred to stop awhile and enjoy themselves.

For hours, men and sometimes their wives arrived, each with a bucket or burlap bag for the meat. At least a sip of coffee, rationing or no rationing, was there for everybody; Madame learned of the affairs of all her friends; the men argued over matters of their own. Something else waited for each caller: "bouillie," a special by-product of the boucherie. Kidneys, heart, and other parts, left over after the apportion-

ment of meat, are made into a rich kind of stew, highly sea-
soned, highly filling. Some call it "cow gumbo." Somebody
is certain to say on boucherie day that the "bouillie" is really
what he joined the arrangement for. Two high platefuls of
the fine stuff, and I wanted no more food for the rest of
the day.

The same feeling for cooperation that produced the boucherie has combined with the family spirit and given rise to
the rassemblée, the Sunday reunion. In mid-morning the children and the grandchildren leave their homes to converge
on that of M'Mère and P'Père in the country, for a visit that
will last through most of the day. Usually it is a matter only
for the immediate kin, but when I expressed curiosity, an
older acquaintance brought me along for one. The house
was a small and simple one on the prairie outside the town;
on this day it overflowed with children, adults, and a sense
of well-being. It was an occasion of pleasant concourse on
the galerie and about the house; of deference to the wishes
of the two grandparents. But the center of the day's events
was clearly the food, and this was a communal enterprise.

From various directions during the morning came the sons
and daughters and their families, each with a pot or series of
pots. Each housewife had prepared in her own kitchen the
dish at which she excelled. One brought gumbo, another a
roast, another a bowl of jambalaya; one a collection of vegetables, and so on. Earlier the M'Mère had prepared only the
background to the food—bowls of rice, coffee, and bread.
Into the kitchen went each wife as she arrived, to set her materials on the fire for a final warming and to remain near them
to see that no bungler interfered in the final stages. As we
arrived, we and our offering of chicken were completely

eclipsed by an uncle who brought over a freezer of home-made ice cream. He was obviously the children's favorite nonc.

All the tables in the old family's possession were gathered, placed end to end; for lack of space, a few were shoved into separate corners. Of necessity, the meal was served in shifts, to about thirty-five persons—the men first, with the children at the side, then the women. The scene was vociferous and fragrant, all things good-humored and well-seasoned. P'Père whispered that he had forgotten Pierre, his youngest son, had quite so many little ones. Only one large plate was spilled, and each tante was properly flustered at the compliments to her dish that we took care to distribute evenly. Small difficulties were quickly smoothed, and all were on smiling terms when the men got up.

The nine men went to the galerie, to smoke and survey the world. The women were not displeased to have this time to themselves, to relay over their food what they had learned of and from their friends during the previous week. Sitting near the window with one of the husbands, I received a nudge. With him I caught the last of the sentence from inside:

"Mais, yes, she is comme ça!"

In the high-pitched excitement that followed at the table, those on the outside exchanged comments of masculine superiority. We talked about the phrase "like that," which some have thought that Walter Winchell invented. P'Père observed gravely that he had heard it as a boy and was well spanked when he asked his mère what it meant. By this time those inside had been listening to us, and found themselves between amusement and annoyance. M'Mère suggested that perhaps a spanking was in order for some of the men, too, old or young; and we retired to our own subjects. "Stop that fighting out there," one of the fathers called to the children in the yard. "Keep away from that pond; they's an alligator in it." The young ones paid little attention to the last warning, and P'Père chuckled: "They use' to tell us the same thing about alligators. Me, I believe' it. We believe' more then than they do now." On that note the rassemblée came to an end.

Here and there in the southern prairie section about such places as Lafayette, I found a pleasant worship of food, in informal organizations of men who are unified by their appreciation of the good French dish and of a special touch in its preparation. Seven or eight of them will meet every week or so for soirees of food and talk of food. One member usually has a camp near the Gulf or on one of the lakes, and here they converge for fishing and cooking and pleasant rest, without concern for shaving or such things as female concern that men's clothes be unrumpled.

One such group was fairly mixed. The members were two farmers, a doctor, a lawyer, a wholesale merchant, and a seller of buggies. Each was an amateur chef, seeking to outdo the other, jealous of his local repute and of his kitchen prerogatives. They took turns at preparing the meals; and they wanted none of the others to help while they worked. Thus no secrets would slip out to curious rivals. They had many disagreements on details, but all concurred that the basis of success in almost every case was the gravy, or roux. It could be dark brown or light; thick or thin; or a sauce piquante that fitted no other classification. But no gravy meant a weak dish, certainement.

A celebrity of this circle had long been noted for his remarkable daube glacé. He achieved a dark color that none of the others could master. At last, the trick came out. He burned the onions slightly before putting in the other ingredients. A fellow-member surprised him during one of the camping parties by coming forth with an identical concoction. He could not eat for the rest of the day. Returning home, he accused his wife of disclosing the treasured formula at one of her coffee parties. Eventually he regained his equilibrium and invented a substitute.

On the night of such a gathering, the chef comes out of the kitchen, to take his place in dignity at the head of the table, and waits silently for the judgment of his peers. There is a tentative sipping and tasting, a professional cocking of the head; a quick glance at one's neighbor, another sample, the adding of a pinch of salt. One waits for the other to speak. The author of the dish finally asks: "Ahn?" Someone suggests that it is very nice, the best cou'bouillon he's had in some months, yes. But if there had been a shade more mustard, a slight . . . well, more lemon . . . The next man says no, that is not it. The tomatoes, they should have been treated a bit in advance; then they would have another savor. A third will smile and shove aside such quibbles. The cou'bouillon is excellent, excellent—as excellent as one can make it with *this* kind of fish. Now the real way, as he always said . . .

§ 17. *Fringes*

TO THE NORTH and to the west are the edges of the prairies, and the soil and the people blend gradually into those of other regions and other nationalities. In one direction the grasslands rise to meet the piny uplands, with their scrawny earth, small ravines, and eroded sections; with their Anglo-

Saxon folk of somewhat sterner mien. In the other, the prairies continue their even expanse to meet the Texas flatlands, and their contrasting civilization in its own special image. At many points, Louisianians tell you, "This is where the West comes in." But there is, instead, a slow shading. Texas mixes with other Anglo-Saxon elements of western Louisiana, and makes itself felt, in twang and in longer stride, at many points within the state. At the same time, groups of Frenchmen have crossed the line of separation and made the Texans wonder and exclaim.

For many years, until the 1920's, the fringes to the north were a well-mixed borderland about which some shook their heads. The other French had many tales, some plausible, others unverified, about things that happened to strangers who ventured into it. It was a place of Gallic elements on a soil that did not appeal to their fellows: English-speaking men who ventured farther toward the French territory than did their compatriots; the descendants of Spaniards and of Irishmen who came under Spain; a scattering of Mexicans, and others. Some of the pockets among the secluded woods became retreats for men who did not fit easily into the disciplines of more stable areas. One element struck out for such places because it knew that there it would find an obscurity such as it wanted. In other cases, black sheep of French and Anglo-Saxon groups were forced from their previous homes and started toward these sections by their neighbors. There is a tradition that one group of settlers included fleeing pirates of Lafitte when they fell into difficulties on the Texas coast after leaving Louisiana. Many who came, of course, were the small and honest farmers and cattlemen who settled down quietly and sought to make a living on their hard soil. But these were not the ones of whom the rest of Louisiana heard. Outlaw gangs, marauders, jayhawkers, and others infested these stretches for many years; after the Civil War, one of the sheriffs of the country gained recognition by chasing a band as far as Mexico and the Illinois country.

French clans developed in the several prairie and surrounding divisions outside the present center of Ville Platte. Branches of one family nursed grudges against others of the same name, and these grew into deadly hatreds. Patriarchal leadership was accentuated; a clan took the name, as one native put it, of the "biggest bull" of its section, some grand-père of particular force. When men of two such groups met each other, outsiders ran to cover. Eventually each clan had a "limit"; if a member moved into that of a rival, he faced a knifing. Men went about with care, and many watched their tongues; a casual slip, the confusion of one distant cousin with another, could bring unpleasant results. Over the whole area there were comparatively few names; within the clans inter-marriage was not uncommon.

Around the rural fais-do-does occurred many of the inter-family hostilities. One clan made strenuous efforts to break up the dances of another. A direct attack was often attempted, men galloping suddenly out of the dark, armed with bricks, ready to use guns or knives. Or more subtle methods were tried, about which they could boast for many weeks. An obscure member might enter a hall and dance once or twice, then leave. He had previously prepared one of his pockets; a small hole in the bottom permitted a handful or so of red pepper to be released as he moved across the floor. In a short time the coughing, choking dancers had to halt. Equally effective, perhaps more diverting, was a practice of cutting up a horse's mane into tiny bits and dropping them to the floor. As the dancers moved about, the pieces climbed up their legs. "That feels worse than a seven-year itch," chuckled a seventy-year-old woodman who told me how he broke up many a fais-do-do in his day.

Through most of the prairies a certain amount of skylarking always took place when buggies were hitched up outside the dances. Horses' tails were shaved or tied to rails, wheels were unscrewed so that the vehicles would wobble. Here matters went further. A family, leaving the dance, might find the saddles of the horses cut apart, its buggy wedged up in a tree, or other vandalisms. A popular night custom, one of the present officials recalled, was that of picking up and removing bridges across the smaller bayous and coulées. Those riding along a dark passage found themselves, at the least, unpleasantly stalled in the middle of the water. Bad accidents occasionally resulted. When automobiles appeared, the owner who left his machine for a short time might come back to find the top removed; and he might or might not get it back.

Every week end brought fights, sometimes several killings. In clashes without weapons, battlers went first for each other's eyes, trying to gouge them out, and kicked at groins and tore at lips. Implements were guns or ten-inch files, the latter sharpened at both ends, with a corncob in the middle for a handle. With such an instrument, adversaries usually sought to accomplish a quick disemboweling. Sometimes, however, there were duels of a frontier variety—"bataille fair-play."

A man bearing several marks of such a battle described a typical one. A referee supervised it, providing a large bandanna handkerchief. Each combatant took an end in his teeth, his knife in his hand. Each held tight with his teeth and slashed at the other, who turned and twisted and did his own hacking. This might go on for many minutes, until one staggered over his prostrate foe, or both collapsed. Because of their native hardihood, both contestants might live. A doctor told me of a case in which a man survived two dozen cuts, several of them deep ones of stomach and chest. His rival was permanently crippled.

On Sunday morning, after the dances, men met each other and asked: "Well, where was the boucherie last night?" Some survivals are found today. A typical Saturday evening conversation, preliminary to blood spilling, is this:

"I wan' see you outside."

"Pourquoi?"

"You dance twice in succeed with my girl. I wan' my satisfied."

Or a youth walks in, red-eyed, hat on back of head, handkerchief hanging jauntily from rear pocket, and announces, in patois:

"Je l'met des hommes, oui." (I'm a man, yes.)

"Te pas mo metre à moin." (You're no more man than I am.)

"Non?"

"Non."

Others draw back or step into position to join the fray, and the women scream and move to safety. A doctor, out on a maternity call, has to leave it for this emergency.

Hostility toward others, particularly town people, showed itself until comparatively late days. A man driving his car into the remote sections found barbed wire across the road from tree to tree, or ground glass at intervals. Some of the citizens of Ville Platte told me that this was "mainly for fun," as a prank upon native and stranger alike. Others declared that certain of the natives feared too inquisitive inquiries into their affairs; bootlegging was sometimes a lucrative business, as it would be in almost any section so located. Another recalled that an additional reason for such elaborate protection was a desire to "protect their girls from strangers," particularly from poachers of the other clans. A driver of a buggy or automobile was halted again and again en route and asked just what he wanted. If his answers were not satisfactory, he was turned back; and it was not often that he argued with the grim men who stood before him.

As would be expected in view of the presence of the Anglo-Saxon element, Protestantism gained recruits. The country was the object of early efforts by a number of religious groups. Joseph Willis, a Baptist and a mulatto, moved to Louisiana in 1804, shortly after it became American. He first tried Vermilionville and several other points in the southern prairies, giving what have been termed the first non-Catholic sermons to be preached in the area west of the Mississippi. "Both his color and his being a Baptist exposed him to violent prejudices," and he was threatened a number of times, according to the Reverend Mr. W. E. Paxton in his history of Louisiana Baptists. He left, but returned a year later and chose a place in the more remote stretches to the north, Bayou Chicot. Here he did well, establishing the first of a series of Protestant churches that dotted the area. Some of his congregation undoubtedly were of the American group, but it is declared that a certain number called him "Father Willis."

One part of this borderland finally incorporated itself, among the last of the state's parishes to be formed, shortly before the First World War; and ironically enough, it took the name of the gentle heroine of the Acadians—Evangeline. Conditions changed but slowly. Robert Gahn, Southwest Louisiana native, in his history of the parish reports that in a twenty-eight-year period, a total of 110 persons were charged with homicides, but only two were sentenced to die. Over two years, fifteen were cited for murder; all escaped punishment. Some felt that the situation was due to the fact that much of the population was related by blood, making it hard to empanel juries. Mr. Gahn blames politically minded officers. Official records reveal that very often—

persons charged with crime were never brought before a jury; and yet persons who were charged and not tried were often not cleared. This would indicate that the unpunished felon and his relatives would have to swear undying loyalty to the officials who protected him. They have written their own indictment by the records they compiled.

In recent years, improvement has been marked in many respects. Roads cut into the far reaches, and the bars began to slip down. Education arrived late, as in other places; yet the parish has seldom if ever voted down a tax for school and other improvements. No railroad ever reached Ville Platte, the parish seat; but the bus eventually arrived, and it has brought increasing contacts with other places. Many things are still informal. Until recently, court was started by the blowing of a cowhorn. The judge is a great hunter; so he has his annual recess in the fall instead of the usual summer period, and everybody understands. In other respects the territory clings to its older ways; and even today I thought I found something of the earlier suspicion and distrust of the caller from outside. The towns lack the easy spirit of the French villages to the south.

Among the English-speaking element, toward the hills, I felt myself in the presence of the true Southern sharecropper—gaunt, sometimes hollow-eyed, men who spoke with slow drawls, friendly yet in another fashion from the Louisiana French. When I heard them talk of terrible months when their few heads of cattle parched in the dust, and when one farmer pointed to an underprivileged stream and called it "our crick," I knew that South Louisiana was in the distance. Yet some of these Anglo-Saxons pick up Gallicisms without knowing it. One of the men in a heavy wool hat told me: "I don't gumbo that French at all."

It is a section of many small graveyards that show the French influence, but also some of the effect of Anglo-Saxonism. A priest in the Ville Platte neighborhood, for instance, has eight burying grounds under his jurisdiction—an unusual number. In earlier days each clan or part of the near-by population had its own cemetery, and they have continued with little change, often within walking distance of each other. One had as many inscriptions in English as in French. A headstone told how the dead man was "killed by lightning while sitting in his bedroom." Another "fell overboard in the river." A third declared: "His lamp was burning bright when his Master called him home." In this place, too, it is said, some of the Lafitte men are interred.

Near-by were the same white grave boxes that are in most French cemeteries of Louisiana; and with them I found eccentricities. Embedded in the mud of one grave was a rusted pot; in the box, beside statues of St. Rita and St. Anthony, were two cups. "That man was a great coffee drinker," a native observed. In another, below a metal wreath and crucifix, were a rubber ball, a toy pistol, and a set of six corroded soldiers, long since fallen upon each other. The child had been buried three years ago; the family had brought his favorite toys, and they would be there as long as the relatives were in the neighborhood, or longer. To the rear, at another grave, a buried fruit jar was partly exposed by the washing away of the soil. Inside was a vague cloth of some kind, and a friend explained: "It was the baby's diaper." At the next resting place, the significance was obvious—a small bottle and a cocktail glass; on others, a man's pipe, the buckle of a woman's dress, a bag of marbles, a once-movable monkey on a string.

Sometimes the priests disapprove and remove the objects. Others at once reappear in their place.

Westward from the prairie center the area slips toward Texas and another Anglo-Saxon culture. Some of the Acadians moved in this direction as the years passed, growing their same small crops, with "a little rice" among them—the "Providence rice" of the low ponds or bayou borders. The patches were largely for their own use; seldom did such farmers raise rice for the market. Through the time of the Civil War and for some years afterward, the western part of the prairies seemed destined to remain as another territory of the Louisiana French habitant. But one of the most dramatic shifts in the history of modern American agriculture was before it.

During the early colonial days on the Atlantic coast, South Carolina and neighboring tidal sections had produced most of the continent's rice. In Louisiana it was planted first along the Mississippi, then about the bayous and prairies, but usually in small amounts. The Civil War brought a sharp decline for the eastern coast cultivation, and slowly Louisiana gained; but the "Providence rice" of the prairies was still an uncertain factor. The early 1880's saw several changes. A few Northwestern and Middle-Western farmers, seeking new lands, heard of these broad and largely uncultivated acres. A story is told of S. L. Cary, who left the North to look over a settlement of his compatriots in Texas. Not entirely pleased there, he started home again. His route was through the western part of the Louisiana prairies; looking about, he liked what he saw. It might have been his own Middle West—with a magnificent difference. Here it was, the depth of winter, with many cattle living off the grass. At home, the thermometer was far below zero, and men were idle and worrying about stock and crops. S. L. Cary was soon in New Orleans, asking anxiously for rights to prairie land. Orleanians grinned and told him not to break his neck over it. He was the only one, apparently, who wanted it.

Mr. Cary and a few friends went there, and, like the Acadians many years before them, they dispatched letters to those whom they left behind. Before many of the French realized what was happening, the Middle West was descending upon them in numbers and in outlook. Large sections of the prairies were "sold" to America in ways that seem oddly in advance of the time. Railroads, farm promoters, and Louisiana officials united to pour over the nation a stream of circulars, pictures, and folders telling of the farmers' heaven that awaited. Mr. Cary and others made constant trips back and forth; cheap-fare transportation was arranged, inspection tours, free barbecues, and other attractions. Any man who wanted to settle in the grasslands was assisted in getting there. "Literature" told of a droughtless land, with plenty of water, warm Gulf breezes, and no snow. Longfellow's "Evangeline" was put to service, with special reprints for the farm family. The "snowdiggers"—the Frenchmen's term for the newcomers—arrived by the trainfuls. The inpouring was the nearest to John Law's Mississippi Bubble dreams that this place ever saw. One slogan which survived was this curious but apparently electrifying one:

> Go West, young man, go West;
> Go West and go to Mamou.

It was more than mere promotion. An unexpected agricultural treasure house was being exploited. The newcomers watched the small Acadian man and his "Providence rice" and saw much to improve. Of all places then known in America, they discovered, this part of Louisiana was best fitted for rice when raised by modern farming methods. Midwestern agricultural machinery provided the key to this wealth. The prairie soil, with its hard clay pan a short distance from the surface, retained the water for the long periods that rice required. The flatness of the ground meant that harvesting equipment could be used with ease. All the water that was needed was available in the near-by bayous. A few adjustments, and the Louisiana prairie began to look like a Midwestern wheat farm.

With each year the new Louisianians learned better how to fit machinery to their ground and crop. Pumping plants were devised for artificial flooding of the fields; men built their own small levees, mounds that kept the water under control and permitted easy flooding and draining at the proper seasons. Canals, small ones and large ones, cut through the prairie. Louisiana was now producing more rice than all other parts of America; the greatest mills in the world were erected here. Mile by mile, little banks of earth curled to the horizon over artificially created lakes bristling with spikes of green and yellow. The old hand methods of the Acadians were gone; "Providence rice" was forgotten.

The Acadian looked on in wonder, unwanted at this new feast in his own land. Many of the sponsors made it clear that they had in mind a "different kind of settler." Like other Anglo-Saxons of other years, they regarded him as unenterprising, set in his old ways; and often they smiled at him because he had not sensed the riches that lay under his nose.

As before, some of the Acadians were persuaded to sell their lands, and strange-looking American farmhouses and strange ways spread over the grasslands. A large alien spur had been thrust into French Louisiana. The towns that arose included an Iowa, a Roanoke, a Kaplan, a Crowley, and others of a ring and manner that are markedly non-French.

"The rice capital" is Crowley; and all the prairie people tell of the way in which it was made to order. Two brothers, C. C. and W. W. Duson, brought it into being almost overnight, out of their own confidence, advertising, and persuasive powers. Two well-established towns had presented bids for the parish seat; the matter seemed simply a choice between them. Then the Dusons produced their idea, in the middle 1880's. The central parts of the American farm belt were visited, inducements were offered, and a great auction of land was arranged on a village site which Acadian families had previously occupied. The Dusons announced that they had money to spend and were ready to spend it. A railroad was being built across the prairie, and a foreman with the name of Pat Crowley persuaded an engineer to run it through this point; in return the settlement took his name. As Velma Lea Hair describes it in her study of the city, lumber yards and other businesses were going up, and wide streets were being laid out, before the land was auctioned. Hundreds came, liked the place, and stayed. For their town-in-the-spawning stage, the two Dusons asked the rank of parish seat, and offered cash to the parish in return; eventually they received it. The new arrivals matched the spirit of the creators. By 1903 they felt certain that they had the five thousand population that would make it possible to declare themselves a city. But no census was due until 1910. So the inhabitants got together, canvassed themselves, made a documented count, forwarded it to the Governor, and had themselves officially declared a municipality.

And yet . . .

The older French Louisiana and the older French Louisianians have not disappeared from this "new" West Louisiana. Many of the Acadians went into rice, as operators, or as tenants and laborers for their own people or for the Americans. Not all the Middle-Westerners have stayed; through the years some have drifted farther West, or back to their earlier homes, or to New Orleans. Here and there the Acadians and other French have moved into the area, and many are still moving in. Clusters of French homes, which the owners declined to give up, have increased, and Acadian towns thrive among the others.

Meanwhile, too, these bland and pleasant people are at work, quietly, on their neighbors. One of the Americans tells me how he "couldn't go those Frenchmen" when he arrived, fifteen years ago; how he perspired and fumed over their attitude. They seemed little inclined to join his drives or his business clubs. Now he finds himself changing. He still cannot understand some of the things about the natives and their lives, but others seem less outlandish. When he came to know them, he learned that all he had heard was not true. Why, now, he had just persuaded two of the Frenchmen to serve on a committee of his own.

The Middle-Westerner's habits are not the same as when he arrived. He almost spat out his first cup of Louisiana coffee. ("I thought something terrible would happen if it went down.") Now he has it, dripped, as often a day as he can get it, and he breaks his morning routine over a cup with Mr. Broussard from the next store. After some years of hesitation, he has come to accept and like crawfish and crabs. He can understand a lot of the French talk about him, and occasionally, when he is in adventurous mood, he can force a sentence out of his mouth and be happy when his neighbors congratulate him. His wife smiles as she tells how he turned from a gravy-hater to one who wants a roux with his rice once a day. As we say good-by, they introduce their son and the little Acadian girl whom he is obviously courting.

Which side will win in the long run? I will accept a bet from you, mister. Not from you, m'sieu.

Final Word

Here, I suppose, is a proper place for a few words about the bayous that I did not include. Many Louisianians have their favorite ones, at the back of their houses, or within hiking distance, or somewhere in that ideal world that they plan to visit in years to come. They may find that their particular choice is not here. One book could not present more than a selection of the twisting waters of the state. Also, some of the streams were eliminated at the start. North Louisiana, the Louisiana of the hills, has some bayous and some handsome ones; but I set 'out to tell primarily of the French country—and so they were passed by. Then Bayou Sara, that richly endowed one of the rolling Feliciana country, and its neighbors—these, too, are not in these pages; they belong to the "English" part of Louisiana. Down toward the mouth of the Mississippi there are bayous; but, as I said at the start, that is a different civilization from the one I am describing: a place dominated by the great central stream of the river rather than by the less determined back waters. In the final analysis, of course, any selection that has been made is a personal one. Here are the bayous that I have known, and liked, and remembered; and here are the reasons for the liking and for the remembering.

One night, on a shrimp trawler, Theodule Martin was talking about the things that had happened one day on a fishing trip. We all listened, impressed. Then Theodule halted and his brother Theophile asked him: Why didn' he tell us about the other things that wen' on, this and that and that other one, ahn? Theodule looked at Theophile a long moment, then answered: Well, and if he put all that in, what would be lef' for Theophile to tell? I hope that there will be others to tell other things about other bayous. Me, I might want to do it myself.

Acknowledgments

Primarily, to Eleonora Waldmann Wharton, for her skillful and sympathetic assistance during all stages of the preparation. To Nilas Young, Ben Kaplan, Rex Laney, Dr. T. Lynn Smith, Elemore N. Morgan, Roger Baudier, Weeks Hall, Florence and Anna Marie Kane, Dr. James Nelson Gowanloch, Dan S. Leyrer, Myron and Roberta Falk, Percy Viosca, Jr., Dr. Richard Joel Russell, Bennett J. Voorhies, Orville E. Priestley and Edith G. Dupre.

To Mel and W. A. Robertson, Emac E. Naquin, Lester Gonsulin, Louise Olivier, Alcuis Fuselier, W. G. Weeks and Edward T. Weeks, Sr., Dr. Thaddeus I. St. Martin, Dr. H. L. Griffin, E. A. Turner, James Marlow, Charles W. Price, Jr., Eugene Dumez, Mrs. Bernice Montégut Buckland, and André A. Olivier.

To Robert Usher, Librarian of the Howard-Tilton Memorial Library, Tulane University, and Marguerite D. Renshaw, Viola Andersen, Elsie Bing and Mrs. Mary Bell Herndon of his staff; James A. McMillen, Director of Libraries, Louisiana State University; Mrs. Ruth Campbell, Curator of the Louisiana Room, Hill Memorial Library, Louisiana State University.

To John Plaisance, Alfred Danziger, Norman Bauer, Dudley LeBlanc, Jake Landry, C. P. Liter, Alfred Hobart, Mrs. Alice Rightor McCall, Isaac D. Chapman, Mrs. Margaret Dixon, Helen Gilkison, S. Sanford and Judge Anna Veters Levy, Harry D. Wilson, Marguerite Watkins, the two Fathers Gubler of Pierre Part and Barataria, Dr. Fred B. Kniffen, Francis T. Knobloch, Elsie St. Martin, Stanley Clisby Arthur, Eugene Delcroix, Fonville Winans, Pauline D. Mizzi, Richard Koch, Wilton P. Ledet, who made available to me some of the unpublished material accumulated during his study of Acadians under a Rosenwald Fellowship, Essae M. Culver of the Louisiana Library Commission and Lyle Saxon, former State Director of the Federal Writers' Project, who together made available a number of the unpublished photographs collected by the staff of the project, now the property of the Library Commission.

Many persons opened to me their collections of data on the

bayou areas, memoirs, family papers and similar materials. A selected list of the more important or more interesting materials which I have used is appended:

BOOKS

Arthur, Stanley Clisby, and Kernion, George C. H. de. *Old Families of Louisiana.* New Orleans, 1931.

Barde, Alexandre. *Histoire des Comités de Vigilance aux Attakapas.* Saint-Jean-Baptiste (Louisiane). Impr. du Meschacébé et de l'Avant-Coureur, 1861.

Baudier, Roger. *The Catholic Church in Louisiana.* New Orleans, 1939.

Bernard, Antoine. *Le Drame Acadien Depuis 1604.* Montreal, 1936.

Brackenridge, H. M. *Views of Louisiana with a Journal of a Voyage up the Mississippi River in 1811.* Pittsburgh, 1814..

Bible, George Potter. *An Historic Sketch of the Acadians.* Philadelphia, 1906.

Cable, George W. *The Creoles of Louisiana.* New York, 1884.

Cable, George W. *Strange True Tales of Louisiana.* New York, 1889, 1917.

Chambers, Henry A. *A History of Louisiana.* Chicago, 1925.

Charnley, Mitchell. *Jean Lafitte, Gentleman Smuggler.* New York, 1934.

Cruchet, René. *En Louisiane, Légendes et Réalités.* Bordeaux, 1937.

Darby, William. *The Emigrants' Guide to the Western and Southwestern States and Territories.* New York, 1818.

Darby, William. *A Geographical Description of the State of Louisiana.* Philadelphia, 1816.

Daubeny, Charles. *Journal of a Tour through the United States and in Canada.* Oxford, 1843.

Deiler, John Hanno. *The Settlement of the German Coast of Louisiana and the Creoles of German Descent.* Philadelphia, 1909.

Dennett, Daniel. *Louisiana As It Is.* New Orleans, 1876.

Ditchy, Jay Karl (ed.). *Les Acadiens Louisianais et Leur Parler.* Baltimore, 1932.

Duvallon, Berquin. *Vue de la Colonie Espagnole du Mississippi.* Paris, 1802.

Fortier, Alcée. *History of Louisiana*. New York, 1904.

Fortier, Alcée. *Louisiana Studies*. New Orleans, 1894.

French, B. F. *Historical Memoirs of Louisiana*. New York, 1853.

Gayarre, Charles. *History of Louisiana*. New Orleans, 1903.

Hearn, Lafcadio. *Chita: A Memory of Last Island*. New York, 1889.

Johnston, Margaret H. *In Acadia—The Acadians in Story and Song*. New Orleans, 1893.

Jones, Howard Mumford. *American and French Culture*. Chapel Hill, 1927.

King, Grace. *Creole Families of New Orleans*. New York, 1921.

King, Grace. *New Orleans, the Place and the People*. New York, 1895.

Lauvrière, Émile. *La Tragédie d'un Peuple*. Paris, 1924.

Leblanc, Dudley J. *The True Story of the Acadians*. Lafayette, 1932.

Le Page Du Pratz, Antoine S. *The History of Louisiana*. London, 1763.

Louisiana—A Guide to the State. American Guide Series. New York, 1941.

Marchand, Sidney. *The Story of Ascension Parish*. Donaldsonville, 1931.

Martin, François-Xavier. *The History of Louisiana from the Earliest Period*. New Orleans, 1827-29.

McIlhenny, E. A. *Bird City*. Boston, 1934.

Olmsted, Frederick Law. *A Journey in the Seaboard Slave States*. New York, 1856.

Paxton, W. E. *A History of the Baptists of Louisiana*. St. Louis, 1888.

Perrin, William H. (ed.). *Southwest Louisiana, Biographical and Historical*. New Orleans, 1891.

Perrin Du Lac, F. M. *Voyage dans les Deux Louisianes*. Paris, 1805.

Ralph, Julian. *Dixie, or Southern Scenes and Sketches*. New York, 1896.

Read, William A. *Louisiana French*. Baton Rouge, 1931.

Read, William A. *Louisiana Place Names of Indian Origin*. Baton Rouge, 1927.

Robertson, James Alexander. *Louisiana Under the Rule of Spain, France and the United States*. Cleveland, 1911.

Robin, Claude C. *Voyages dans l'Interieur de la Louisiane*. Paris, 1807.
Russell, William Howard. *My Diary North and South*. London, 1863.
Saxon, Lyle. *Lafitte the Pirate*. New York, 1930.
Smith, J. Frazer. *White Pillars*. New York, 1941.
Sparks, William Henry. *The Memories of Fifty Years*. Philadelphia, 1870.
Spratling, William, and Scott, Natalie. *Old Plantation Houses in Louisiana*. New York, 1927.
Stephenson, Wendell Holmes. *Alexander Porter, Whig Planter of Old Louisiana*. Baton Rouge, 1934.
Surrey, Nancy M. Miller. *The Commerce of Louisiana During the French Regime, 1699-1763*. New York, 1916.
Taylor, Richard. *Destruction and Reconstruction*. New York, 1879.
Viosca, Percy, Jr. *Louisiana Out-of-Doors*. New Orleans, 1933.
Voorhies, Felix. *Acadian Reminiscences*. Boston, 1907.
Whitfield, Irène Thérèse. *Louisiana French Folk Songs*. Baton Rouge, 1939.
Williamson, Frederick W. *Yesterday and Today in Louisiana Agriculture*. Baton Rouge, 1940.

PERIODICALS AND PAMPHLETS

Allen, R. L. "Letters from the South," No. 9. In Allen, A. B., ed., *American Agriculturalist*, Vol. VI. New York, 1847.
Arthur, Stanley Clisby. "The Fur Animals of Louisiana." Bulletin No. 18, Louisiana Department of Conservation. New Orleans, 1928.
Cable, George W. "The Pirates of Barataria." *Century Magazine*, April, 1883.
Dart, Henry P. "A Louisiana Indigo Plantation on Bayou Teche." *Louisiana Historical Quarterly*, October, 1926.
Daniels, R. L. "The Acadians of Louisiana." *Scribner's Monthly*, January, 1880.
Dickson, Harris. "The Promotion of Bird City." *Saturday Evening Post*, February 10, 1934.
Fortier, Alcée. "The Acadians of Louisiana and their Dialect."

Publications of the Modern Language Association of America. Baltimore, January, 1891.

Gilmore, H. W. "Family Capitalism in a Community of Rural Louisiana." *Social Forces*, October, 1936.

Gilmore, H. W. "Social Isolation of the French-Speaking People of Rural Louisiana." *Social Forces*, October, 1933.

Ginn, Mildred Kelly. "A History of Rice Production in Louisiana to 1896." *Louisiana Historical Quarterly*, April, 1940.

Gould, Harley N. "The Acadian French in Canada and in Louisiana." *American Journal of Physical Anthropology*, September, 1941.

Griffin, Harry Louis. "History of Lafayette." Lafayette, 1936.

Hall, Weeks. "Louisiana Parish Cookery." *Harper's Bazaar*, February, 1941.

Howe, H. V., and Moresi, C. K. "Geology of Iberia Parish." Louisiana Department of Conservation, Geological Bulletin No. 1, 1931.

Howe, H. V., and Moresi, C. K. "Geology of Lafayette and St. Martin Parishes." Louisiana Department of Conservation, Geological Bulletin No. 3, 1933.

Howe, H. V., Russell, R. J., and McGuirt, H. H. "Physiography of Coastal Southwest Louisiana." Louisiana Department of Conservation, Geological Bulletin No. 6, 1935.

Kelly, Minnie. "Acadian South Louisiana." *Journal of Geography*, March, 1934.

Kniffen, Fred B. "The Historic Indian Tribes of Louisiana." *Louisiana Conservation Review*, July, 1933.

Kniffen, Fred B. "Louisiana House Types." *Annals of the Association of American Geographers*, December, 1936.

Lafargue, André. "Louisiana Linguistic and Folklore Backgrounds." *Louisiana Historical Quarterly*, July, 1941.

McAllister, R. S. "Last Island Hurricane." *Southwestern Presbyterian*, April 9, 1891.

McCloy, Shelby T. "French Charities to the Acadians, 1755-99." *Louisiana Historical Quarterly*, July, 1938.

Parenton, Vernon J. "Notes on the Social Organization of a French Village in South Louisiana." *Social Forces*, October, 1938.

Pierce, G. W. "Historical and Statistical Collections of Louisiana: Terrebonne." *DeBow's Review*, December, 1851.

Post, Lauren C. "The Rice Country of Southwestern Louisiana." *Geographical Review*, October, 1940.

Pugh, W. W. "Bayou Lafourche from 1820-5." *Louisiana Planter and Sugar Manufacturer*, September-October, 1888.

Russell, Richard Joel, and Howe, H. V. "Cheniers of Southwestern Louisiana." *Geographical Review*, July, 1935.

Russell, Richard Joel. "Flotant." *Geographical Review*, January, 1942.

Russell, Richard Joel; Howe, H. V.; and others. "Lower Mississippi River Delta." Louisiana Department of Conservation, Geological Bulletin No. 8, 1936.

Russell, Richard Joel. "Louisiana Stream Patterns." Bulletin of American Association of Petroleum Geologists, August, 1939.

Sandoz, William J. "A Brief History of St. Landry Parish." *Louisiana Historical Quarterly*, April, 1925.

Scroggs, W. O. "Rural Life in the Mississippi Valley About 1803." Proceedings of the Mississippi Valley Historical Association, VIII, 1915.

Smith, T. Lynn. "An Analysis of Rural Social Organization Among the French-Speaking People of Southern Louisiana." *Journal of Farm Economics*, October, 1934.

Smith, T. Lynn. "The Growth of Population in Louisiana, 1890 to 1930." Louisiana Bulletin No. 264, Louisiana State University, July, 1935.

St. Martin, Thaddeus I. "Cajuns." *Yale Review*, June, 1937.

Stephens, Edwin Lewis. "The Story of Acadian Education in Louisiana." *Louisiana Historical Quarterly*, July, 1935.

AND

Inventories of the Parish Archives of Louisiana, prepared by the Historical Records Survey Projects of the Work Projects Administration, 1938-42.

Issues of the *Louisiana Conservation Review*, published by the Louisiana Department of Conservation.

Issues of the *Louisiana Tourist*, published by the Louisiana Department of Commerce and Industry.

Files of the *Item*, *Times-Picayune* and *States* of New Orleans; the Baton Rouge *State Times*; Crowley *Signal*; Lafayette *Advertiser*; Ville Platte *Gazette* and others.

THESIS MATERIAL

NAME	SCHOOL	YEAR	SUBJECT
Father Edward J. Kammer	Catholic University of America	1941	Ph.D. thesis: On marsh-dwellers of four Louisiana parishes.
Marjorie S. Bordelon	Tulane University	1936	M.A. thesis: On a rural town in Louisiana.
Helen Margaret Bowie	Louisiana State University	1935	M.A. thesis: On Bayou Lafourche.
Velma Lea Hair	Louisiana State University	1941	M.A. thesis: On the history of Crowley.
C. L. Folse	Louisiana State University	1935	M.A. thesis: A social study along Bayou Lafourche.
Frances Marion Hickman	Louisiana State University	1939	M.A. thesis: On the French speech of Jefferson parish.
Dorothy Elizabeth King	Tulane University	1935	M.A. thesis: On bayou life.
Mrs. Louise Westfeldt McIlhenny	Tulane University	1935	M.A. thesis: On the retention of French cultural traits by rural Acadians of Louisiana.
Marguerite A. Pecot	Louisiana State University	1931	M.A. thesis: On *The Cajun.*
Irene M. Petitjean	Columbia University	1930	M.A. thesis: On Acadian folk-songs.
Pamela Elizabeth Robertson	Tulane University	1942	M.A. thesis: On welfare activities in St. Landry parish.
Marcelle Schertz	Louisiana State University	1940	M.A. thesis: On the plays of Judge Felix Voorhies.
Marguerite Watkins	Louisiana State University	1939	M.A. thesis: On Terrebonne parish.
Robert Gahn	Southwestern Louisiana Institute	1940	M.A. thesis: On Evangeline parish.